# Delta Raiders

# Delta Raiders

D Company, 2nd Battalion, 501st Infantry
101st ABN Division

Compiled by the
Delta Raiders of Vietnam Association

Southern Heritage Press
St. Petersburg, Florida

## Southern Heritage Press
Byron Kennedy, Publisher
P. O. Box 10937
St. Petersburg, Florida 33733
1-800-282-2823

Copyright 1998 Delta Raiders of Vietnam Association
All rights reserved.

This book may not be reproduced
in whole or in part,
by mimeograph or any other means,
without permission from the publisher.

Limited edition
ISBN:0-941072-34-7

Printed in the United States of America
Book Design by
Voshardt/Humphrey Artworks, Inc.
St. Petersburg, Florida

# Foreword

The Delta Raiders of Vietnam Association (DROVA) was established in concept by Mr. John Palm. Mr. Palm wanted to locate those Delta Raiders (Raiders) who served in Vietnam with his son, Terry. Mr. Palm located several members of the First Platoon, who then held the first Raider Reunion in the early 1980s. With the continuing efforts of Rod Soubers and others, DROVA was born. The goal of DROVA was to locate as many Raiders as possible and put together a photo history of the Company. DROVA has nine board members, who meet once a year to plan the activities of the Raiders for the next year. The Board has been working on the Chronology/Photo history for the past twelve years and what is contained in this book is the culmination of their work. Many hours have been spent putting together this Raider history.

This chronology/photo history is formatted to give a day by day accounting of the activities of the Raiders in Vietnam. It contains intermingled stories and accountings of specific battles, such as PK17, the Battle for Hue, Hill 805, Hamburger Hill and many more, that the men of Delta Company participated in during their four plus years in Vietnam. It also contains selected photos that are representative of: the Areas of Operation we all worked in during our stay in Vietnam; group pictures of Platoons, Squads, or just friends; firebases; jungles and lowlands; and other activities that we all remember, and can relate to. This book contains a listing of all the men who served with the "Raiders" during the Vietnam War and a list of all the Raiders killed in action (KIA) giving their lives for their nation.

We wish we could have put every photo, letter, correspondence, or thought that we have collected over the last twelve years in this book. With time and money being a factor, we elected to go with those photos and stories that we felt all Raiders could relate to as being a part of their Tour of Duty. This history can give you the insight of what those Raiders who came before or after you did to maintain the Raider spirit and tradition. It will also let you better understand what was happening on a certain day that today might be a little hazy to remember. Many Raiders were not able to preserve any of their time in Vietnam on film to keep as a remembrance. The photos in this book were taken by your friends who were in the field at the same time.

This photo history would not be possible if it were not for the work of many Raiders who spent endless hours accumulating, researching, writing, remembering and documenting the activities of the Raiders in Vietnam. Special thanks to: Rod Soubers who spent countless hours in the National Archives in Washington, D.C., reviewing Army records to establish the day-by-day activities of the Delta Raiders; Ray "Blackie" Blackman who spent endless days collecting and cataloging photos, and contributed art work to the project; and Cleo Hogan, Wayne McMenamy, Mike Allen, Dan Michener, Terry Moore, Gene "Raider Rob" Robertson, Chuck Leshikar and many others who sent photographs or contributed to the successful completion of this Raider History. Special thanks go to all of the KIA families for the time that you have spent with the organization and for the contribution of photographs of our Special Raiders. They will always be remembered. Above all, this history of the Delta Raiders is a labor of love and respect and is dedicated to all those men who served with Delta Company, 2/501, of the 101st Air Borne Division in Vietnam. It is dedicated to the memory of all those "Raiders" who gave their lives to exemplify the true meaning of Honor, Duty, and Sacrifice. It is dedicated to all those unsung heroes, who, by their gallantry, made the Raiders one of the most decorated infantry companies in the history of the United States Army. Delta Company has the distinct honor of being the only company in the Vietnam War to have two medal of honor recipients, Joe Hooper and Clifford Sims. It is to these brave "Raiders" and to those who gave all for their comrades and country that this book will be dedicated as a lasting memory of their sacrifices.

Paul Grelle, President (1984-1996)<br>
Delta Raiders of Vietnam Association

# Acknowledgement

The Delta Raiders would like to gratefully acknowledge the hours and hours of effort given by Terry Byfield, Lori Bailey and Darlene Henson. These ladies organized, typed, checked, cross-checked and, most importantly, read the pages which follow so that this book could be produced in a clear and readable fashion. They devoted more than just time to the work, they cared — about the men, about the stories and about the Delta Raiders. Thank you, ladies, we could not have done it without you.

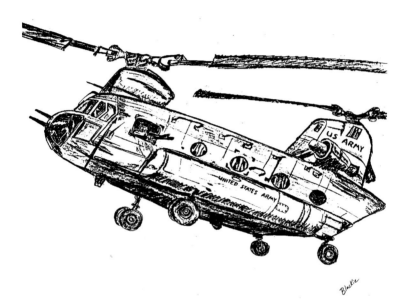

# Table of Contents

| CHAPTER | PAGE |
|---|---|
| 1. Dedication and List of Those Killed in Action | 11 |
| 2. Background Notes on the Birth of the Delta Raiders | 21 |
| 3. Chronology: December 13, 1967 – February 23, 1968 | 39 |
| 4. February 21, 1968 by Cleo Hogan | 51 |
| 5. Congressional Medals of Honor | 59 |
| 6. Chronology: February 24, 1968 – October 30, 1968 | 63 |
| 7. The Days of Blue Falcon Ridge by Chuck Leshikar | 101 |
| 8. Chronology: October 31, 1968 – May 31, 1970 | 113 |
| 9. The Introduction by Ray Blackman | 167 |
| 10. Chronology: June 3, 1970 – June 26, 1970 | 179 |
| 11. July 11, 1970 by Rod Soubers | 183 |
| 12. Chronology: July 1, 1970 – July 15, 1970 | 199 |
| 13. A Combat Assault! by Terry Moore | 203 |
| 14. Chronology: July 16, 1970 – January 4, 1971 | 207 |
| 15. Going Out on an Ambush by Michael B. Allen | 219 |
| 16. Chronology: January 5, 1971 – February 12, 1972 | 231 |
| 17. A Father's Story by Erin Policz | 263 |
| Faces, a poem by Roy Moore | 273 |
| Roster of Delta Raiders | 275 |
| Glossary | 313 |
| Index | 320 |

# 1.
# Dedication to the Delta Raiders Killed in Action

The Vietnam War was a unique war in American History. The War left many emotional scars that have been with us since that time and will continue to be with us for many years to come. In the past years, the Delta Raiders have come together for reunions every two years. The reunion is a constructive activity where Delta Raiders, their families and the families of the Delta Raider KIAs can come together to remember and renew old friendships and to form new ones. These reunions are proof that those serving with the Delta Raiders have maintained traditional values and their commitment to each other.

Everyday, let us pause to remember the Delta Raiders who sacrificed for us and for the United States of America — those who gave their lives to preserve freedom for us. We are honored to pay tribute to the sacrifices of our fellow Delta Raiders and we honor them with our remembrance by recalling the beautiful notes of "Taps" and repeating the words of that simple melody:

DAY IS DONE
GONE THE SUN
FROM THE LAKE
FROM THE HILL
FROM THE SKY
REST IN PEACE
SOLDIER BRAVE
GOD IS NIGH.

## Ch. 1 / Delta Raiders Killed in Action

**KIA LIST**  **KIA DATE**

| | | | | | |
|---|---|---|---|---|---|
| Dec. 2nd | 1967/68 | SP4 | Anslow | Walter Harold | (3/22/68) |
| Dec. Unl. | 1971 | SSG | Bales | Ronald Eugene | (4/15/71) |
| Dec. 1st | 1967/68 | SP4 | Begody | Harold L. | (2/14/68) |
| Dec. 1st | 1969/70 | SP4 | Beyl | David R. | (7/18/70) |
| Dec. 2nd | 1967/68 | PFC | Brockman | Robert David | (6/15/68) |
| Dec. 3rd | 1967/68 | 2LT | Brulte | Robert Francis | (2/15/68) |
| Dec. 3rd | 1967/68 | SP4 | Burroughs | Emanuel Fero | (2/15/68) |
| Dec. 3rd | l967/68 | SGT | Cash | David Manfred | (2/15/68) |
| Dec. 3rd | 1971 | 1LT | Church | Ralph Lee | (6/12/71) |
| Dec. Unk. | 1968 | SGT-Medic | Cleveland | James Arthur | (7/20/68) |
| Dec. 2nd | 1969 | PFC | Courtney | Jimmy Darrell | (7/25/69) |
| Dec. 2rd | 1971 | SP4 | Daniels | Rex Martin | (4/16/71) |
| Dec. Unk. | 1969 | SGT | Dunn | Robert Terrence | (10/24/68) |
| Dec. 2nd | 1968 | PFC-RTO | Eller | Lawrence William | (4/10/68) |
| Dec. Unk. | 1968 | SGT | Gillard | Michael | (5/20/68) |
| Dec. 3rd | 1967/68 | SSG | Gingery | John Bernard | (4/28/68) |
| Dec. Unk. | 1971 | PFC | Greene | Terry Willard | (4/15/71) |
| Dec. 2nd | 1967/68 | SSG | Gregory | Eulas Fay | (3/23/68) |
| Dec. 1st | 1967/68 | 2LT | Grimsley | Lee Eldrige | (4/16/71) |
| Dec. 1st | 1969/70 | SP4 | Guimond | Paul Gerald | (7/14/70) |
| Dec. 2nd | 1970/71 | SP4 | Hein | Robert Charles | (4/15/71) |
| Dec. 2nd | 1969/70 | SSG | Hembree Jr. | James Thomas | (7/14/70) |
| Dec. 2nd | 1967/68 | PFC | Holmes | Ernest Paul | (2/15/68) |
| Dec. 1st | 1970 | SSG | Jones | Willam Edward | (7/14/70) |
| Dec. 1st | 1969/70 | PFC | Keister | John Lay | (7/14/70) |
| Dec. HQ | 1969 | CPT | Kelly Jr. | John Edward | (7/25/69) |
| Dec. 1st | 1970 | PFC | Knickerbocker | Robert J. | (12/25/70) |

12 • Delta Raiders

## KIA LIST

## KIA DATE

| | | | | | |
|---|---|---|---|---|---|
| Dec. 2nd | 1968 | PFC | Marron | Bruce A. | (7/20/68) |
| Dec. Unk. | 1969 | PVT | Martinez | Alex Esequiel | (7/20/69) |
| Dec. Unk. | 1970 | PFC | Maynard | Richard Lee | (12/14/70) |
| Dec. 2nd | 1971 | | McGinnes | Charles Dennis | (4/16/71) |
| Dec. 2nd | 1971 | 1LT | McKenzie | Paul | (4/15/71) |
| Dec. 3rd | 1971 | PFC | McKinney | Robert Dale | (6/1/71) |
| Dec. 1st | 1970 | PFC | Muncey | Jay Allen | (7/28/70) |
| Dec. Unk. | 1968/69 | SP4 | Nordell Jr. | John E. | (2/5/69) |
| Dec. 1st | 1970 | 1LT | Palm | Terry Alan | (7/14/70) |
| Dec. 1st | 1969/70 | SP4 | Rollason | William David | (7/18/70) |
| Dec. 2nd | 1969/70 | 1LT | Rufty | Joe Hearne | (1/29/70) |
| Dec. 3rd | 1968 | PFC | Saunders | Michael Joseph | (4/28/68) |
| Dec. 2nd | 1969/70 | SSG | Schneider | Gary Lee | (7/15/70) |
| Dec. Unk. | 1968 | SP4 | Sheldon | Leroy Eldan | (2/24/69) |
| Dec. 2nd | 1967/68 | SSG | Sims | Clifford Chester | (2/21/68) |
| Dec. 2nd | 1969 | PFC | Sommer | Douglas John | (5/23/69) |
| Dec. 2nd | 1970/71 | SGT | Stearns | Jerry Sheldon | (4/15/71) |
| Dec. 3rd | 1967/68 | SP4 | Tabet | Henry Marsial | (2/15/68) |
| Dec. Unk. | 1968 | PFC | Terrell | Robert Earl | (4/26/68) |
| Dec. 3rd | 1967/68 | PFC | Thackrey Jr. | Wade E. | (2/15/68) |
| Dec. 2nd | 1970 | PFC | Utter | Keith Edward | (7/14/70) |
| Dec. 1st | 1971 | SP4 | Vandiver | Harry Melborn | (11/30/71) |
| Dec. 2nd | 1967/68 | PFC | Wagner | David Frederick | (4/9/68) |
| Dec. 2nd | 1971 | PFC | Ward | William James | (4/15/71) |
| Dec. 3rd | 1969/70 | SP4 | Warner | Wilfred Wesley | (7/23/70) |
| Dec. Unk. | 1968 | PFC | Williams, Jr. | Arthur | (12/2/68) |
| Dec. Unk. | 1968 | | Williams | Clifford Leroy | (3/27/68) |

## Ch. 1 / Delta Raiders Killed in Action

Ronald Eugene Bales

Harold L. Begody

David R. Beyl

Robert Francis Brulte

*David Manfred Cash*

*Jimmy Darrell Courtney*

*John Bernard Gingery*

*Paul Gerald Guimond*

## Ch. 1 / Delta Raiders Killed in Action

James Thomas Hembree, Jr.

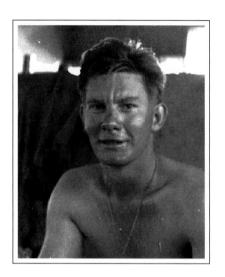

John Lay Keister

John Edward Kelly, Jr.

Charles Dennis McGinnes

*Jay Allen Muncey*

*Terry Alan Palm*

*William David Rollason*

*Joe Hearne Rufty*

## Ch. 1 / Delta Raiders Killed in Action

*Gary Lee Schneider*

*Clifford Chester Sims*

*Henry Marsial Tabet*

*Robert Earl Terrell*

Wade E. Thackrey, Jr.

Keith Edward Utter

Harry Melborn Vandiver

*David Frederick Wagner*  *Arthur Williams, Jr.*

# 2.
# Background Notes on the "Birth" of The Delta Raiders

### D Company, 2nd Battalion, 501st Infantry
### 101st ABN Division

### Prepared for the
### Delta Raiders of Vietnam Association
### 1990

### C. Wayne McMenamy
### "Raider 6"

*"From the soul that haste given you life, you have honed your skills well, proven your gallant spirit and molded a character of strength and the willingness to show compassion and love for your fellow soldier.*

*With your blood you have forged a tradition of valor and pride and through this a brotherhood is born.*

*Thus, you are bound forever, one to another, by this, your baptism a fire.*

*Arise Raider, no longer the bastard child."*

PK17 (Outside Hue)<br>15 Feb. 1968

The above words are from my notes made following the first major engagement of the Delta Raiders which took place in I Corps, Republic of Vietnam, during the 1968 enemy Tet offensive. Over time, many words have been spoken and written about the unit during this phase of their proud history. However, these words keep coming back to me summarizing what I observed and felt about the Raiders as its first Commander.

It is with a great deal of pride that I find that the spirit that was born on the parade fields of Ft. Campbell, that took roots in the founding of its name and insignia and matured in the ricefields and hills of Vietnam, continues on today. It's hoped that the following background will put into perspective some things and events that took place during this very special period in our lives. Some things may be known, some things may be unknown, or simply, some things may be forgotten.

In September 1967 I was assigned to the 101st Airborne Division, Ft. Campbell, Kentucky. I had already served in Vietnam from 1965 to 1967 with the Army's Special Forces. During the end of this period, I had been listed as MIA following a long-range reconnaissance mission in Cambodia. After returning to "friendly control," I had been assigned to Ft. Sill, Oklahoma, to recover and serve as a Special Warfare Instructor at the Artillery School. It was during this time that I was contacted by the Infantry Branch in Washington, D.C., to see if I was ready for a special assignment. My answer was yes.

The 2nd and 3rd Brigades of the 101st were being brought up to full combat strength in preparation for deployment to Vietnam. Within the 2nd Battalion, 501st Infantry Regiment, a fourth rifle company was to be formed. My mission: To organize, equip and train an Airborne Infantry Company from scratch, and then to deploy that unit into combat. I was given less than 90 days to accomplish the task.

When we talk about "from scratch" I mean SCRATCH! We had four empty offices (no tables, chairs, filing cabinets or even files) and two empty company bays (no beds or wall lockers). A, B and C Companies had to provide five men each to help start us off. I was little surprised that the men provided came from the "bottom of the resource pool" — several replacements coming directly from the stockade. From the start it was clear that in the eyes of the other units within the Battalion, we were just a "bastard child" and would never attain the level of efficiency they enjoyed after many years of concentrated training and effort. As such, there was no great emphasis on providing us with, what they considered, their better "talent."

There were, however, some good points to this situation. LTC Richard Tallman, who commanded the 2/501st had come up through the ranks. He had been an enlisted infantryman during WWII, graduated from West Point, served as a Platoon Leader during Korea and already had one tour in Vietnam. LTC Tallman knew the importance of leadership and the ability to relate to the situation of the common soldier. Aside from my combat experience, I had been given this assignment because I also had come up through the ranks and had been an NCO prior to commissioning. As such, to assist me in this mission, I was assigned one of the finest 1st Sergeants the Army ever turned out, 1st Sergeant Arthur Scott (Scotty). Scotty had been molded in the "old Army." He was a soldier's soldier. Aside from myself, he would be the only other combat veteran in the unit and would prove an invaluable asset to not only the unit but the tasks that lay ahead.

During the next two weeks we prepared for the arrival of the rest of the replacements who were due by the first of October. We ordered equipment (much of which would not arrive until time for us to deploy), put wall lockers and beds together and generally "scrounged" any basic equipment we could find that wasn't nailed down. Some of the more less-appreciated "talents" of our initial group, significantly contributed to the accomplishment of our mission.

During the first part of October 1967, our "infantrymen" arrived. We had cooks, bakers, clerks, engineers, drivers, artillerymen and a small segment of what could be loosely termed, infantrymen. Overall 97% of the unit was non-infantry. We had more of a Combat Service Support Company than a Rifle Company. The only thing that they had in common was basic training and jump wings. While the overall IQ and attitude of the men was higher than average, more than that was going to be needed to get them through what was to come. From the beginning, both Scotty and I recognized that we needed something to draw them together as soon as possible, not just as a unit or team, but something stronger.

Shortly thereafter, while in discussion with the Battalion Commander one day, he referred to the "raiding" of one of the other Company's supply rooms, allegedly by members of Delta Company and that such a reputation was unbecoming. I left after offering assurances that there must have been either some mistake in identification or the possibility of an over zealous interpretation of instructions and dedication to the needs of the unit on the part of the men involved.

The rest of the Battalion didn't know it, but they had given us a name and early reputation for resourcefulness. A reputation that would be molded in a positive sense and built upon, and a name, "The Delta Raiders," which offered a unique identification of the men involved. Developing a sense of pride from this basis was the next step.

Given the shortness of the time available before deployment we needed to find out as quickly as possible who was going to make the grade and who wasn't. Our training program developed as sort of a cross between AIT, the NCO Academy, and pre-season football training. Individual training was long and hard, sometimes 20 hours a day, 7 days a week. Early on I had a cot put into my office. There was neither the time nor reason to go to the BOQ. This was now my family and my home was with my unit.

Whatever the Battalion requirements, the unit always strived, and usually succeeded, to do better. They were after all, Raiders. If the Battalion ran one mile, the Raiders ran two. If the Battalion ran two miles, then the Raiders ran three, and so on. Extra push-ups and the "front leaning rest," in

formation, was a part of the daily routine. At every opportunity I tried to instill into the unit a sense of unique identification and pride. Everyone shared in the workload, from the CO to the most junior Private. There was no black or white, rich or poor, regular or draftee. Only Raiders. When called to attention in company formation or when being dismissed, all would sound off in unison "Raider, Sir." While initially this brought a few chuckles from some of the other companies, especially when in Battalion formation, it was not long before the Raiders were showing that they had what it took and that they were more than just a "rag tag" collection thrown together to boost the numbers within the Battalion. More than just the "bastard child."

Our weapons platoon, under the leadership of SFC Robert Benoit, showed that it was the best in the Division by beating all other units in local competition. At the same time our medics, radio operators and administration personnel were also proving their high level of efficiency during the numerous inspections we had to endure during this period. The individual rifle squads were improving rapidly and overall the Raiders were coming together as a smooth and aggressive fighting machine. They were also starting to prove a bit of embarrassment to the other companies within the Battalion in the quickness that this was taking place.

While it's easy sometimes when you're recounting such events to overlook some of the important contributions, I would at this point like to highlight the tremendous job done by SSgt. Charlie Wyatt as Mess Sgt. and his team of cooks. There is no doubt they played a special part given our unit's daily training schedule. It should be noted that all officers and NCO's ate in the Mess Hall with the rest of the unit on a daily basis. This was just another part of the continuing effort to forge a strong "brotherhood" within the unit.

Even though the individual requirements that we set within the Raiders were much higher than those in the rest of the Battalion, it was also one of the easiest to get out of. All you had to do was quit and a transfer could be arranged to another Company in the Battalion. No one did! In fact, by the end of November 1967, there was a long list of people requesting transfers to the Raiders from other Companies, not only within the 2/501st but the rest of the Division. It was at this point that we "snared" one of the shining lights at Battalion Headquarters, 1st Lt. Cleo Hogan. Cleo had been banging on our door for several weeks. I needed an Executive Officer but I had a responsibility to my men to ensure they got the best, for the XO is just a heartbeat from Commanding the unit. As such to that point, I had not found someone I felt could do the job. Cleo more than measured up to the responsibility. Hell, he was born a Raider.

The Raiders were already starting to make a proud name for themselves, even while at Ft. Campbell. It's difficult to fully appreciate the esprit de corps that was now existing within the Raiders. A good example was SFC Hines, Platoon Sgt. 2nd Platoon. He was just over a year from having his 20 years in and he could have been excused from deploying with the unit, but Sgt. Hines was a Raider and wouldn't even entertain the thought of the unit deploying without him. That was pride! Even Corporal Joe Hooper was coming back from pass on time. (I'd have to give consideration to making him a Sgt. again).

It should be noted at this point that discipline within the rest of the Battalion was going through some rough times. Court martials and Article 15's were all too common an occurrence. I wouldn't say that a Raider never did any thing to warrant an Article 15 or worse, but having "been there," I knew that a soldier, even an excellent soldier, may sometimes stray a bit. I didn't like to "paper" anyone for something I felt was out of character. The first time, depending upon the infraction, would usually cop a severe warning. The second time, discipline of a more "restricting and physical" nature would result. Although discipline was usually handed out with the same severity as required under an Article 15, nothing was ever recorded at this point. It was just a "gentlemen's" agreement between Raiders. As such there was never an incidence of the third time.

In early December 1967 our training was over. Key equipment had already been shipped to Vietnam and an advance team deployed to assist with the arrival of the rest of the Company. On the 11th of December 1967, during a dark and wintery night, the Raiders moved out of their barracks and turned the lights off for the last time, assembled on the parade field and checked their individual weapons and equipment. Shortly thereafter we moved to the Airfield where two C-141s were waiting to airlift the entire unit directly to Vietnam. The Raiders were as ready as they could be. Their training had been more demanding than many had ever known. They had all come a long way in a very short time. They had all met the test. Christ, I was proud of every one of them. That pride was to increase even more over the coming period. Next stop, Vietnam.

On the 13th of December 1967 we landed at Bien Hoa, came off the aircraft with full basic load and three day's rations. We loaded into trucks and proceeded to our new home at Cu Chi in III Corps. Over the next few weeks the Raiders would get their first taste of combat and the life of a "grunt." Operations at that time were primarily around Cu Chi and the Hobo Woods area. It was during this time that the Raider Patch came into being.

I was seeing a lot of changes in the mood of our forces from that of the early injection of combat troops in 1965. We were beginning to become too "base camp bound." The Army in its effort to ensure that the "troops" got the best support available were in fact developing a "cancer" of dependence

that was robbing the soldier of his confidence, spirit and general self-esteem. Pride and esprit de corps were basically being discarded. Evidence of this was the increased use of subdued unit patches, all in the name of camouflage. It was like robbing a soldier of his soul, his identification, his respect. I was not going to let that happen to the Raiders. They had worked hard and deserved better. I discussed these things on several occasions with Scotty and he was of the same mind. So on Christmas Eve 1967, while having a quiet Christmas drink with Scotty, I drew a rough sketch of what was to be the Raider patch. It was to be a clear message to the enemy on the battlefield that this was a unit to be respected, and a clear message to everyone else that this was a unit with a special pride. For the men in the unit, it would be kept in the forefront of their minds, who they were and what they were: Raiders.

In early January we were on a joint operation with the 17th Cav. outside the Minh Tanh rubber plantation. I had promoted Joe Hooper to Sergeant and replaced him as my radio operator because every time the shooting started, he would drop his radio, leaving me with two to carry, and move directly into the action. So I promoted him and assigned him as a squad leader with the 1st Platoon under command of LT Lee Grimsley. I knew that Lee and his Platoon Sgt., George Parker, would appreciate the extra "help." This would later prove to be one of my better decisions. It was during this period that we received orders that we were to be extracted and redeployed up north.

Our new mission, as I understood it, was to redeploy to I Corps along with the rest of the Brigade and engage in combat operations designed to relieve some of the pressure on the Marines holed up in Khe Sanh. During this period the Marines were being hit pretty hard several times a day by 122 rocket fire from a large NVA force that had completely surrounded the camp. The only way in was by air. They were like bottled-up "rats." How could our leadership allow something like this to develop? Nonetheless, our mission was clear, or so I thought.

We flew by C-130 aircraft to Phu Bai, just outside of the old imperial capital of Hue. There we were lifted by chopper to the Brigade staging area located in a large ancient graveyard. It had a bad feeling about the place, but the many large concrete headstones and tombs offered excellent natural (or in this case unnatural) cover. The unit took its place in the Brigade perimeter and awaited its turn to be airlifted further north into combat.

Over the next few days, one by one the Companies of the Brigade were extracted. For those of us left, we would adjust the perimeter which was getting smaller and smaller. Up until this time our NDPs and patrols had received little contact. Then on January 30 things changed. We were down to only two Companies left in the Graveyard. The day started with the reports of several of our lift choppers being shot down while enroute to our position. Under normal circumstances we would have dispatched a patrol to the area, but we were starting to come under both mortar and sniper fire. It was clear that something big was happening. Radio communications were being jammed, and when you did get through, it was clear that things were becoming confused and critical. The situation at this time was that part of the Brigade was somewhere between Quang Tri and Khe Sanh. The Battalion Headquarters was located at a place called Camp Evans, about 25 miles north of the Graveyard and located halfway between Quang Tri and Hue. C and D Companies were on their own in the Graveyard.

The NVA's Tet offensive could not have been better timed as far as catching the Brigade all strung out. It was taking a big bite of I Corps. Everyone was being hit at the same time. Thus our ability to regroup quickly was greatly reduced. However, it was to prove too big of a bite for the enemy to digest.

Given the severity of the situation, as well as the poor defense our position provided should a large force engage us, the decision was made to try to reach the Marine Camp at Phu Bai. The airstrip there would provide a ready means for us to link up with the rest of the Battalion — that was, if any choppers were still flying. At least 12 were reported lost on the first day of the offensive within the local area.

The Raiders then performed one of many admired feats to come. Under constant sniper and mortar fire they led the way in a daylight withdrawal from the Graveyard, eight miles back through the mountains to the Camp at Phu Bai. The unit arrived in tact, no casualties and no equipment lost.

After arriving at Phu Bai, we set up our NDPs while I tried to arrange some sort of transport to Camp Evans where the rest of the Battalion was located. During the next 48 hours the unit was subjected to constant 122 Rocket fire. But once again our luck held and there were no major casualties. Finally we were able to get a Chinook helicopter driver from the 1st Cav. to ferry us to Camp Evans. There we joined the rest of the Battalion on February 2, 1968.

The situation was not good and I knew that soon the Raiders would have to face the ultimate test. I thought I'd learned during my previous tours how not to become too close to your men. Every casualty is a part of yourself and when one dies, a part of yourself dies with them. I had lost all of my classmates from Special Forces early in the war and had no close ties by the time I joined the Raiders. I had been determined not to let anyone or thing get too close, to tune out any feeling of emotion in order to maintain some form of sanity. It didn't work. By now the Raiders were a part of me and I of them. These initial fears were finally realized when our first major casualty occurred. While on patrol outside Camp Evans, PFC Brad (Gunship) Gagne "kicked" a mine and lost his leg. While it hurt that one of my men was so seriously injured, I knew it was not to be the last. However, that hurt was offset to some degree by the spirit shown in Gagne's parting request. Disregarding the seriousness of his wound, he made but one request as he was put on the medevac chopper: "Don't forget to forward my CIB and Raider patch." A Raider with class.

The next day we were moved to a small Vietnamese checkpoint called PK17, located just outside the city of Hue. 1st Platoon was positioned on the first highway bridge north of the city. Their mission was to keep this key bridge out of enemy hands. The 2nd and 3rd Platoons would run patrols south of PKl7 to intercept any reinforcements coming into Hue which by now was almost completely in enemy hands. Both the bridge and PK17 were hit on a nightly basis, but we were here to stay. On 14 February, the first Raider lost his life.

While on a sweep east of the bridge, Sp/4 Harold Begody, who was point man for the 1st Platoon, triggered an enemy ambush and was killed in the initial volley of fire. The fact that the Raiders were able to quickly overcome the enemy position without further loss was directly attributable to Sp/4 Begody's actions in forcing the enemy to prematurely launch their attack. He had learned his skills well. Rest well raider.

The next day, February 15, 1968, was to be the first major "trial by fire" for the unit. It would be where the brotherhood of the Raiders was truly forged. It was to be their first major action. It would not be their last.

Intelligence had reported the sighting of an enemy platoon moving towards Hue, just south of PK17. Our mission was to intercept that unit. The area south of PKl7 was open ricefields for about 1km. It then turned into heavy woods that offered good concealment. I left PK17 at first light with 2nd Platoon under the command of LT Dave Loftin and 3rd Platoon under the command of LT Bob Brulte. The Headquarters Section included LT Michael Watson, FO, Sp/4 Lawrence Marunchuck, RTO and myself. Total field strength was 56 men. It was shortly before 7 a.m. when the unit entered the woods. We were about 100 meters into the woods when LT Brulte notified me that Sgt. David Cash, who was on point, reported sighting several NVA regulars. LT Brulte and I moved forward to assess the situation. We were just short of Sgt. Cash's position when the unit came under extremely heavy fire. Sgt. Cash was hit immediately, but we could not tell how seriously. He was lying in a small clearing, and from our position, it was hard to tell if he was still alive. Nonetheless, we had no intention of leaving him. The 2nd Platoon came on line and we consolidated our position. I was soon concerned as to the steadily increasing volume of fire being received as well as the coverage. This was an awful large Platoon. LT Watson was instructed to call Artillery onto the enemy position. The first volley of rounds hit home but seemed to have little effect on what was fast becoming a major enemy assault. LT Watson then called for a second "fire for effect."

There are some things that are forever etched on one's mind — like the sound that a volley of rounds from a 105 Battery makes upon impact. It's a very distinct sound. The second "fire for effect" sounded different. In that moment, my fear was recognized. The first 5 rounds were on target, a split second delay, then the 6th round landed in the middle of the 3rd Platoon position. "Short round, cease fire." One of the rounds had "cooked off" and was slow and late coming out of the tube. It's one of the tragic things that sometimes happens in combat. It was unavoidable and no one was to blame. The results, however, were devastating: two killed, including LT Brulte, and eight wounded. Almost half of 3rd Platoon was now out of action, including all officer and key NCO positions.

By now the enemy fire was increasing and many of those wounded by the "short round" were now coming under direct enemy fire since they were unable to offer much resistance. An LZ was set up by Sgt. Clifford Sims to medevac out the wounded, but this was quickly under enemy fire. The unit was now completely surrounded. Later, intelligence reports would show that the "enemy platoon" that we were supposed to intercept would turn out to be the lead unit for a reinforced Battalion on its way into Hue. During the next few hours the Raiders were to prove that they were no longer the "bastard child" of the Battalion.

Our problem was two-fold: one, to hold our lines and two, to recover our wounded, now almost completely exposed to enemy attack. Two of our next casualties were as expected under the circumstances, our medics. With complete disregard for their own personal safety, Sp/4 David McKieghan and PFC Alex Spivey moved among the wounded, treating their wounds and were responsible for saving several lives. But this had its price. Exposed as they were, it was only a matter of time until they both themselves became casualties. But, in true Raider fashion, others carried on.

The difficulty continued to be the recovery of those wounded by the "short round." At about noon I received word that two Companies from the 1st Cav. had been deployed to the enemy's flank to try and relieve some of the pressure on our unit so that we could possibly break contact. Two hours later I received word that they had been withdrawn due to heavy enemy pressure and the fact that command did not want them to become decisively engaged at this time. We were once again on our own.

Our position was becoming difficult to defend against such a superior force and the Command at PK17 was recommending I withdraw and cut my losses. Any withdrawal at this time would have meant leaving behind several of our seriously wounded to the enemy. My reply was short and simple:

I refuse to leave any of my men on the battlefield. The decision was mine and mine alone, and I accept full responsibility for the fact we refused to retreat and the additional casualties that occurred as a result of that decision. They weren't just soldiers — they were family, they were Raiders. I had brought them here and I was damn well not going to abandoned them, wounded and dying, to the enemy.

During the next few hours the fighting continued at a heavy pace. The enemy continued to probe for weakness in our positions, but the Raiders held firm. LT Loftin along with Sgts. Washington and Gregory and PFC Miles, repeatedly exposing themselves to heavy enemy fire, provided critical cover for the recovery of our initial wounded. Sp/4 Flores temporarily became the "acting Platoon Leader for 3rd Platoon after LT Brulte was killed. He along with PFC Hendricks stayed on the radio and provided a critical link with 3rd Platoon while Platoon Sgt. James Deland moved among his men with encouragement and determination.

There were many acts of gallantry and courage on that day, but the courage displayed that day was not limited to just the men on the ground. It was also during this time that our ammo supply was becoming critical. I had requested a resupply earlier, but had been told that the LZ was too hot for them to get in. Fortunately it wasn't too hot for everyone.

From out of nowhere Scotty showed up with a chopper he had "highjacked" and under heavy enemy fire, brought us some badly needed ammo. Unconfirmed reports say he threatened to pull his "45" on an officer and pilot unless he flew him in. It was left unconfirmed. The important thing was that we got our resupply. As the aircraft came in unannounced, it was unable to touch down because of the volume of enemy fire. While Sgt. Sims and his men provided as much covering fire as possible, the aircraft made a short and nervous hover. Scotty kicked the ammo off and left with an aircraft that had several new holes in it and, I'm sure, a much relieved pilot.

Several times during the day the enemy tried to tighten the "noose" around our position, but the Raiders just dug in a little more. By 5 pm I was wondering how much longer we could hold. PFC Wade Thackrey, 3rd Platoon, had been killed and Sp/4s Billy Barnett and Gene "Raider Rob" Robertson wounded trying to recover one of their wounded comrades. PFC's Lorin Johnson, Glenn Williamson, James Jenkins, Sp/4 Kyle Tucker and SSgt. John Gingery continued to repeatedly brave heavy enemy fire in attempts to rescue our wounded. These were not isolated incidences but part of a continuing display of the gallantry and unselfish sacrifice shown for a fellow Raider and repeated several times during this, our "longest day."

It was shortly after 6 p.m. and it was starting to get dark when the last of our wounded were recovered. The last to be recovered was Sgt. Cash. He had died.

Enemy fire was starting to ease for the first time that day. We were able to clear a path through the enemy position and while LT Loflin and I, along with several members of 2nd Platoon, provided covering fire, LT Watson with the remaining members of the unit, and carrying our dead, moved out of the woods. The enemy tried to make one last assault on our position, but once again was beaten off with the loss of several soldiers. LT Loflin and I were the last to leave the woods. Once clear, LT Watson called in a heavy artillery barrage that finally silenced all enemy fire.

While the enemy killed was put at over 50 with an unknown number wounded, none of us cared too much about making a detailed body count or determining who killed whom. We left that to the Command at PK17. Too much emphasis was always being placed on body count during the war. I had always been taught that the final results of the battle were more important. The Raider's resolve and determination had been tested to the limit. They had withstood what another force of much greater size and strength could not. They had stood their ground against a much larger force and ended the battle with their honor intact. But it was not without its costs. In addition to those already noted, also wounded were Sp/4s Walker, Medina, and Rainwater from the 2nd Platoon, Sgts. Hacker and Hinz, 3rd Platoon, PFC Simmons, 3rd Platoon, and myself.

Nothing had been left on the battlefield for the enemy. Neither equipment nor, most importantly, a Raider. The Raiders had shown courage and compassion that would mark them forever as one of the most truly gallant units ever assembled. They, by their actions, had seriously damaged the combat effectiveness of a far superior enemy force. They were "bent," but they refused to break. For those enemy soldiers who may have gotten close enough to see our patch and survived, I'm sure the 101st Airborne and the Delta Raiders would not be quickly forgotten.

During the next two days we continued to patrol, but never again encountered a major force. Then on the 19th of February 1968, the Battalion was ready to make its assault into Hue. 1st Platoon was brought in from the An Lo bridge and LZ Sally was set up in the ricefields outside PK17 to receive the rest of the Battalion which arrived early in the morning. Later that day as we pushed through the same general area were the battle of the 15th took place, my luck ran out when an enemy sniper shattered my left knee. Moments later while trying to take the sniper out, I was again wounded, this time in the groin. A few minutes later the sniper was silenced. As I was being loaded onto the medevac chopper, I turned command of the Raiders over to LT Dave Loftin and requested that Cleo Hogan be put in command as soon as possible.

Because of the severity of my wounds I was medevaced out of the country. I then spent a month in a hospital in Japan, just down the hall from several other Raiders, including "Doc" Spivey. After getting "put back together," enough to be medevaced to the States, I was moved to the hospital at Fort Ord, California, for recovery. It was during this time that I received a letter from Cleo Hogan outlining the events that followed my departure. The actions of Joe Hooper and SSgt. Sims, the death of SSgt. Gregory and the wounding of LT Loftin. Most important, it outlined the continued gallantry by the unit as a whole. God, I loved them all!

After six months in hospital and several more months of recuperation, I volunteered for flight school, became a "Cobra Driver," and returned to Vietnam as commander of an Air Cav Troop in the 1/9 Cav., 1st Cavalry Div. It was to be my last tour of duty.

A lot of time has now passed since then. Over the years as I look back to that unfortunate time in our country's history and remember the times spent as an advisor with Omega Project during my early years to the time when I finished my last tour as a pilot, there is but one time held most special. A time when a group of men with diverse backgrounds and skills, of different races and character, came together as one. A time when a brotherhood was formed that would bind us always, one to another. A time that I was fortunate enough to share with the members of the Delta Raiders.

*Raider 6*

Footnote:
The spirit of the Raiders continues to this day. It was one of the last units to be withdrawn from Vietnam in 1972. In 1986 The Delta Raiders of Vietnam Association was formed. It has over one hundred former Raiders in its membership along with a large group of KIA family members. Among its many activities, the Association holds a reunion every two years to renew friendships and honor those Raiders "who gave their all."

# 3.

**Delta Raiders
Co. D. 2/501, 101st ABN. Div.**

# Historical Chronology
## December 13, 1967 – February 23, 1968

Delta Company of the 2/501 was reactivated as a combat unit at Ft. Campbell, Kentucky, on Oct. 1, 1967, under the command of Captain Charles W. McMenamy (Captain Mac). The Company, along with the 2nd and 3rd Brigades of the 101st Airborne Division (the 1st Brigade had been in Vietnam since 1965), was airlifted to Vietnam in December, 1967. The Division airmove (Operation Eagle Thrust) was the largest airlift of troops from the United States directly into a combat zone.

The Company, transported in C-141 Starlifter transports, landed in Bien Hoa, Vietnam on December 13, 1967. Although the entire Company that arrived in Vietnam was airborne qualified, it was never involved in an airborne operation. The Division operated as an airmobile infantry unit, similar to the 1st Cav. Division. The 101st Airborne Division was officially redesignated the 101st Airborne Division (Airmobile) on July 1, 1968. Beginning in early 1968 most replacement personnel assigned to the Company had the standard 11-B infantry MOS and were not airborne qualified.

Delta Company, along with the remainder of the 2/501 and the 2nd Brigade, was initially based at Cu Chi (30 miles northwest of Saigon) before moving north to Phu Bai in I Corps on Jan. 26, 1968. The Company departed Vietnam from Cam Ranh Bay on March 1 and 2, 1972.

The following chronology of events, spanning over four years in Vietnam, unfolds the proud and amazing story of the Delta Raiders — one of the most highly decorated combat units of the war. Most chronology entries are brief, while major engagements and situations are described in a more detailed narrative format. The chronology is primarily based on the records of the 101st ABN DIV located at the National Archives, as well as the personal input from numerous Delta veterans.

## Dec. 13-17, 1967

The 2-501 (including Co. D), along with the remainder of the 2nd BDE and the 3rd BDE, arrived at Bien Hoa. The battalion, along with the remainder of the 2nd BDE, moved from Bien Hoa to the Cu Chi base camp by truck convoy and initiated in-country training and "close in" patrols which continued into the month of January.

## Dec. 18, 1967

**0811H** Co. D located 3 tunnels at XT665172, XT685182, and XT663172. All tunnels appeared to be old with no signs of recent use.

## Dec. 29, 1967

**1400H** Co. D had 1 man medevaced for heat exhaustion.

## Dec. 30, 1967

**0200H** Co. D had 2 trip flares tripped by the enemy and at 0255H sighted movement to their front. The Company employed M-79 fire and grenades with unknown results.

## Jan. 1, 1968

2nd BDE remained at the Cu Chi base camp, with elements of the 2-501 (inc. Co. D) manning defensive positions in sector C of the base camp.

## Jan. 3, 1968

**1106H** (XT665237 - LZ Hook): Co. D and Recon Platoon CA'd from Cu Chi to LZ Hook, complete at 1111H. Mission: to conduct search and destroy operation in the area of Eagle Beak.

**1144H** (XT630196): Co. D reported finding a pit composed of green bamboo stakes, and at 1202H the Company reported locating a bunker at the same location. Results: all destroyed.

**2320H** A Co. D patrol reported sighting a sampan which was engaged by the element with M-79 and small arms fire.

## Jan. 4, 1968

**0510H** Co. D fired M-79 rounds at suspected movement to their front with unknown results.

**0950H** (XT666240): Co. D located 2 tunnels, 1 tunnel 3' in diameter and 1 tunnel 6' deep; with 3 more tunnels off the main one. Also located were 4 60mm mortar casings. The tunnels were destroyed with C-4.

**1005H** Co. D continued a search & destroy mission in AO Cobra.

**1255H** (XT668241): Co. D spotted and fired upon 2 VC floating down a river on a raft.

## Jan. 5, 1968
**0758H** (XT665236): 2-501 patrols (md. Co. D) returned from ambush sites and began air move to Cu Chi at 0830H, completed at 1128H.

## Jan. 10, 1968
Beginning at 1020H, the 2-501 (md. Co. D) CA'd from Cu Chi to LZ Whiskey (YT029170) for staging into multiple company ambushes in AO Uniontown. Co. D's ambush in position at 1845H, after CA from YT029170 to XT683114 (LZ Yellow).

## Jan. 15, 1968
**0845H** (XT733119): Co. D while working to the southeast located a sampan, 2 VC were reported still in the area.

**0920H** (XT708128): Recon Platoon located a hootch containing fresh food and fresh footprints leading from the hootch: Co. D investigated.

**1020H** (XT715126): 2-501 requested permission to go into 1-501 area since Co. D and Recon Platoon had 3 VC spotted, 2 possibly wounded by gunships. At 1027H Co. D also found knapsacks containing toilet articles and fatigues.

**1057H** (XT715126): Co. D and Recon Platoon found a cache of approximately 1900 lbs. of rice on a dike, and at 1107H Co. D discovered rocket pads at XT713127.

**1140H** Co. D(-) moved by air from their field location to Cu Chi base camp, complete at 1202H.

**1235H** (XT703114): Co. D(-) while moving to search 2 VC bodies (KIA by gunships) spotted 2 VC who were engaged by the element. Of the 2 VC bodies searched by Co. D(-), 1 was wearing black PJ's and the other in shorts with 1 good AK-47. Results: 4 VC KIA (2 by Co. D), 1 IWC

**1304H** Co. D(-) unable to locate the 2 VC engaged by the element at 1235H. Co. D(-) moved by air from their field location to Cu Chi base camp, closed at 1320H.

## Jan. 16, 1968
Co. D is designated as the Ready Reaction Force (RRF) at Cu Chi.

## Jan. 18, 1968
2-501 (Co's A, C, & D) were given the mission to Cordon and Search Tan Hoa (XT695145). Co. A departed Chu Chi at 171759H to secure the road

from the base camp to XT687145. Co's C and D moved by road to that location beginning at 0030H, with all units in position at 0325H. The battalion commenced a search of the village at 0730H, finishing at 1150H. The search resulted in 23 detainees turned over to the Province HQ). The 2-501 then returned to Cu Chi base camp and resumed its role as the BDE Reaction Force.

## Jan. 19, 1968

**1937H-1945H** (XT6615): 2d BDE received approximately 12 rounds of 75mm recoilless rifle fire. Arty was employed. A Co. D ambush patrol detected gun positions that fired on the base camp at 1937H. FAC 2-501 also detected the same positions, artillery was adjusted. Results: 3 US KIA, 6 US WIA (none from Co. D), enemy casualties unknown.

**2150H** Co. D ambush patrols located at following locations: 1/D XT644177, 2/D XT634177, 3/D XT628169.

## Jan. 21, 1968

2d BDE departed the Cu Chi base camp in support of Div. OPORD 3-68 (Operation Casey); a mission to conduct search and destroy operations in AO Attala, to locate and destroy the 165th VC Regt.

## Jan. 22, 1968

**1845H** Co. D requested a dustoff for 1 man with a severe allergy case, medevac complete at 1902H.

**2325H** (XT728635): Co. D received 1 round of 60mm mortar fire with negative casualties.

## Jan. 23, 1968

**0915H** (XT728638): Co. D located a camp site used by 2 or 3 personnel. A search of the area was made with negative results. At 1005H Co. D followed the forward battalion element 600m north of PL Green (XT729642), and was held up between 1145H and 1233H as a tank lost a track, which was repaired.

**1310H** Co. D heard automatic weapons fire in the vicinity of XT702662, arty was employed into the area. At 1315H Co. D found 3 pressure-type antipersonnel mines at XT734667, which were destroyed in place.

## Jan. 24, 1968

2-501 (including Co. D returned to Cu Chi by air and road during the afternoon to re-equip in preparation for the move to Phu Bai in I Corps.

## Jan. 26, 1968
2d BDE moved by air at 1305 to Phu Bai airfield to participate in Operation JEB STUART under the OPCON of the 1st Air Cav. Div. Co. D closed at the Phu Bai airfield at 1415H. The Company was then air lifted to a Brigade staging area located in a large cemetery, approximately 3 miles from Phu Bai.

## Jan. 27, 1968
**1340H** Co. D completed exchange with 1-5 Cav. as the 2-501 assumed security of LZ El Paso (YD810154).

**2230H** Co. D heard movement to their right front. A trip flare was activated and M-79 fire employed. Negative contact reported.

## Jan. 28, 1968
**1000H** The Arty FO with Co. D observed an unknown number of personnel carrying weapons in the vicinity of YD799143 and requested fire on that location.

**1255H** (YD805147): In Co. D's area, the D/1/44 Arty duster detonated a pressure-type mine, resulting in minor damage to the vehicle (the track and 1 road wheel blown off) and creating a crater 2' wide and 1' deep. Results: 4 US WIA (not serious), dustoff completed.

**1557H** (YD807149): Co. D located and detonated an 81mm dud mortar round.

## Jan. 29, 1968
**1730H** Co. D received sniper fire from 1 person believed to be at YD808157. Arty was adjusted in, with mission complete at 1758H. Jan. 30, 1968 1540H Co. D observed 2 personnel at YD803153 who upon seeing the unit walked away over a hill. The Company sent out a patrol to investigate with negative results.

## Jan. 31, 1968
**0345H-0425H** LZ El Paso was under mortar attack, receiving 50 60mm mortar rounds. B/326 Med reported receiving 4 KIA and 9 WIA. Mortar fire came from YD790176, with arty employed on that location.

**1425H** (YD787145): Co. D found and evacuated 11 82mm mortar rounds.

## Feb. 1, 1968
BN CP located at LZ El Paso.

**0540H** 2/D received sniper fire from their left flank. The platoon returned automatic weapons fire with negative results. At 0904H (YD811147) Co.

D found 1 wounded VC who had apparently been firing at them earlier, but he died before he could be questioned. Results: 1 VC KIA.

## Feb. 3, 1968
1540H (Phu Bai airfield): Co. D(-) moved by CH-47s to Camp Evans, one of the last companies in the battalion to move.

## Feb. 4, 1968
BN CP located at Camp Evans. Co. D(-) and Co. B assumed perimeter defense of Camp Evans. The weather was foggy, rainy, and damp.
2430H 2-501 became OPCON to the 1st Air Cav. Div.

## Feb. 5, 1968
0900H (Phu Bai airfield): The remainder of Co. D moved by CH-47 to Camo Evans.
1130H Co. D reported finding an unknown type dud round.

## Feb. 6, 1968
1440H Co. D spotted several suspected enemy, one of whom was thought to be carrying a weapon. One of the suspects ran away into nearby hootches.

## Feb. 7, 1968
0920H (YD557333): Co. D suffered 1 WIA when a man stepped on a boobytrapped anti-personnel mine while on patrol outside of Camp Evans; medevac completed 0949H. Results: 1 US WIA (E: Bradford Gagne, the first combat casualty of Delta Company in Vietnam). The site of the boobytrap was near the same location that 2 arty fire for effect missions were fired on huts. A secondary explosion occurred near the site of the rounds impacting.
1605H (YD567338): A search of the area revealed 5 mortar positions and 8-9 two man positions, with some completed and some still in preparatory stages. Also observed were 5 individuals fleeing south, who were engaged with small arms fire, with negative results. In the same area the Company discovered a stream capable of handling sampan traffic. Drag tracks were also discovered near the stream; it appeared that something had been dragged along two paths toward the positions found earlier.
1630H Near the above stream, Co. D found fuse cans, cover plugs (82mm), and empty boxes that housed mortar rounds; the Company also observed one male fleeing south toward the railroad tracks, and in the same location found 18 spider holes and 4 mortar positions.

## Feb. 9, 1968

**1350H** (YD547295): Co. D found ruins of houses 1 old bomb without fuse, and 1 155 shell without a fuse.

**2300H** (YD550282): Co. D spotted 4 suspected VC, 2 wearing light colored shirts and 2 wearing dark colored shirts. Arty called in the location.

## Feb. 10, 1968

Camp Evans Co. D improved defensive positions along their sector the defense perimeter.

## Feb. 11, 1968

**0300H** (YD543302): Co. D received sniper fire from suspected location YD541298. The area was checked out with negative results.

## Feb. 12, 1968

**0100H** 2-501 became OPCON to the 3rd BDE, 1st Air Cav. Div. Co. D moved from Camp Evans to PK 17 (YD649280). 1/D secured the Lo Bridge (YD623304), while the remainder of the Company provided base security at PK 17.

## Feb. 13, 1968

**0600H** While sweeping through a village near PK 17, Co. D(-1/D) engaged an enemy force, resulting in 1 VC KIA and several maintainees, mostly children and one old man. BDE scouts had pinned down the enemy while Delta Company moved into the village. The area, which had many tunnels, was sealed off and searched by Company. The Company captured 3 Ml Garand rifles, 5 carbines and assorted items of equipment.

**1530H** Co. D requested a medevac for 1 man who was wounded by a boobytrap. Results: 1 US WIA (E: Frank H. Wingo).

## Feb. 14, 1968

**1520H** (YD633312): Co. D received small arms fire, machine gun fire M-79 fire from an estimated VC Platoon from YD635316. Gunships were requested. At 1530H Co. D reported they were still receiving sniper fire from the trees, and requested ETA on gunships.

**1615H** (YD633312): Co. D indicated that the area where enemy fire came from was beyond their limits of march. Asked whether they could continue or return to their location of the previous night. 1655H Co. D had moved back, about 500m from the bridge. Results of contact: 1 US KIA (Harold L. Begody - first Co. D man killed in action in Vietnam), the KIA was picked up from the Company by log bird at the An Lo Bridge; 1 US WIA; captured 5 M1 carbines, 3 M1 rifles, 60 30cal rounds, 12 mm mortar rounds, and 4 BAR magazines.

## Feb. 15, 1968

Co. D (- 1/D) had the mission of proceeding from PK 17 (vic. 645285) to conduct a Search and Destroy operation with an objective in the area of YD650252. At 0903H Co. D was located at 648270 and reported finding freshly dug positions in the Company. They moved overland from the east toward the enemy position; upon reaching the enemy position the two companies came under heavy enemy fire and were withdrawn at approximately 1500H, since the BDE did not want the companies to become decisively engaged. After contact was finally broken at 1730H, Co. D was ordered to return to PK 17.

Delta Company suffered a total of 6 KIAs (Robert Francis Brulte, 3rd Platoon Leader, David Manfred Cash, Ernest Paul Holmes, Wade E. Thackrey, Jr., Emanuel Fero Burroughs, and Henry Marsial Tabet); 17 serious WIAs that were evacuated (Michael Kopay, Billy Barnett, Bernard Hacker, William J. Hinz, Julio D. Medina, Robert Rainwater, Eugene Robertson, Kurtland Walker, Joe W. Dunlap, Ronald Hendricks, David McKieghan, Alex D. "Doc" Spivey, John W. Wheat, Dennis C. Simmons, Barry Rainey, Glen Pechacek, and Robert A. Gould); and 5 minor WIAs that were not evacuated (Lester Heiserman, James Jenkins, Richard Ryan, and Captain Charles McMenamy).

The total NVA body count was 56; 8 killed by Co. D, 24 by ARA, 22 by arty, and 2 by 5/7 Cav.

## Feb. 16, 1968

Co. D continued to provide security for PK 17, with one platoon providing security at the An Lo Bridge.

## Feb. 17, 1968

1008H (YD662268): Co. D, about 1-1.5 clicks from PK 17, found ten 25 lb. bags of rice and 15 100 lb. bags of rice; also found were some manuals on mines and some maps. The element found all of this inside of the hootches in the area. The element continued to search the area with negative results.

## Feb. 18, 1968

1645H Co. D reports locating a dud 82mm mortar round in front of their CP.

## Feb. 19, 1968

Companies A and C moved by CH-47 from Camp Evans to LZ Sally while Co. D moved overland to secure the LZ. Co. B remained at the An Lo Bridge for security. The 2-501 completed movement to LZ Sally (YD636285) at 1330H. The battalion then moved to attack an objective, vic YD650250, with the mission of clearing all approaches into Hue from the northwest in conjunction with the 5-7 and 2-12 Cav. The objective was to be prepared with arty fires and an airstrike.

**1500H** (YD645250): Moving southeast, Companies A and C followed by Co. D engaged an estimated enemy reinforced company. The enemy allowed Companies A and C to pass, then engaged Co. D and the BN CP with heavy weapons fire. The enemy, wearing khaki uniforms, was dug in their positions. The engagement was broken at 1730H. Results: 5 US KIA,16 US WIA ( including Captain Charles McMenamy, who was wounded in the leg), 4 US WIA (M), 17 NVA KIA, 1 RPG MG captured.

## Feb. 20, 1968

**1100H** 1LT Cleo C. Hogan, Jr. assumed command of Delta Company, succeeding Captain McMenamy who was wounded the day before.

**1225H** (YD642238): Co. D engaged 1 enemy who was shooting an AK-47 at a C-130: negative results.

**1430H** (YD652246): Co. D engaged a platoon size enemy force. They received fire from 2 automatic weapons; negative assessment.

## Feb. 21, 1968

The 2-501 continued search and destroy operations southeast of LZ Sally with Companies C and D moving toward Hue from the northwest and west with Co. A in reserve, while Co. B acted as a reaction force and secured LZ Sally.

It was on this day that two Delta Raiders (SSgt Joe R. Hooper and SSgt Clifford C. Sims) earned the Congressional Medal of Honor in two separate actions for "conspicuous gallantry and intrepidity in action at the risk of his life above and beyond the call of duty," and one Delta Raider (Sgt Dale A. Urban) earned the Distinguished Service Cross for "extraordinary heroism" in the much of the same action as Hooper.

At 1000H Co. D began to find articles that had apparently been discarded by the NVA, and located an area where an estimated 100 NVA had recently spent the night. At 1330H Delta Company crossed a rice patty along a small stream, with Co. C to their left. As the Company approached the stream or river they encountered a withering hail of fire from rockets, machine guns and automatic weapons from a series of bunkers lining the opposite shore. The barrage caused the company to halt and take cover. SSgt Joe R. Hooper (a squad leader in 1st Platoon) and Sgt Dale Urban (a team leader in Hooper's squad) rallied several men and stormed across the river through chest-deep water, overrunning several bunkers on the opposite shore. Inspired by the move, the rest of 1st Platoon along with 3rd Platoon (on the right flank) moved to the attack and assaulted a heavily fortified enemy position concealed within a dense wooded area. As the two platoons advanced deeper into the dense woods, the hostile fire increased from the strategically placed bunkers and fortified villages. The deadly cross fires again caused men to falter and take cover as the casualties mounted. The 2nd Platoon, which had been in reserve, then advanced filling in the position between the 1st and 3rd Platoons. SSgt Clifford Sims, a squad leader in 2nd Platoon, led his squad in a furious attack against the enemy force which had pinned down 1st Platoon, providing the platoon with freedom of movement and enabling it to regain the initiative.

With utter disregard for his own safety, SSgt Hooper moved out under intense fire again and pulled back the wounded, moving them to safety. During this act Hooper was seriously wounded, but he refused medical aid and returned to his men. With the relentless enemy fire disrupting the attack, Hooper and Urban assaulted several enemy bunkers, destroying them with hand grenade and rifle fire, and Hooper shot 2 enemy soldiers who had attacked and wounded the Battalion Chaplain (CPT William W. Erbach). Leading his men forward in a sweep of the area, Hooper destroyed 3 buildings housing enemy riflemen. At this point he was attacked by a NVA officer whom he fatally wounded with his bayonet. Finding his men under heavy fire from a house to the front, he proceeded alone to the building, killing its occupants with rifle fire and grenades. By now his initial body wound had been compounded by grenade fragments, yet despite the multiple wounds and loss of blood, he continued to lead his men against the intense enemy fire.

As Hooper's squad reached the final line of enemy resistance, it received devastating fire from 4 bunkers in line on its left flank. SSgt Hooper and Sgt Urban gathered several hand grenades and raced down a small trench which ran the length of the bunker line, tossing grenades into each bunker as they passed by, killing all but 2 of the occupants who were captured. With these positions destroyed, they concentrated on the last bunker facing their men, destroying the first with an incendiary grenade and neutralizing 2 more by rifle fire. Hooper then raced across an open field, still under enemy fire, to rescue a wounded man (Tex W. Gray) who was trapped in a trench. Upon reaching the man, he was faced by an armed enemy soldier whom he killed with a pistol that had been tossed to him just moments before by SSgt Lonnie Thomas (another squad leader in 1st Platoon). After moving Tex Gray to safety and returning to his men, Hooper and Urban neutralized the final pocket of enemy resistance by fatally wounding with rifle fire 3 NVA officers, located in high brush 30 meters to their front. SSgt Hooper then established a final line and reorganized his men, not accepting medical treatment until this was accomplished and not consenting to evacuation until the following morning.

After leading the assault to relieve the pressure on 1st Platoon, SSgt Sims was ordered to move his squad to a position where he could provide covering fire for the company command group and to link up with the 3rd Platoon, which was under heavy enemy pressure.

After moving no more than 30 meters SSgt Sims noticed that a brick structure in which ammunition was stocked was on fire. Realizing the danger, Sims took immediate action to move his squad from this position. Though in the process of leaving the area two members of his squad were injured by the subsequent explosion of the ammunition, Sims' prompt actions undoubtedly prevented more serious casualties from occurring. While continuing through the dense woods amidst heavy enemy fire, SSgt Sims and his squad were approaching a bunker when they heard the unmistakable noise of a concealed boobytrap being triggered immediately to their front. Sims warned his men of the danger and unhesitatingly hurled himself upon the device as it exploded, taking the full impact of the blast. In so protecting his fellow soldiers, he willingly sacrificed his life.

During the heat of the battle Charlie Company maneuvered through the woods on Co. D's left and fired on NVA coming out of the woods. Near the end of the battle the BN CO (LTC Tallman) attached Recon Platoon to Co. D, which relieved some of the pressure on the 3rd Platoon (right flank) side. Results of the contact: 1 US KIA (Clifford Chester Sims, who received the Congressional Medal of Honor); 22 US WIA (Hubert L. Davis, James B. Bowman, John B. Gingery, James L. Martin, James Calhoun, Jody Gravett, Tex W. Gray, David R. Leaf, Alfred M. Mount, James C. Rachell, Thomas A. Hopkins, Ava A. James, Thomas Miles, Noah N. Rockel, Davis Wallace, Frankie Gains, Victor A. Holmes, Joe R. Hooper (evac on the 22nd), Lonnie Thomas, Ernest McManus, Samuel Ayala, and Henrie L. Delaney); 24 NVA KIA.

**1700H** (YD693226): Co. D captured 1 Chicom 2 watt radio type 71B (5N55-05302) and documents which were evacuated.

## Feb. 22, 1968

After the battle of the day before Delta Company was placed in reserve so it could reorganize. Co. C began a sweep of the area of yesterdays contact and encountered heavy resistance. Companies A and B were committed into the area. Results: 6 US KIA (none from Co. D), 30 US WIA, 43 NVA KIA (24 by Co. D).

**2225H** Co. D from their perimeter engaged 7 enemy at approximately 75m with small arms fire. Results: 2 NVA KIA.

## Feb. 23, 1968

**0700H** Companies A, B, and D of 2-501 attacked to the south against light to moderate enemy resistance, then turned east and attacked Hue on the south flank of 2-12 Cav. During the sweep Delta Company encountered a lot of abandoned NVA equipment and supplies. They also found, to their surprise, evidence of a brutal massacre of 30 Vietnamese civilians who had apparently been held by the NVA. Apparently before the NVA left, they shot each of the civilians one time in the head.

**1305H** The 2-501 received several mortar rounds from YD710221 resulting in 2 WIA for Co. D.

**1400H** Captain Cleo Hogan (Co. D CO) captured a NVA hiding under some roots of an uprooted tree along a river.

**1600H** Co. D located at YD709230, along with the BN CP, Companies A and C.

# 4.
# 21 February 1968
# Day of Infamy

## Cleo Hogan

I was awakened at 0600 hrs and after a quick check of the perimeter of Company D, I went to a concrete block building to meet with the other Company commanders and the battalion commander. The order for the day was D Company on the right and C Company on the left, followed by Battalion Headquarters and Company A providing rear security. The Battalion, as part of a multi-battalion force, was to move southeast to the vicinity of 705200, the north bank of the Song Huong River.

As the Company moved out, we began to find evidence of a large North Vietnamese force having been in the area in the past 24 to 36 hours. Evidence included discarded equipment, such as blankets, rifle clips, helmets, ammunition container and some uniforms. At 1000 hrs members of Company D found where at least 100 North Vietnamese had spent the night. The estimate was based upon sleeping positions, discarded personal items and trampled vegetation. Shortly thereafter, members found two large cooking fires with pots of rice. The fires had been extinguished, but the rice was still warm. It was evident that the North Vietnamese had been there earlier this same morning. I informed LTC Tallman of the items found and was advised to proceed with caution, keep the point element well in front and be prepared for a North Vietnamese ambush or delaying action.

At 1100 hrs Company D broke out of the woods in the vicinity of the SHOE LAKE (670235) and proceeded south to the Khe Soi River. I directed 2LT Bischoff to find a place where the Company could cross the river. 2LT Bischoff turned east along the river for approximately 500 meters and then entered the wood line and found a place that the Company could cross in the vicinity of 684232. As the Company entered the wood line, more enemy items were discovered and it was evident that the Raiders were very close to the enemy. LTC Tallman halted the Battalion, order the Companies to form a defensive position and summoned the Company commanders to his location. LTC Tallman stated that Chaplain Erbach (the Battalion chaplain) was in route to the Company D location to talk to anyone who wished to talk with him. Chaplain Erbach initially visited in the 1st Platoon area and then proceeded to the 3rd Platoon area. At the briefing, I was advised that intelligence had information of the presence of the North Vietnamese 90th Regiment in the area and would likely fight a delaying action while most of its units moved into the city of HUE, and the mountain area to the west. LTC Tallman stated that the Battalion would likely remain here overnight while more intelligence was evaluated and a final plan was formulated and coordinated with other units on our left. At 1315 hrs, while the men were still eating C Rations, changing socks, writing letters home, and doing all the things soldiers do each time they stop. I received the order to move out of the wood line at 1330 hrs and proceed to the vicinity of 705200. Company D moved out with 3rd Platoon on the right and 1st Platoon on the left. As the point and lead element of 1st Platoon reached the vicinity of 685223, a soldier in the center of the lead element was thrown backwards violently and was floundering around in the rice paddy. I halted the Company and reported to HQ that a member of 1st Platoon was having a seizure. Upon reaching the man, it was clear that he had a gunshot wound to the left shoulder above the heart, with the bullet exiting his back just below the shoulder blade. As I requested a Medivac for the wounded man, Battalion Headquarters asked the whereabouts of Chaplain Erbach. I stated that he was still with 3rd Platoon. With the evacuation of the wounded man complete, the Company began moving again. The 1st and 3rd Platoons had only gone about 150 meters when a tremendous volley of gunfire was directed at Company D from the vicinity of 693228. 1st and 3rd Platoons were in an open rice paddy and immediately moved to find cover among some grave mounds some 200 meters to the East. The Company was ordered to attack toward the village to the East. I asked what I should do with Chaplain Erbach since he was still with 3rd Platoon and would not be in an attack. I was informed that Chaplain Erbach would have to stay with Company D until he could be brought back to Battalion Headquarters. Just as 1st and 3rd Platoons began the attack, heavy volumes of fire prohibited Chaplain Erbach from returning and he was forced to go in the attack with 3rd Platoon.

    The attack route was mostly open rice paddy with a few small grave mounds. 3rd Platoon supported while 1st Platoon maneuvered toward the wood line. As 1st Platoon crossed the rice paddy, it appeared as though every tree in the wood line 300 meters to the east was firing at Company D. Under tremendous fire, members of 1st and 3rd Platoons charged across the rice paddy and crossed the waist deep stream (693226) and disappeared into the wood line. I moved Company Headquarters and 2nd Platoon (under the command of 2LT Dave Loftin), to the grave mounds vicinity of

'689227. Heavy volumes of automatic weapons fire was coming from the vicinity of a building with a red roof (693229). As I evaluated the situation and reported to Battalion HQ, PSG Parker reported that the wood line was filled with North Vietnamese in well-concealed, well-fortified positions. PSG Parker estimated that his element was up against a much larger force and stated that heavy equipment and cases of ammunition were everywhere, just inside the wood line. I advised LTC Tallman and was ordered to continue the attack. He stated that Company C, on my left, had advanced into the woods and had not encountered any enemy in their sector. Within minutes contact with 2LT Grimsley and PSG Delany had ceased and I no longer could reach either of them. 2LT Bischoff on the right flank reported that he was pinned down in the vicinity of a pink pagoda vicinity 694226. Not being able to communicate with 2LT Grimsley, I contacted PSG Parker and directed him to take action to neutralize the machine guns in the vicinity of the building with the red roof. LTC Tallman, who had been listening to the conversation, stated that an air rocket artillery gunship was overhead and gave me the call sign and frequency of the ARA. I requested that the ARA take out the building with the red roof, to which the pilot reported that he could see 50 buildings with red roofs, which one did I want taken out. Realizing that he might not see the humor, I quickly gave him a magnetic heading from a yellow smoke grenade, a distance, and asked him to fire a marker round to which I could adjust his fire. His first round was on target and only missed the main area by perhaps 25 meters. After firing an additional 10 or 12 rockets, all fire from the building with the red roof ceased. I thanked him for a job well done and left his radio frequency.

Extremely heavy volumes of small arms fire continued from the area around 693226. Much of the fire was still directed at the Company Headquarters and was impacting in the rice paddy in the vicinity of 2nd Platoon. Within 30 minutes communication with everyone except 2LT Bischoff had been lost. Realizing that I had to find out what was going on inside the wood line, I advised members of Headquarters element to spread out, charge toward the wood line, ford the small stream and assemble across the stream, in the vicinity of the archway at 693228. As 2LT Watson (artillery forward observer) Sgt. Bohn (Company interpreter) and the six other members of the headquarters element charged across the rice paddy, a heavy volume of automatic weapons fire was directed at them in the rice paddy. As the men and myself reached the small stream, the lower elevation afforded excellent cover as the bullets were passing well over our heads. I pointed out the archway and directed the men to follow me through the archway and take cover. As I entered the archway, I immediately noticed the trench line and bunker system along the wood line and took cover among some fallen bamboo trees some 25 meters inside the wood line, to the left of the foot path leading from the archway. While waiting for the other members of the Headquarters element to reach my position, I could see massive amounts of North Vietnamese supplies and equipment in the immediate area. It took about 15 minutes for everyone to reach my location, and when the RTO reached my location, LTC Tallman was waiting for an assessment of the situation. I gave a very bleak and dismal preliminary report. I told LTC Tallman of the tremendous amount of equipment, and that at least a half dozen North Vietnamese bodies were just inside the tree line. I told him there was tremendous fire some 50 meters to my front, and that I had lost contact with everyone except my 3rd Platoon. I told him that the village was thick bamboo, banana plants and thick vegetation. The heavy firepower, and well-developed trench bunker system gave rise to speculation that major portions of 1st and 3rd Platoons may have been wiped out. It was about this time that I confided in 2LT Watson that D Company may well end up like Custer at the Little Big Horn. Members of HQ element crawled 25 to 30 meters forward but could not make voice contact with any other members of D Company. Fearing that the HQ element might now be alone, and knowing that I had to find out what had happened to 3rd Platoon, I directed 2LT Loftin to send me one element (a squad) to join the HQ element inside the wood line. As the battle continued to rage, PSG Parker appeared on the left. Relieved to see anyone from 1st Platoon, I asked for an assessment of his area. PSG Parker stated that he had about two or three men slightly wounded, none serious, and that everyone needed ammo. He reported that his radio and 2LT Grimsley had both been knocked out and would not work. I asked if 2nd and 3rd Platoons were still linked but he did not know. The members of HQ element gave PSG Parker all the ammo they had and PSG Parker disappeared back into the thick bamboo. Just then Sgt Joe Hooper appeared on the left half carrying a severely wounded man and asking where he could take him for evacuation. Behind Sgt Hooper was two other less seriously wounded but requiring evacuation. I reported the wounded to Bn HQ and directed Sgt Hooper to the grave area where 2LT Loftin was handling the medivac. I directed Sgt Hooper to take the men back and bring all the ammo that he could carry on his return. Just as Sgt Hooper left, SSG Sims and his 10 men came running into the area, each carrying large quantities of ammo.

    Sgt Hooper showed the men where to go, gathered all the ammo he could carry, and disappeared into the thick vegetation. SSG Sims asked what I wanted him to do, and I asked him to take his men and see if he could find any members of 3rd Platoon on the right. AS SSG Sims moved across the foot path to the right, he noticed that a concrete block building some 35 meters across the trail had caught fire and was burning. SSG Sims looked inside and yelled that it was full of mortar ammo and was likely to

explode. Sims quickly moved his men to the left, and began receiving fire from a bunker 25 to 30 meters to our front. As SSG Sims began to maneuver against the enemy soldier, a loud pop indicated that a hand grenade exploded, lifting SSG Sims' body 3 or more feet into the air. The enemy soldier fired again and a member of Sims, squad killed him. I rolled SSG Sims over and discovered that major portions of his lower body had been blown away. He was alive, bleeding badly, but not conscious. Four of his men carried him back to the grave area and he was evacuated.

All this time a fierce battle was also raging on the right flank in the vicinity of the pink pagoda. 2LT Bischoff reported that his unit was still pinned down and that the Chaplain, CPT Erbach, had been wounded and had to be evacuated. He also reported that three other men had been evacuated. I ordered 2LT Bischoff to rally his men and continue the attack to the 1st Platoon or Sims' squad. At this point, I was very much afraid that a gap had developed in the center of the Company between 1st and 3rd Platoons, and that the North Vietnamese were concentrating in this area.

About this time, LTC Tallman asked if I could use the Recon Platoon (commanded by 1LT Ken Buch). I stated affirmatively and 1LT Bush came up on my command net. He stated that he was 400 meters south of the grave area where the medivac choppers were landing. I asked if he could see the pink pagoda across the small stream (693226). I directed 1LT Bush to flank the pagoda and attack north until making contact with 3rd Platoon of D Company. 1 LT Bush acknowledged and stated that he was now moving to the objective area east of the pink pagoda.

Just as I had finished directing Recon Platoon, CPT Denny Gillem (Commander of Company C) came up on the BN net and told me to keep pushing through the village and that the North Vietnamese were attempting to flee east across the rice paddy. Members of Company C were picking them off as they attempted to run across the open rice paddy. After a dozen or more North Vietnamese had tried to cross the open area, the remainders decided to fight it out with Company D in the thick village.

Suddenly once again Sgt Hooper showed up at my position, again carrying a wounded and requesting additional ammo. Sgt Hooper seemed to be everywhere. He was charging bunkers, throwing grenades and generally inspiring all the men around him. Sgt Hooper had the best assessment of the situation and I relayed to LTC Tallman that D Company likely had 1 killed (SSG Sims) and perhaps as many as 20 wounded and evacuated, but that the situation was not as dire as first reported and that the Company was continuing the attack to the east. By now the fighting was at 15 to 20 meters with North Vietnamese in the trenches and bunkers and members of Company D crawling and assaulting their positions. Company C continued to envelop the enemy from the rear, and by now Recon Platoon was attacking from the right flank in front of 3rd Platoon. The battle was virtually hand to hand for nearly an hour and then Recon Platoon found the North Vietnamese trench line where the enemy had concentrated and attacked them from the right flank, wiping out the last of the resistance. As 1LT Bush reached my position, 1st Platoon had broken out of the village to the east and linked up with Company C. 3rd Platoon had linked with 1st Platoon and the Company minus 2nd Platoon had made it through the village, and the major part of the battle was over.

LTC Tallman then directed Company C, Company D and Recon Platoon and the following had been wounded: Hubert Davis, James Bowman, John Gingery, James Martin, James Calhoun, Jody Gravett, Tex Gray, David Leaf, Alfred Mount, James Rachell, Thomas Hopkins, Ava James, Thomas Miles, Noah Rockel, Davis Wallace, Frankie Gaines, Victor Holmes, Joe Hooper, and Henrie Delaney.

In just a little over three hours, Company D had over ran a major North Vietnamese Headquarters unit, captured several chicom radios with supporting documents and began to rebuild the unit esprit de corps which had been so evident only one week earlier. This victory had restored the confidence of Company D, and I was proud to be their commander. Little did we know that the final results of this battle would be two Medal of Honors, SSG Sims and Sgt Hooper, one Distinguished Service Cross, Sgt Dale Urban, and several other awards for valor.

LTC Tallman decided to encircle the battle area with Company C on the North, Company D on the East and South and Company A on the West. Company B would provide security for Battalion Hq in the north portion of the village. During the night a few North Vietnamese who had hid in the village fired a few rounds and almost started a fire fight between members of Company A and Company D. As Company A returned fire, the rounds were impacting in the Company D area causing members of Company D to think they were under attack and return fire which would impact in the Company A area causing them to again return fire. I ordered everyone to stop firing unless they had a definite visible target and the firing from both companies stopped. The night was relatively quiet but everyone was so tense that no one slept. The cold damp air made for a miserable night.

# 5.
# Congressional Medals of Honor

*The President of the United States*

*in the name of*

*The Congress*

*takes pleasure in presenting the*

*Medal of Honor*

*to*

## JOE R. HOOPER

Citation: For conspicuous gallantry and intrepidity in action at the risk of his life above and beyond the call of duty. Staff Sergeant (then Sgt.) Hooper, U.S. Army, distinguished himself while serving as squad leader with Company D. Company D was assaulting a heavily defended enemy position along a river bank when it encountered a withering hail of fire from rockets, machine guns and automatic weapons. S/Sgt. Hooper rallied several men and stormed across the river, overrunning several bunkers on the opposite shore. Thus inspired, the rest of the company moved to the attack. With utter disregard for his own safety, he moved out under the intense fire again and pulled back the wounded, moving them to safety. During this act S/Sgt.

Hooper was seriously wounded, but he refused medical aid and returned to his men. With the relentless enemy fire disrupting the attack, he singlehandedly stormed 3 enemy bunkers, destroying them with handgrenade and rifle fire, and shot 2 enemy soldiers who had attacked and wounded the Chaplain. Leading his men forward in a sweep of the area, S/Sgt. Hooper destroyed 3 buildings housing enemy riflemen. At this point he was attacked by a North Vietnamese officer whom he fatally wounded with his bayonet. Finding his men under heavy fire from a house to the front, he proceeded alone to the building, killing its occupants with rifle fire and grenades. By now his initial body wound had been compounded by grenade fragments, yet despite the multiple wounds and loss of blood, he continued to lead his men against the intense enemy fire. As his squad reached the final line of enemy resistance, it received devastating fire from 4 bunkers in line on its left flank. S/Sgt. Hooper gathered several handgrenades and raced down a small trench which ran the length of the bunker line, tossing grenades into each bunker as he passed by, killing all but 2 of the occupants. With these positions destroyed he concentrated on the last bunkers facing his men, destroying the first with an incendiary grenade and neutralizing 2 more by rifle fire. He then raced across an open field, still under enemy fire, to rescue a wounded man who was trapped in a trench. Upon reaching the man, he was faced by an armed enemy soldier whom he killed with a pistol. Moving his comrade to safety and returning to his men, he neutralized the final pocket of enemy resistance by fatally wounding 3 North Vietnamese officers with rifle fire. S/Sgt. Hooper then established a final line and reorganized his men, not accepting treatment until this was accomplished and not consenting to evacuation until the following morning. His supreme valor, inspiring leadership and heroic self-sacrifice were directly responsible for the company's success and provided a lasting example in personal courage for every man on the field. S/Sgt. Hooper's actions were in keeping with the highest traditions of the military service and reflect great credit upon himself and the U.S. Army.

*The President of the United States of America, authorized by*
*Act of Congress, March 3, 1863, has awarded in the name of*
*The Congress the Medal of Honor posthumously to*

## STAFF SERGEANT CLIFFORD C. SIMS
## UNITED STATES ARMY

for conspicuous gallantry and intrepidity in action at the risk of his life above and beyond the call of duty.

 Staff Sergeant Clifford C. Sims distinguished himself on 21 February 1968, while serving as a squad leader with Company D, 2nd Battalion (Airborne), 501st Infantry, 101st Airborne Division, near Hue, in the Republic of Vietnam. Company D was assaulting a heavily fortified enemy position concealed within a dense wooded area when it encountered a strong enemy defensive fire. Once within the woodline, Sergeant Sims led his squad in a furious attack against an enemy force which had pinned down the 1st Platoon and threatened to overrun it. His skillful leadership provided the platoon with freedom of movement and enabled it to regain the initiative. Sergeant Sims was then ordered to move his squad to a position where he could provide covering fire for the company command group and to link up with the 3d Platoon, which was under heavy enemy pressure. After moving no more than thirty meters Sergeant Sims noticed that a brick structure in which ammunition was stocked was on fire. Realizing the danger, Sergeant Sims took immediate action to move his squad from this position. Though in the process of leaving the area two members of his squad were injured by the subsequent explosion of the ammunition, Sergeant Sims' prompt actions undoubtedly prevented more serious casualties from occurring. While continuing through the dense woods amidst heavy enemy fire, Sergeant Sims and his squad were approaching a bunker when they heard the unmistakable noise of a concealed booby trap being triggered immediately to their front. Sergeant Sims warned his comrades of the danger and unhesitatingly hurled himself upon the device as it exploded, taking the full impact of the blast. In so protecting his fellow soldiers, he willingly sacrificed his own life. Staff Sergeant Sims' conspicuous gallantry, extraordinary heroism and intrepidity at the cost of his own life, above and beyond the call of duty, are in keeping with the highest traditions of the military service and reflect great credit upon himself and the United States Army.

# 6.
# Chronology
## February 24, 1968 – October 30, 1968

**Feb. 24, 1968**

**0607H** (YD718210): 2-501 received mortar rounds, rockets, and M-79 rounds with negative results. The battalion continued to attack east against moderate resistance, moving southeast and then east to attack on the right flank of 2-12 Cav. to relieve pressure.

**2155H** The battalion received 20-30 rounds of small arms and 3 rounds mortar fire from YD749214. The battalion asked if there were any friendlies at that location. Reply from 3rd BDE (1st Cav.) was uncertain, "but you are very close to friendlies"; the BN was advised to return with direct fire weapons at muzzle flashes, firing selectively.

**2240H** The 2-501 received 3 60mm mortar rounds and heavy Arty fire, as well as a few rounds from the Battleship USS New Jersey, was called in on the suspected mortar location at YD707216.

The 2-501 moved east against little enemy resistance in the populated area north of the Perfume River. The battalion seized a bridge at YD710219 and uncovered enemy fortified positions in the path of the advance.

**Feb. 25, 1968**

BN CP located at YD733215.

**1215H** (YD736209): Co. D at a crossroad noticed many people carrying banners saying "Long Live Ho Chi Minh." BN S-3 apprehended the people carrying the banners.

**1400H** A small Vietnamese boy (age about 10) was captured after firing a few rounds from a C-54 carbine, with negative casualties.

**1530H** (YD742212): Co. D, along with tanks of the 3-5th, received fire from a brick building near the wall around Hue. Two of the M-43 tanks fired on the building, completely destroying it. The Company located a trench system at YD741214 with a building that appeared to be a mess hall. The whole deserted complex appeared to be a headquarters area. Several signs were located that said "Shoot the American and Vietnamese Aggressors, for a better Vietnam, Long Live Ho Chi Minh."

**1630H** Delta Company moved into Hue and occupied several bombed out buildings along the west wall around Hue.

**2155H** Co. D reported receiving 20-30 rounds of small arms fire.

## Feb. 26, 1968

**0055H** Co. D received M-79 rounds and some small arms fire from across a moat, 3 or 5 rounds landing 15-20 feet from their position. The rounds were believed to have come from the ARVN at YD747216.

**0105H** Co. D reports M-79 rounds coming from YD748216, from the Company's side of the river near the citadel wall. The Company did not return fire since they could hear the M-79 being fired, with the rounds landing in the moat in front of them.

**0730H** 1SGT Arthur Scott flew in eggs, spam, biscuits, and coffee, Delta Company's first hot meal in 7 days.

**1300H** (YD744213): During a sweep Co. D found 1 .31 cal rifle, 1 AK-47, 1 RPG-2, 3 RPG-2 pouches, 120 AK-47 rounds, and 1 US pyrotechnic pistol 1-7 Cav. secured an area in the vic of YD705228 in which Co. D found 30 civilians murdered by the NVA during the US advance in Hue. The 2-501 continued to search in the area south of Hue.

Delta Company spent the night in an old French building that contained several beds.

## Feb. 27, 1968

**1000H** (YD738215): During a sweeping operation Co. D captured 2 SKS, 250 7.62 rounds, and 1 PRC 10 radio.

## Feb. 28, 1968

Co. D searched the area of the battle of the 21st. A few weapons and some equipment were located. The NVA had apparently not returned to the area, since the NVA bodies were still in the area unburied.

## Feb. 29 1968

Co. D provided security for mine sweep teams on Highway 1 (QL 1); with their night ambush position located at YD675253.

## March 2, 1968

2nd BDE reassumed OPCON of 2-501 from 3rd BDE, 1st Cav. Div.

BN CP located at FB Pinky (YD636253).

Company D conducted search and destroy operation south along Highway 1 from FB Pinky to Hue, and provided a security element for mine sweeping operation from FB Pinky southeast along Highway 1.

**0655H** (YD671266): A Co. D element, while returning from an ambush, detonated a booby trap while moving along railroad tracks. Results: 3 US WIA.

**1325H** (YD693246): Co. D found 4 bodies in a bunker, 2 were wearing khaki uniforms. The bodies appeared to be 10-12 days old.

## March 3, 1968
**1020H** (YD677274): Co. D located a bunker complex.
**1107H** (YD680280): Co. D received automatic weapons and small arms fire from an unknown size enemy element. ARA and Arty were employed on the suspected enemy location. The Company searched the area with negative results.
**2110H** (YD674273): Co. D fired on an enemy soldier who stumbled into a Delta Company ambush. Results: 1 NVA KIA

## March 5, 1968
**1220H** Co. D requested their dog be put on a log ship to have it checked for rabies. A man in Co. D was bitten on the hand by the dog.

## March 6, 1968
**2007H** Co. D's ambush in position at YD705270.

## March 7, 1968
**0925H** Co. D requested a medevac for 2 Vietnamese children who stepped on an ARVN mine; medevac complete at 0956H. At 1040H the Company was located at YD689271.
**2010H** (YD685288): A Co. D ambush patrol heard what sounded like personnel shouting orders in Vietnamese. At 2130H the Co. D ambush patrol engaged an estimated 8-10 enemy at YD687289, ambushed one more person crossing the bridge at 2142H, and at 2255H ambushed another enemy swimming in the river at the same location. Results: 6 VC KIA.

## March 8, 1968
**1820H** A Co. D man shot himself in the foot with a .45 pistol; medevac completed at 1842H.

## March 9-14, 1968
Co. D provided security for FB Pinky.

## March 10, 1968
Co. D secured FB Pinky and one platoon provided security guards for a convoy from Hue to Camp Evans along Highway 1.

## March 11, 1968

**2140H** (FB Pinky): 3/D spotted 2 figures 10-20 meters from wire and engaged with hand grenades. At 2210 3/D detected additional movement and fired hand flare. At 2217H Co. D heard 2-3 M-79 rounds which were believed to have come from 81mm mortar squad or Engineer Platoon who claimed they saw 3 individuals in starlight scope. Co. D advised Engineers of ground rules.

## March 14, 1968

Co. D provided security for minesweep operation from FB Pinky to CPN, and provided local security for FB Pinky.

**1530H** (YD683284): Co. D captured 1 VC with 3 grenades. Results: 1 VC POW, 3 grenades.

**1615H** Co. D became OPCON of 1-501.

## March 15, 1968

**1400H** Co. D released OPCON of 1-501.

**1510H** Co. D requested a medevac for a heat casualty.

**2040H** Co. D ambush in position at YD663232.

## March 18, 1968

**0845H** Co. D received mortar rounds from suspected enemy location at YD675243. Co. D sent two squads to check out the area with negative results.

**2027H** (YD645235): Two 8 man patrols of Co. D, on the way to set up an ambush, encountered a smaller enemy force which jumped the patrol swinging machetes. The patrols scattered with negative casualties and later regrouped to set up their ambush.

## March 19, 1968

**0853H** Co. D in searching the area of contact the previous night, found a pack with 20 lbs. of explosives and 1 pick with a short handle. Both VC and US elements appeared to have surprised each other.

**1645H** One of the men in Co. D's ambush of the previous night purposely shot himself in the foot. The man read Article 31 and statements were taken by witnesses at the time of the incident. The man was taken in by log bird for medical attention, and then taken to Bien Hoa for court martial.

**2135H** A Co. D ambush observed 46 personnel, in steel helmets with no packs and with weapons carried squirrel hunting style, moving northeast up a trail toward Co. D's position; but the observed group did not reach the ambush position.

## March 20, 1968

**2200H** (YD679220): A squad size ambush position from Co. D engaged an estimated 20 VC with small arms, automatic weapons, and claymores, with arty in support. The VC were moving north down a trail when 10-12 of the enemy in line were engaged by two claymores, killing at least five. Three or four VC then gathered around the VC KIAs and were killed by small arms fire and hand grenades. The remaining VC returned small arms fire, automatic weapons fire, and grenades. The VC were dressed in brown to khaki uniforms and were wearing packs. Results: 2 US WIA (M), 8 VC KIA.

## March 21, 1968

**0925H** Co. D found a knapsack containing a green uniform and other military equipment; and at 1222H Co. D found a body at YD680234.

**1358H** (YD693228): With 3rd Platoon in the lead, Co. D received heavy small arms, automatic weapons, and mortar fire from an estimated reinforced NVA platoon located atop Hill 309. Co. D, Co. C, and the Recon Platoon maneuvered against the enemy element within a located bunker complex. TAC air was flown in support with air strikes made against an enemy location at YD652202. Results: 7 US WIA (E), 1 US WIA (M), 2 NVA KIA.

## March 22, 1968

BN CP located at FB Geronimo.

Artillery blasted Hill 309 during the night and at 0700H TAC air began bombing the hill for nearly two hours.

**0855H** (YD653203): With 2nd Platoon in the lead, Co. D attacked Hill 309 and received heavy small arms and automatic weapons fire from an estimated reinforced NVA platoon in bunkers on the hill (YD653202). Fire was returned with organic weapons, arty and navy TAC air. At 1145H 2nd Platoon maneuvered around behind the hill with the remainder of the Company providing covering fire. By 1212H, after over three hours of contact, the enemy was finally forced from their positions and fled. Results: 5 US WIA, 19 NVA KIA, 4 NVA KBA, 4 AK-47 and 1 LMG captured, 3 bunkers destroyed and 5 bunkers damaged.

**1315H** (YD653203): Co. D received 10 rounds of unknown type mortar fire. No fire was returned since location of the source could not be determined. There were negative US casualties and negative damage. At 1615H (YD653202) Co. D received 8-10 more rounds of 60mm mortar fire, killing Walter Anslow and wounding 3 others. Shortly after, 1 helicopter bringing in 6 new replacements also received heavy mortar fire, severely disabling it. One of the new men jumped from the chopper to take cover and landed on the poncho containing Anslow's body. The new man was covered with blood and he went berserk. Despite CPT Hogan trying to talk him out of it, he had to be medevaced out. Arty was employed on the suspected mortar position, YD640185. Results: 2 US KIA (Walter Harold Anslow and Eulas Fay Gregory died on March 23), 2 US WIA.

**1500H** MG Olivito Barsanti (101st Abn Div CO) and LG Stillwell landed on top of the hill accompanied by a newsman. At 1600H, MG Barsanti returned to present 3 Silver Star awards.

## March 23. 1968

**0530H** (YD653202): Co. D received small arms and automatic weapons fire, grenades and RPG fire from an estimated platoon size enemy force. Fire was returned with small arms and automatic weapons, with arty firing in support. At 0600H the enemy fled and a sweep of the area was made. Results: 3 VC KIA, 2 AK-47s, 1 RPG launcher and 1 RPG round captured. There were negative US casualties.

**0818H** Co. D requested a medevac for 1 man with a high fever, medevac complete at 0330H.

**0945H** (YD642201): Co. D received 13 rounds of unknown type mortar fire and sporadic small arms fire from the top of the ridgeline (YD645195). An airstrike was placed on the suspected position.

**1205H** (YD661201): Co. D found 4 NVA bodies. Results: 2 NVA KIA, 2 NVA KBA.

Co. D then received small arms and automatic weapons fire from an estimated NVA squad. Fire was returned with organic weapons. Results: 5 NVA KIA, 4 AK-47s and 1 LMG captured

These incidents occurred in the same general area where a new trail system had been discovered running north and northeast from New NVA Base Area 114. The BDE S-2 indicated that enemy forces would probably continue to defend this vital supply route in order to rapidly resupply VC/NVA forces in a proposed attack against Hue City.

## March 24, 1968

**0001H** (YD651202): Companies B and D received 4 rounds of 60mm mortar fire, 30-40 AK-47 rounds, and 4-5 RPG rounds. Fire was returned with mortar, small arms, and automatic weapons fire. At 0045H the enemy fled. Results: negative US casualties, enemy casualties unknown.

**0412H** (YD652200): Co. D received 10-12 rounds of 60mm mortar fire. Counter mortar and arty fire was employed at the suspected mortar position, YD646195. Results: 2 US WIA (E: Jody Gravett and Craig Sturgess), enemy casualties unknown.

## March 25, 1968
**0640H** Co. D has 1 NVA with an AK-47 who gave himself up. He was picked up and sent to LZ Sally; he was from the 9th BN, 90th NVA Regt.

## March 26, 1968
**0605H** (YD638196): Co. D received 5 rounds of small arms fire. No fire was returned as the source could not be determined.

**1129H** (YD638193): Co. D received 2 grenades followed by small arms, automatic weapons, and 60mm mortar fire from an estimated company size NVA force located in 4-5 bunkers. Fire was returned with organic weapons and arty. At 1217H Delta Company knocked out an NVA mortar position at Y0636194 by 5 hits with a LAW. At 1500H Co. D located a well used trail in the vicinity of previous contact. Results: 2 US WIA (E: Franklin Grant, Jr. and unknown), 5 NVA KIA.

## March 27, 1968
**0920H** After heavy arty preparation Co. D moved from their NDP towards an objective at YD637195.

**1215H** (YD633192): Co. D engaged an estimated NVA company size force, well dug in within a bunker complex, later confirmed as the HQ of the 9th BN, 90th NVA Regt. Heavy volumes of small arms and automatic weapons fire were employed by the enemy. Small arms and automatic weapons fire, arty, ARA, and TAC air were placed on the enemy positions. Results: 1 US KIA (Clifford Leroy Williams), 7 US WIA (E: George P. Parker (1st Platoon SGT, Nicholas Saxiones, David W. Martin, Robert B.

Washington, 2Lt William D. Loftin (2nd Platoon Leader), Richard Buzzini, Robert Brockman), 2 US WIA (M), 14 NVA KIA.

## March 28, 1968

BN TAC CP located at YD653203 (along with Co. C).

Airstrikes employed in support of Co. D on objective area (YD637196) at 0925H, 1220H, 1405H, 1517H, and 1620H. The airstrike at 1220H exposed an extensive bunker and trench system. The airstrike at 1405H produced 10 secondary explosions. Arty prep was also fired into the objective area between 1230H and 1325H, producing 3 secondary explosions. At 1315H Co. D started moving towards the objective area, arriving at 1450H. The Company found many trails, trenches, 4 bunkers (destroyed), and signs of many personnel in the area.

At 1618H (YD637196) Co. D and Recon Platoon engaged 2 NVA with small arms and automatic weapons fire. The element also found 1 can of black powder, 2 AK-47, and 2 RPG-2. Results: 2 NVA KIA, 2 AK-47s and 2 RPG-2 captured.

2Lt Ronald Phillips joined Co. D to replace 2Lt Loftin as 2nd Platoon Leader.

**1823H** (YD637195): Co. D found a medical record identifying unit as the 2nd Co., 9th BN, 90th NVA Regiment.

**2230H** (YD640135): Co. B and Co. D received 4 hand grenades. Fire was returned with grenades and M-79 fire. Results: negative US casualties, enemy casualties unknown.

## March 29, 1968

BN CP located at LZ Sally.

**1110H** (YD637195): A sweep by Co. D of yesterdays contact area produced the following results: 31 NVA KIA; captured and evacuated the following equipment: 15 B-40 rockets, 31 60mm mortar rounds, 2 AK-47s, 1 SKS, 11 RPG charges, 7 Soviet gas masks, 1 CHICOM claymore, 6 stick grenades, 25 60mm fuses, 1500 rounds of small arms ammo, 105 lbs. of documents, and 1 pair of goggles.

Co. D CA'd from YD637195 to YD653240.

**1955H** (YD647237): A Co. D ambush while moving to their ambush location engaged 7 VC with claymores and small arms fire. Results: 3 VC KIA, negative US casualties.

## March 30, 1968

**0300H** Co. D witnessed a B-52 strike on the area of the March 23 contact, 2 miles away.

**0807H** (YD647237): In checking the ambush location of the previous night Co. D located a small pool of blood, 1 poncho, and 1 grenade.

**1031H** (YD655248): Co. D located an old mortar position that did not appear to have been used during previous two weeks. The Company also located 6 bunkers in the vicinity, which were all destroyed. At 1047H the Company reported what appeared to be burning houses to the front of their location, and at 1325H they located 3 more mortar positions at YD644257.

## March 31, 1968
Co. D moved by air to Utah (Wunder) Beach.

## April 1, 1968
Operation JEB STUART ended and Operation CARENTAN II began.

**0801H** The 2-501 returned to OPCON 2nd BDE from 3rd BDE, 82nd Abn. Div. (312001H - 010800H): at 1800H the battalion became OPCON to 2nd BDE. 1st Air Cav. Div.

## April 4, 1968
BN CP and Co. D located at Utah (Wunder) Beach. Co. D pulled security for Wunder Beach, the name used by the Navy for their supply depot at that location. The 101st, however, referred to it as Utah Beach.

**2145H** (YD475556 - Utah Beach): Co. D observed 3 individuals inside the wire to the front of their west perimeter. Illumination was fired and the enemy fled to the southwest.

## April 5, 1968
**0230H** (YD479559 - Utah Beach): Co. D received 4 rounds of 122mm rocket fire from the southeast, with negative casualties. At 0315H the Company received 5 more rounds of 122mm rocket fire from suspected location YD525536, and at 0330H the Company received 7 82mm mortar rounds from suspected location YD514533: all with negative casualties.

**1240H** (YD460588): Co. D found and destroyed 20 punji pits (hardwood with metal tips) and 3 boobytrapped Chicom grenades attached to a plank.

## April 7, 1968
Co. D remained at Utah Beach where they improved defensive positions, pulled security, and established local ambushes.

## April 9, 1968
Co. D provided security for a minesweep team from Wunder Beach to FB Hardcore and then returned to Utah Beach. At 1100H (YD463492) the

Company found and destroyed 1 mine containing 40 lbs. of explosive charge.

## April 10, 1968

**1145H** Co. D was placed on alert for a CA into Thon Phuoc Dien to assist Co. A, which had encountered heavy contact in the area.

Their initial mission was to pin down the enemy while Company A removed their WIAs and KIAs. Most of Co. D was inserted without resistance; however, 2nd Platoon was inserted to close to the woodline and came under fire as they landed.

**1325H** (YD475487 - Thon Phuoc Dien): As Company A (on the left) and Company D (on the right) moved into the village of Thon Phuoc Dien they received small arms, automatic weapons and RPG fire from an estimated reinforced company in bunker positions. The two Companies maneuvered against the enemy employing heavy organic weapons fire with ARA support. At 1530H the Companies pulled away from the village and called in artillery and 8 TAC airstrikes (with napalm and 500 lb. bombs), as well as mortar tear gas canisters, against the enemy position.

Co. D captured a NVA POW who stated that a large NVA force was going to attack FB Hardcore the night of April 10. Companies A and D were ordered to break contact and force march to FB Hardcore. When the two companies had moved approximately halfway to the firebase, they were ordered to return to the village of Phuoc Dien. The 2/17 Cav. was moved to secure FB Hardcore, although no attack came.

At 1900H Co. B was moved to the area by helicopter and the 3 companies cordoned off the village. Numerous ambush positions were established to prevent the enemy from escaping. Results: 3 US KIA (1 from Co. D: Lawrence William Eller), 10 US WIA (3 from Co. D Evac), 6 NVA KIA, 1 AK-47 captured.

The area was illuminated by flare ships and artillery was fired throughout the night. The enemy used small arms, automatic weapons, RPG and mortar fire against the cordon in attempts to leave the village. At 2301H (YD477434) Co. D observed 1 NVA crawling out of the village and engaged him with small arms fire. Results: 1 NVA KIA.

At 2358H Co. D observed and fired at an additional NVA trying to escape the tight cordon. Results: 1 NVA KIA, 1 9mm pistol captured.

## April 11, 1968

**0001H-1645H** (YD475487): Companies A, B, and D continued the cordon around the village in which heavy contact occurred on April 10. The enemy force, estimated to be a reinforced NVA company, continued their attempts to escape the village throughout the night. Arty fire from LZ Jane and FB Hardcore supported the 3 companies through the operation. During the morning Co. A and one platoon from Co. B moved into blocking positions.

3/D observed several NVA firing from bunkers and attempted, unsuccessfully, to silence them using a LAW. CPT Hogan requested a 106RR rifle be airlifted to the area. The 106RR arrived at 1130H and fired 5 rounds. A loud speaker unit then demanded that the NVA surrender or face additional 106RR, artillery, and air strikes. Approximately 5 minutes later, a NVA came out of the woodline with a white flag tied to his rifle barrel, and asked to talk to the officer in charge. CPT Hogan moved with an interpreter to the area of 3rd Platoon and the NVA stated that there were only 25 NVA still alive in the village and that they would surrender if the US forces would stop firing. Approximately 20 minutes later, about 20 NVA marched single file out of the village to a point about 200 yards from the Co. D perimeter. The NVA stopped, formed a platoon formation, neatly stacked arms, and then marched to the 3/D area with their hands on their heads. The NVA were air lifted to Utah Beach and classed as POWs.

Beginning at 1312H, Company D and the remainder of Company B swept the village. Co. B met no resistance. Co. D, however, came under heavy fire approximately halfway through the village. 1st Platoon was sent to help 2nd Platoon neutralize a complex of bunkers. While the fire fight was raging, B.G. Clay (Asst Div Commander) radioed that he was overhead and wanted to land and observe the mopup operations. CPT Hogan requested that B.G. Clay delay coming into the area until the fighting had reduced. Within 5 minutes, however, B.G. Clay was on the front lines of Co. D. After receiving several bursts of automatic weapons fire from the NVA positions, B.G. Clay was convinced to return to the Co. D rear until the operation was complete. At 1645H the sweep was completed and the Companies returned to FB Hardcore. As the Companies cleared the objective area a 4.2" mortar barrage was placed on the objective area at 1720H. Co. D arrived at FB Hardcore at 1756H and then moved by truck to Utah Beach, closing at 1909H.

Total Results for the 3 companies: 67 NVA KIA (primarily by Co. D), 20 NVA POWs and 11 detainees captured; 3 US KIA, 12 US WIA (Evac, including Dave Bischoff, 3rd Platoon Leader of Co. D), 5 US WIA (M); 8 AK-47s, 6 EKS, 3 M-16s, 1 45 cal pistol, 2 RPGs and 3 LMGs captured and evacuated.

## April 13, 1968

**1125H** Co. D found 30 punji pits, 2'x3'x3' deep. Each pit contained approximately 10 stakes that were 10" long. All destroyed in place.

## April 14, 1968

1Lt Aranow became acting Co. D CO while CPT Hogan went on R&R in Hawaii.

**1305H** Co. D moved by truck from Wunder Beach to bridge sites YD437433, YD460400, and YD476376, with one platoon at each site to reinforce security of paramilitary forces.

**2100H** (YD481369): While enroute to an ambush location a squad from 2/D received small arms fire from an unknown size enemy force. Small arms and automatic weapons fire was returned and the enemy fled. The 2/D ambush moved out from bridge with PF element. With PF leading, the PF wanted to go through the village although US (2/D) protested; but when the PF moved into the village 2/D followed. As the 2/D element was almost clear of the village the lead man was fired on and wounded in the chest, medevac completed at 2135H. Results: 1 US WIA (E: Dwight E. Peterson), enemy casualties unknown.

## April 15, 1968

2105H (YD450432): A squad size ambush from 3/D (with PF element) observed 8 enemy across the river about 75m to the west. The ambush element initially engaged the enemy with small arms and automatic weapons fire followed by all 8 hiding in a rice paddy. The element then engaged the area with M-79 fire and at 2125H observed 3 persons attempting to escape, who were engaged with small arms, claymore, and automatic weapons fire.

## April 16, 1968

**0700H** (YD450432): Co. D in checking the ambush site of the previous night discovered 1 VC KIA.

**1515H** (YD474486): Co. D found and destroyed 20 bunkers, 1000 rounds of small arms ammunition and 6 60mm mortar rounds. Also found and evacuated were 2 rucksacks containing medical supplies.

## April 17, 1968

BN TAC CP moved from Wunder Beach to LZ Sally. Co. D moved by air from bridge security to LZ Sally.

## April 21, 1968

**1445H** (YD753311 ): Co. C observed and engaged 2 VC with arty and organic weapons fire. As Co. C pursued the enemy, contact increased to an estimated reinforced enemy company located in the village of Thon Kim Doi. Co. D moved to reinforce, while heavy volumes of organic weapons fire, Arty and TAC air were placed on the target area.

**1350H** (YD75331 1): Companies A and B were CA'd into blocking positions completing the cordon around the village. Moderate fighting continued throughout the night as the enemy force employed small arms and RPG fire in vain attempts to escape the village. Continuous illumination was employed throughout the night with arty providing supporting fires. Results: 5 US WIA (E; none from Delta Co.), 18 NVA KIA, 3 NVA KBA.

## April 23, 1968

**0001H** (YD75331 1): Companies A, C, and D, assisted by the 1st ARVN Div. Panther Force and the 222RF Company maintained the encirclement of the village of Thon Kim Doi. At 0053H 3 NVA attempting to escape the cordon encountered heavy volumes of organic weapons fire. During the night the enemy employed sporadic small arms and RPG fire. Following a heavy artillery preparation, Co. A commenced to sweep the village from the north as Co. D swept from the west. At 0830H Co. C captured 1 NVA POW attempting to escape. At 1045H Co. A engaged 3 NVA with organic weapons. Results: 6 NVA KIA, 2 US WIA (E: Frank D. Gains and Stan T. Riley of Co. D), 2 AK-47s and 1 sniper rifle captured.

**1530H** The 1st ARVN Div. Panther Force was airlifted to Hue. Companies A, C, and D established extensive ambush positions in the vicinity of the village to interdict any further enemy movement. Preliminary interrogation of the POW captured revealed him to be from the 3d Co., 4th BN, 812th NVA Regt. (also known as the Thu Ben Regiment).

## April 24, 1968
**1125H** (YD744302): Co. D found 2 NVA bodies killed by air strikes approximately 2 days before. Results: 2 NVA KIA.

## April 25, 1968
**1230H** (YD730294): Co. D picked up 2 detainees (30 years old) who were turned over to the ARVN for interrogation. The ARVN commander advised that there are 2 or 3 NVA companies in the area Co. D is moving.
**1450H** (YD720310): Co. D observed 5 NVA with weapons and engaged them with small arms and automatic weapons fire.

## April 26, 1968
**1733H** (YD713314): Co. D CA'd from YD714314 to YD719342, complete at 1740H; the second lift received sporadic small arms fire on liftoff from LZ, with negative results.
**1812H** (YD722343): Co. D had one man detonate a boobytrap (with tripwire) located on the side of a grave. Results: 1 US KIA, 1 US WIA.

## April 27, 1968
**1035H** (YD716329): Co. D found 500. lbs. of rice, which was destroyed.
LTC James A. Heiter took over as 2-501 Commander from LTC Richard Tallman.
**1115H** (YD716333): While conducting a sweep through the village of Xam Thu Le, Co. D engaged 1 VC with small arms fire. At the same time, 3 other VC who had been hiding in a nearby bunker, turned themselves over to Co. D, asking for Hoi Chanh status. The detainees were then evacuated for interrogation and classified returnees. They stated that they were members of a 30-man guerrilla platoon operating out of Xam Thu Le with a mission of conducting guerrilla activities in Quang Dien (YD6934). Results: negative US casualties, 1 VC KIA, 3 returnees, 1 M-1 carbine, 1 M-16 rifle, and 1 SKS captured.
Co. D NDP located at YD666336.

## April 28, 1968
**1527H** (YD648372): Co. D received report from FAC that 20-25 persons in khaki green uniforms were spotted at YD653366. The area was engaged with arty and naval gun fire. The Company moved into the area at 1615H and received small arms and RPG fire from an estimated NVA squad,

resulting in 2 US KIAs. Co. D returned fire with organic weapons and placed artillery on the suspected enemy position (YD649368). Contact was broken at 1716H when the enemy fled. The 2 US KIAs were evacuated by the BDE CO's helicopter. Results: 2 US KIA (John Bernard Gingery and unknown).

## April 29, 1968

1545H (YD654366): Co. D received sniper fire, negative casualties. In the area Co. D found and destroyed 4 rounds of 82mm mortar ammo and 2 AK-47 magazines (60 rounds). Also found in the area was 300 lbs. of rice which was turned over to the District Headquarters.

1910H (YD687273): 2/D received small arms fire from an unknown size enemy force across a river (YD691282), with negative casualties. The platoon returned organic weapons fire with unknown results.

## April 30, 1968

1055H (YD689287): Co. D discovered 1 NVA KIA, killed as a result of arty fire during the night as the 2nd BDE cordon operation continued. Throughout the day, heavy volumes of arty were placed on the enemy positions, and a total of 15 TAC airstrikes were flown in support of the cordon operation. At 1830H Co. D received 20 60mm mortar rounds in the vicinity of YD690287, and at 2135H received 2 60mm mortar rounds, all with negative casualties.

## May 1, 1968

Co. D (OPCON of 1-501). along with B/2-501 , A/1-501 , B/l-501 , A/i- 502, and 3 PR platoons, continued the containment of enemy forces in the hamlets of Thon Duong Son (YD637273) and Thon Phuoc Yen (YD690277). At 0440H Co. D and Co. A 1-502 engaged an unknown number of the enemy attempting to cross the river. Throughout the day arty and TAC air supported the cordon. Results: Co. D had 6 US WIA, 121 NVA KIA (killed primarily by arty and airstrikes), 95 POWs, 34 AK-47s and numerous other weapons.

## May 2, 1968

Co. D continued to participate in the cordon of Thon Phuoc Yen, conducting local patrols in the northern sector of the cordon. Throughout the previous night the enemy made numerous unsuccessful attempts to escape the cordon. Throughout the day arty and 8 air strikes supported the cordon. At 1530H Co. D was released OPCON of 2-501.

**1546H** Co. D CA'd from YD696288 to YD727337, complete at 1620H. At 1825H (YD729330) the Company found and evacuated 1 SKS and 1 Soviet carbine.

## May 3, 1968

**1030H** (YD731327): Co. D passed through the center of a village with negative contact.

**1305H** (YD724314): Co. D received ineffective sniper fire from 1 VC who fled immediately as organic weapons fire was returned. At 1334H Delta Company received a heavy volume of small arms fire and 1 round of 60mm mortar fire from an estimated enemy squad. Organic weapons fire and arty were employed against the enemy force. Contact terminated at 1500H, as the enemy dispersed and fled and the Company withdrew to permit 5 airstrikes to support. Results: 1 US WIA, enemy casualties unknown.

**1705H** Co. D CA'd from YD731311 to YD695296, complete at 1740H; and assumed a blocking position to cordon an unknown size enemy force in the vicinity of YD690303.

## May 4, 1968

**0335H** (YD693298): While participating in a cordon of the village of Pho Nam, Delta Company received 1 RPG round with negative casualties. At 0416H Co. D received 25-30 60mm mortar rounds and counter mortar arty was immediately employed against the enemy firing positions, YD702305 and YD699318. Most of the enemy mortar rounds passed over Co. D's position and impacted in cordon location. Results: 1 US WIA (M).

**0745H** (YD693298): A log ship attempting to land at an LZ in Co. D's area received intense automatic weapons fire from woodline to the north, resulting in the door gunner being slightly wounded.

**1200H** (YD693298): Co. D relieved in place by Co. B 1-502, and Co. D moved to the Hue Water Plant.

## May 5, 1968

**0327H** Co. D, located on bridge at Hue, observed heavy rocket and mortar fire in northeast corner of Hue, at 0340H observed the northwest corner of Hue under ground attack, and at 0353H observed mortar firing from YD732211 (arty called in on village).

## May 6, 1968

Co. D provided security for Hue bridges at YD749210, YD780209, and YD771222. From 0320H to 0506H 3/D at YD749210 received 12 RPG rounds resulting in 2 US WIA. Fire was returned with organic weapons. A first light sweep resulted in 1 VC WIA suspect, evacuated on a log bird. Results: 2 US WIA, 1 VC WIA suspect.

## May 7, 1968

BN CP located at FB Pinky.

**1145H** Co. D was relieved of security mission for Hue bridges and moved by vehicle to YD670270.

## May 9, 1968

**0130H** (YD659245): A Co. D ambush engaged with organic weapons fire an estimated 20 NVA moving southwest. The enemy fled without returning fire. Results: negative US casualties, 1 NVA KIA 1 AK-47 captured.

## May 9-12, 1968

Co. D provided security for FB Pinky.

## May 10, 1968

Co. D provided security for FB Pinky, with ambushes in the area, provided minesweep security from FB Pinky to YD733236, and 1 platoon provided security for MEDCAP (Medical Civil Action Program) at YD656283.

## May 12, 1968

Co. D continued to provide security for FB Pinky.

**1136H** (YD660241): Co. D found 6 buried NVA bodies killed by small arms fire about 3 days earlier. Near the graves, the Company also located along a trail a sleeping position, gear, and a bag of rice. At 1210H (YD660242) Co. D sustained 1 WIA from a boobytrapped hand grenade, and at 1330H (YD654245) Delta Company found 1 NVA body wrapped in a hammock, killed by small arms fire 2 days earlier. Results: 1 US WIA, 7 NVA KIA.

**2034H** (YD645237): A Co. D ambush position engaged 6-10 VC moving northeast on a trail, whistling and singing. The enemy were engaged with small arms and claymores. The VC attempted to break contact immediately. Results: 2 VC KIA, 1 VC POW WIA, 1 AK-47 and 1 SKS captured.

## May 13, 1968
**2220H** (YD649242): Co. D received approximately 25 rounds of 82mm mortar fire. Counter mortar fire was placed on the suspected enemy location, YD631222. Results: negative US casualties, enemy casualties unknown.

## May 15, 1968
**1745H** (YD665251 ): Co. D had 1 man seriously cut his finger while cutting bamboo, medevac completed at 1300H.

**1845H** (YD662245): Co. D while enroute to an ambush location observed 3 NVA carrying individual weapons. Arty was adjusted on the enemy location (YD651239) with the enemy immediately dispersing.

## May 16, 1968
**0002H** (YD661245): Co. D received 20 rounds of 60mm mortar fire. Counter mortar fire was adjusted on the suspected enemy firing position, YD658244. At 0653H (YD658245) Delta Company found and destroyed in place 3 boobytrapped Chicom grenades and 2 1/4 lb. blocks of TNT. At 1203H (YD643255) Co. D apprehended 2 detainees who were later classified civil defendants and turned over to district.

## May 17, 1968
Operation NEVADA EAGLE began.

## May 18, 1968

**0255H** (YD660245): Co. D engaged 1 NVA carrying a M-16 weapon. Results: 1 NVA KIA, 1 M-16 captured.

Co. D moved back to the Hue bridges.

## May 19, 1968

**2219H** (YD750210): Co. D at the Hue bridge received 2 mortar rounds and approximately 50 rounds of small arms fire from the vicinity of Highway 1. Fire was not returned as the enemy location could not be determined. Results: negative US casualties.

## May 20, 1968

Co. D continued to provide security for Hue bridges.

**0745H** Co. D had 1 man on the main Hue bridge who was crushed against the bridge rail and killed by a civilian truck; the driver of the truck had apparently lost control.

**0920H** Co. D moved by vehicles to YD677265 and conducted platoon size training in the attack of fortified villages at YD674254, and then the village at YD674243 following an arty prep. The Company returned to Hue bridges at 1423H. At 1430H Co. D was relieved in place by Co. A, and moved by vehicles to YD668260.

## May 22, 1968

**0140H** (YD642257): A Co. D ambush position reports hearing 25-30 M79 rounds in the vicinity of YD640259.

**0750H** Co. D CA'd from YD635255 to YD581259, closing at 0827H, 1640H (YD603264): Co. D received 4 rounds of 32mm mortar fire, with negative casualties. Arty was fired on suspected mortar position. At 1715H (YD604268) 1/D engaged approximate)y 30 NVA with small arms and automatic weapons fire. The enemy fled to the northeast as gunships continued the engagement. Results: 16 NVA KIA (10 by Co. D, 6 by ARA), 1 AK-47, 2 RPG-7 rounds.

At 1907H (YD596254) 3/D engaged 1 NVA with small arms fire. Results: 1 NVA KIA. At 2024H (YD605265) 3/D observed 8-10 NVA cross a river (YD602266) and move toward ambush position where they were engaged with small arms fire. The enemy returned fire and fled to the southwest. Results: negative US casualties, 2 NVA KIA.

## May 23, 1968

**1258H** Co. D (3/D) CA'd from YD597260 to YD600273, closed at 1318H. At 1320H (YD595253) 3/D found 1 bunker containing 3 60mm mortar rounds, 125 lbs. rice, 1000 AK-47 rounds, 1 hammock, 2 ponchos, 1 NVA rucksack and miscellaneous clothing.

**1955H** Co. D received 7 rounds of 82mm mortar fire from YD598266. Co. D had received resupply at YD596276 and moved to NDP at YD596271, leaving 2 fires burning. The rounds impacted where Co. D had departed. Arty fired on suspected enemy mortar position.

## May 24, 1968

**0600H** (YD596271 ): Co. D received 3-10 60mm mortar rounds near their position (where they were resupplied on the 23rd), with negative casualties. The 1st Platoon moved to the suspected enemy mortar position at YD597265. At 0731H contact was made with 25- 30 enemy and ARA was requested. One squad attacked the enemy position and the enemy fled to the south and was engaged with small arms fire, arty, and ARA. Results: 6 NVA KIA, 1 60mm mortar tube, 1 AK-47, 1 SKS, and 1 Chicom carbine captured.

**0310H** (YD596264): Co. D sustained 1 US WIA from a boobytrapped Chicom grenade (with tripwire device) and at 0925H sustained another WIA from a buried boobytrapped grenade with pressure type device. At 1025H (YD590270) Co. D had 2 more WIA from a boobytrapped large bag of explosives, medevac completed at 1033H. Results: 4 US WIA.

## May 25, 1968

MG Barsanti came out to the Co. D's location to award a silver star to 2Lt Trabert and bronze stars to 4 other 1st Platoon men.

**2000H** (YD595268): Co. D observed enemy mortar fire landing in the vicinity of YD598268. Fire was not returned as the enemy location could not be determined.

**2005H** (YD602263): A Co. D ambush engaged 4 VC carrying individual weapons while wading across a river. Results: 4 VC KIA, 4 1W destroyed.

## May 26, 1968

**2025H** (YD602267): A Co. D ambush position observed 2 individuals climb from a hole, vic. YD603268, and run toward the river. The ambush element then moved to YD603263 and continued to observe.

**2150H** (YD597267): Co. D received 12-15 rounds of unknown type mortar fire. Arty was adjusted on the suspected enemy firing position, YD604264. Results: negative US casualties, enemy casualties unknown.

## May 27, 1968
**1223H** (YD599263): Co. D sustained 1 US WIA when a man stepped on a boobytrapped grenade (with trip wire device) placed in a C-ration can. Results: 1 US WIA.

**1823H** Co. D reports 50-75 personnel moving west at YD532278. Arty fired on location.

## May 28, 1968
**1157H** Co. D reports that RF in sweeping a village at YD605267 had found 1000 lbs. of rice, 100 gal of milk, 200 gal of cooking oil, 100 lbs. of rolled oats, 6 new AK-47s, 50 lbs. of soap, and 200 lbs. of sugar; all evacuated to district headquarters. Co. D established a blocking position from YD607278 to YD605268 while RF searched the cordoned village.

## May 29, 1968
**0837H** (YD595291): Co. D captured and destroyed in place 1 boobytrapped cylinder packed with explosives.

**0915H** (YD595285): Co. D sustained 1 US WIA from a command detonated 105 round. A sweep of the area uncovered 2 additional rounds that were then destroyed in place. Results: 1 US WIA (E: PSGT George Parker, Jr., 1st Platoon SGT).

**1050H** (YD595234): Co. D captured and destroyed in place 13 boobytrapped 105 rounds. The rounds were located in a hole with pull type device.

**1823H** Co. D CA'd from YD600280 to YD642257, closing at 1902H.

## May 31, 1968
**0920H** Co. D CA'd from YD644258 to YD595230.

**1349H** (YD602228): Co. D had 1 man go into a bunker and come out with a white substance on his face which caused it to swell. A medevac was initially requested and later canceled.

## June 1, 1968
**1106H** (Y0603233) Co. D reported finding an ARVN helmet floating down the river, the helmet had the name Smith written on it.

**1718H** Co. D CA'd from YD599235 to YD656256, closed at 1745H.

## June 2, 1968
Co. D moved to FB Pinky and assumed security for the firebase. At 0310H 1/D moved by CH-47 to OP T-Bone and assumed security mission, and 1 platoon with 1 PF Platoon provided security for MEDCAP at YD724264.

## June 3, 1968
One platoon from Co. D provided security for MEDCAP at YD693243.

## June 4, 1968
Co. D (-1/D) provided security for FB Pinky and secured minesweep from FB Pinky south to Hue, and 1/D provided security for OP TBone.

**0306H** (FB Pinky): Co. D reported a trip flare went off around bunker #19, but nothing was sighted. 1/D near FB T-Bone found and destroyed 2 Chicom grenades, 1 NVA canteen, 3 carbine magazines, and 1 charge of 0-4 wrapped in bamboo.

## June 5, 1968
Co. D(-1/D) continued security mission for FB Pinky and 1/D continued security mission for OP T-Bone, with both elements conducting RIFs in the adjacent area.

## June 6, 1968
**1032H** (YD637191 ): 1/D found 6 bunkers with concrete sides (2 large enough to hold 6-3 personnel), 3 well camouflaged huts (2 of which were partially built), 1 rucksack, and 1 pair of PJs. Results: 1 rucksack and 1 pair of PJs captured and evacuated, bunkers and huts destroyed.

**1850H** (YD681711 ): 1/D at OP T-Bone observed 3 mortar flashes outside their AO. This information was passed on to the 1st BDE.

## June 10, 1968
**1040H** (YD646216): A Co. D patrol found a 250 lb. bomb.

## June 11, 1968
**1145H** (YD693275): The Pathfinders with Co. D received small arms fire from the east as they swept down from the northwest. Small arms fire was returned silencing the enemy fire. A sweep of the area met with negative results.

**1330H** (YD678288): The Pathfinders engaged an estimated VC squad with small arms and automatic weapons fire. The enemy force returned 1 M-79 round and automatic weapons fire before fleeing west.

**1408H** (YD680282): Co. D while sweeping the area of the 1330H Pathfinder engagement received 8-10 rounds of M-79 fire. The company returned small arms and automatic weapons fire silencing the enemy fire. Results: negative US casualties, enemy casualties unknown.

2125H (YD653203): 1/D received 2 unknown type mortar rounds (both duds) impacting 200m outside their NDP. Fire was not returned since the source could not be determined.

## June 12, 1968
**0001H** The battalion reports they are unable to contact Co. D by radio, finally establishing contact at 0030H through artillery channels. They were informed that the Co. D RTO had fallen asleep.
**1130H** (YD682282): Co. D found 2400 lbs. of rice.
**1320H** 1/D moved by air from OP T-Bone to Co. D OP location, YD646247.
**1700H** Co. D returned to FB Pinky.

## June 13, 1968
**0200H** Acting on a tip from an NVA informer and under orders from LTC Heiter, Co. D, along with an ARVN Platoon (Pathfinders), followed an NVA informer into the hills where he said 5 other NVA were located. At 0712H (YD628196), the Pathfinders with Co. D engaged and killed 2 VC running from a bunker while sweeping southwest from their NDP. 1 AK-47 and 1 SKS were also captured. At 0945H at the same location, Co. D received small arms and automatic weapons fire from an estimated enemy squad to the southwest (vic. YD625191). Organic weapons fire was returned silencing the enemy fire at 1015H. A sweep of the area was conducted with negative results. Results: 1 Pathfinder WIA, 2 VC KIA, 1 AK-47 and 1 SKS captured.

## June 15, 1968
**0605H** (YD683260): A Co. D ambush enroute to their NDP spotted 1 NVA hiding in the bushes. He was engaged with small arms fire resulting in 1 NVA POW WIA, evacuated to LZ Sally at 0643H. His pack had 1 US .45 pistol and a NVA flag.
**0830H** 2d BDE requested a Dog Tracker team to assist Co. D in searching for traces of a VC force in their area. Also have a Chieu Hoi to assist in the search.

**2230H** (YD660260): Co. D ambush spotted 3 VC and approached their position from the rear. The rear security element of 3 men engaged the VC with small arms fire and the VC returned fire. One Co. D man with a starlight scope tried to maneuver across a trail and was hit in the head (KIA). The ambush also set off 4 claymores and fired arty. Results: 1 US KIA (Robert David Brockman), enemy casualties unknown.

## June 16, 1968

**2245H** (YD660256): An ambush patrol from Co. D executed an ambush on 10-15 VC, engaging them with small arms and automatic weapons fire, claymores and illumination, as they moved southwest to northeast along a trail. The remnants of the enemy fled to the southwest, where they returned small arms fire on the ambush position. The ambush was relocated and the former ambush area was registered for arty. Results: negative US casualties, 6 VC KIA, 1 AK-47 and several grenades captured.

## June 17, 1968

**0625H** In checking the contact area of the previous night, Co. D found evidence that other wounded VC were dragged from the location.
**0740H** Co. D arrived at LZ Sally for showers and change of clothes.

## June 18, 1968

**0906H** Co. D CA'd from YD633247 to YD6400257, closing at 0930H. 1 of the lift ships while landing on the LZ had a tail rotor hit some shrubs resulting in damage. An element of Co. D secured the Huey until it could be extracted.
**1150H** (YD605222): Co. D discovered 13 bunkers with overhead cover while sweeping the area on the west bank of the Song Bo, into which they conducted a CA at 0930H. The following items were found at the location: 1 60mm mortar tube, 16 60mm mortar rounds, 3 RPG rounds, 500 rounds of 7.62 ammo, 45 gallons of cooking oil and 1 wallet with a south Vietnamese ID card.
**1705H** Co. D moved by air from YD598225 to YD677245, from where they establish night ambushes.

## June 19, 1968

**0005H** (YD664256): A Co. D ambush patrol engaged 4 VC moving to the northeast with small arms fire and claymores. A sweep of the area was conducted with the aid of illumination, which resulted in 4 VC KIA; 2 drag tracks were also discovered. Simultaneously, movement was heard and engaged with small arms fire. The patrol was then relocated and arty was fired into the area with negative results. Results: negative US casualties, 4 VC KIA.

## June 21, 1968
BN OP located at FB Pinky.
**0027H** (YD639242): A Co. D ambush patrol engaged 7 VC with small arms fire and illumination. Upon coming under fire, the enemy force entered a nearby trench line and fled to the south without returning fire. Arty was not employed due to the close proximity of Co. B's NDP. A first light sweep of the area met with negative results.
**0753H** 1/D began moving by log bird to OP T-Bone, closing at 0820H.
**1038H** (YD642202): Co. D while conducting a RIF 2 KM west of FB TBone, found 2 graves containing 2 VC bodies. Results 2 VC KIA.

## June 23, 1968
**0505H** Co. D received mortar fire and at 0513H came under ground attack receiving grenades and RPG rounds. The Company returned organic weapons fire under illumination. Results: no US casualties, enemy casualties unknown.

## June 24, 1968
BN CP located at OP T-Bone.
Co. D (-) provided security for OP T-Bone and established platoon ambushes in the area.

## June 26, 1968
Co. D continued to provide security for FB T-Bone and conduct ambushes in the area.

## June 27, 1968
**1235H** (YD632195): Co. D found old bunkers and at 1253H found 26 meters of 4 strand commo wire while conducting RIF operations to the south. The wire was evacuated to LZ Sally.

## June 28, 1968
**1210H** (YD628190): Co. D found several notebooks, miscellaneous spare parts for AK-47, and 3 RPG-2 rounds while conducting a RIF operation to the southwest of their NDP. The notebooks were evacuated to LZ Sally. A further search of the area revealed 1 AK-47 and 1 unidentified Chicom carbine, both of which were in unserviceable condition. Results: 1 AK-

47, 1 unidentified Chicom carbine, 3 RPG-2 rounds, spare parts for AK-47, and several notebooks captured.

**June 30, 1968**
**0827H** (YD616179): Co. D found two empty huts, and at 1150H found a hootch (5'x5'x7') with a grass roof in the same area.

**July 1, 1968**
**1645H** (YD604166): Co. D found 1 LMG with an extra barrel while conducting a RIF operation to the southwest. Results: 1 LMG with spare barrel captured and evacuated.
The 101st AIRBORNE DIVISION was redesignated (General Order 325) the 101st AIRBORNE DIVISION (AIRMOBILE).

**July 2, 1968**
**1144H** (YD598163): 1/D during a RIF operation to the southwest of their NDP, discovered a grave containing 1 VC body. Results: 1 VC KIA.

**July 5, 1968**
**1255H** (YD589183): Co. D found 10 bunkers (with 3 showing signs of recent use) near a trail with a water buffalo track on it and barefoot tracks heading north.
**1530H** (YD584177): Co. D had 1 US WIA when an M-79 accidentally discharged (the weapon was on safe). Results: 1 US.

**July 6, 1968**
**1306H** Co. D CA'd from YD577174 to YD793191, complete at 1430H, at which time Co. D became OPCON of 1-501 (thru 7/13).

**July 7, 1968**
**1338H** (YD828178): 1/3/D searched for a sniper who had fired at a vehicle on Highway 1. Search was made with negative results.
**1901H** 2/D had a man go berserk at the LCU ramp in Hue, when he fired his M-16 into the river hitting a small child in a sampan.

**July 8, 1968**
Co. D (OPCON to 1-501) discovered 3 bullet holes in the Pipeline at YD815186. A repair team was notified to repair it.

## July 9, 1968
**0158H** (YD808189): Co. D while in an ambush position heard a man shouting in Vietnamese and 2 or 3 shots fired at YD813190. A check of the area at first light produced negative results.

## July 13, 1968
**2013H** (YD823182): Co. D observed an explosion 50-75m south of their position. The explosion believed to be by grenade, a check of the area revealed no damage.

## July 14, 1968
**0845H** Co. D returned to OPCON of 2-501 from the 1-501.
**1029H** (YD640170): 1/D found and destroyed an old bunker with about 50 rounds of .50 cal and about 150 rounds of NVA 7.62.
**1108H** Co. D had 1 man medevaced with a high fever, complete at 1137H.

## July 18, 1968
**1135H** Co. D had 1 man medevaced with an unknown sickness.
**1525H** (YD629146): Co. D found a dead water buffalo (apparently of natural causes) and tracks of a "big" cat.
**1625H** (YD630145): Co. D found 10 122mm rocket canisters.

## July 19, 1968
Co. D(-1/D) searched area of Hill 246 (YD624144) which showed signs of about 40-50 bunkers which used to be on the hill but were apparently destroyed by airstrikes.
**0902H** (YD617139): 1/D patrol spotted 1 NVA wearing an OD shirt and US pistol belt. The platoon engaged the NVA with small arms fire, resulting in 1 NVA KIA and 1 AK-47 captured. Results: 1 NVA KIA, 1 IWC.

**1314H** 3/D moved by air from YD624144 to COL CO Beach for R&R standdown.

## July 20, 1968

**0808H** (YD614140): Co. D found 5-6 bunkers in the area, along with two blue sweat shirts, 1 OD-type jacket, and 1 sign in Vietnamese pointing the way to a latrine.

**0905H** (YD613193): Co. D's point man received a burst of AK-47 fire from about 400m to the southwest, with negative results.

**1244H** (YD615140): Co. D while conducting search operations received AK-47 fire from 3 persons. Fire was returned with small arms, automatic weapons, and arty, with the enemy fleeing south. A sweep of the area had negative results. Results: 1 US KIA, enemy casualties unknown.

## July 22, 1968

**0845H** (YD602139): Co. D while conducting a RIF operation received AK-47 fire from an estimated enemy squad at YD600137, resulting in 1 US WIA (E). The enemy was engaged with small arms and automatic weapons fire, and arty with unknown results. Results: 1 US WIA.

## July 24, 1968

**1100H** (YD614138): Co. D found 80 bunkers dispersed over the following 3 locations, YD614138, YD617139, and YD621141.

**1253H** (YD619138 - 5 KM north of FB Bastogne): Co. D while conducting a RIF discovered an ammo cache in a bunker and the nearby area consisting of: 72 RPG-2 rounds with charges wrapped in plastic, 104 rounds of 57mm RR, 14 60mm mortar rounds, 18 82mm mortar rounds, 50 lbs. of explosives, 200 rounds of 7.62 ammo, and 1 unknown type round. Results: samples of each round evacuated, rest destroyed.

**1705H** (YD619138): Co. D located some documents in a bunker, including 5 copy books, a rice and tax collection book (no names), 1 newspaper, VC propaganda, and 1 diary about a man with 2 uncles. 1 uncle who went north with the Viet Minh and came back to the Huong Tra district as a cadre to set up cells along Highway 1, and 1 uncle at Hue. All documents were evacuated to LX Sally on a log bird. One of the documents (dated July 15, 1968) indicated the village chief (Nguyen Van Mau) of Huong Tranh received 30,000 peos to buy rice for the VC. Also, on June 20 the VC collected rice and taxes from Lieu Thuong hamlet and gave the money to Le Thi Hoa and Le Thi Ke of that hamlet to keep for the VC.

## July 25, 1968
**0815H** (YD619138): Co. D while conducting a RIF found and destroyed 33 bunkers. Results: 33 bunkers destroyed.

**1645H** (YD620144): Co. D discovered and destroyed 1 hut containing 200 rounds of AK-47 ammo.

## July 27, 1968
**1000H** (YD635155): Co. D while on a search and destroy mission found 1 SKS in a bunker. Results: 1 SKS captured and evacuated.

## July 29, 1968
**0755H** (YD624158): 3/D found and destroyed 17 82mm mortar rounds laying on the floor of a hootch, and at 0835H at the same location found 2 SKS, 1 Ml rifle, and 1 B-40 along with about 60 hootches with bunkers.

**1703H** Co. D(-) moved by air from YD619153 to YD653330, closing at 1803H, at which time the Company became OPCON to 1-502.

## July 30, 1968
**0735H** Co. D medevaced 1 man that had fallen on an engineer stake and injured his back.

**1055H** Co. D moved by OH-47 from YD667303 to LZ Sally, closing at 1128H.

## Aug. 1, 1968
BN CP located at FB T-Bone.
Co. D received a class on mines and boobytraps.

## Aug. 2, 1968
**1140H** Co. D completed a medevac for 1 heat casualty.

## Aug. 4, 1968
**0747H** Co. D competed a medevac for 1 man with a high fever.

## Aug. 5, 1968
**0645H** The Co. D CO reported that the PF element with his 2nd Platoon ambush refuses to move and his 2nd Platoon will not stop for them since they have a mission to complete. At 0921 the PF element was released from Co. D.

## Aug. 7, 1968

**0804H** Co. D(-1/D), along with 60 RF/PF forces, CA'd from YD628224 and YD637247 to YD577171, complete at 0917H. At 1805 the elements were extracted from YD577171 to YD628224 and YD637247, closing at 1843H. 1/D occupied an OP at YD608211 during the day.

## Aug. 8, 1968

Co. D became OPCON to the 1st BDE.

## Aug. 16, 1968

**1033H** 2/D completed a medevac for 1 man with a sprained ankle.

**1840H** 2/D requested a medevac for another man with a sprained ankle, medevac completed at 1917H.

## Aug. 17, 1968

**1605H** (YD613211): Co. D requested a medevac for 1 man with a machete wound of the hand, medevac complete at 1620H.

## Aug. 20, 1968

**1210H** (YD597196): 2/D engaged 2 NVA in khaki's with small arms fire, 200m from their position. The enemy fled to the southeast. The area was swept with negative results. At 1355H (YD598182) a man with 2/D received a bullet that bounced off his helmet. At 1453H 3/D at YD559195 received sniper fire from approximately 200m west of their position. At the same time 2/D, located at YD599191, received small arms and RPG fire from an estimated enemy squad approximately 200m south of their position. Arty was called on grid Y0599190 and ARA was on station.

The unit attempted to move back into the area and received 3 RPG rounds. Arty was again adjusted into the area, complete at 1535H. The unit moved into the area and at 1814H received a few rounds of small arms fire and 1 RPG round. Arty again adjusted into the area. 2 US were WIA, including 1 man with a broken leg requiring a medevac. When the medevac came in at 1935H it received small arms and RPG fire and was unable to land, although it took no hits. The medevac was completed the following morning. Results: 1 US WIA, 1 US WIA (M), enemy casualties unknown.

## Aug. 21 1968

**0805H** A medevac for 1 WIA (with broken leg) with Co. D was completed on the second try of the morning; the first attempt at 0730H had to be aborted due to a bad hoist.

**1045H** (YD600191-6 KM east of FB T-Bone): 1/D made contact with an estimated reinforced enemy squad, receiving heavy small arms fire from the southwest at 20-30 meters. The platoon returned organic weapons fire; Arty, Gunships and TAC air were also employed. Contact completed at 1055H, with 2 US WIA (medevac completed at 1135H). At 1546H while making a check of the area of contact the Company received small arms and RPG fire, resulting in 1 US WIA (E). The Company pulled back, and Gunships and TAC air were again employed. At 1614H the Company again received automatic weapons fire, resulting in 3 US WIA (E). Contact completed at 1755H. At 1959H 3/D requested a medevac for 1 man who accidentally shot himself in the hand, medevac completed at 2035H. At 2002H Co. D reported a Starlight scope was lost during the contact. Results: 6 US WIA, 2 US WIA (M), 10 VC KIA.

## Aug. 22, 1968

**1255H** (YD596192): Co. D received a burst of automatic weapons fire from YD599190, The company pulled back, called in Arty and swept the area with negative results. Negative US casualties.

**1435H** (YD565040): Co. D while on a RIF found 8 bunkers (7'x7' with overhead cover) and 7 fighting positions. Nearby were 4 graves about a month old, 27 empty ammo boxes, and 1/2 case of mortar ammo, all of which were destroyed. At 1510H the Company found 53 1-2 man fighting positions at YD568038, the positions were about 2 months old and not recently used. Results: 4 NVA KIA.

## Aug. 23, 1968

**1200H** (YD599192): Co. D found 6 spider holes, 3 bunkers and 3 trenches; all of which appeared to have been recently used. All positions were destroyed. The Company also recovered the Starlight scope that had been lost during contact on Aug. 20; the scope was found all shot-up.

## Aug. 24, 1968

**0955H** (YD597188): 2/D engaged 2 VC with small arms fire. The VC returned fire and fled to the southwest. Arty was called in with negative results. Results: negative US casualties.

**1150H** (YD598185): 1/D heard Vietnamese voices in the woodline. The company reconnoitered the area by fire; a sweep proved negative.

## Aug. 25, 1968

**0920H** (YD595187): 1/D while on a RIF received 1 round of small arms fire which hit their point man. Direction of fire was unknown and a sweep of the area proved negative. Results: 1 US WIA (E: Lawrence Brewer, Jr.).

**1315H** (YD596181): 1/D on a RIF found a day old grave with 1 NVA body. Negative weapons or documents. Results: 1 NVA KIA.

## Aug. 26, 1968

**1356H** (YD594191): 1D engaged an unknown size enemy force and the enemy fled south. At 1531H 1/D reported it had 1 man fall down and cut his eye, medevac completed at 1743H. At 1610H Co. D(-1/D) engaged 3 enemy (point for a larger force) resulting in 2 VC KIA and captured 1 SMG while occupying blocking positions 6 KM west of FB T- Bone (YD595183). An enemy force of about 15 returned fire with small arms fire and grenades, resulting in 2 US WIA, medevac completed at 1758H. The Company pulled back and Arty was employed. Results: 2 US WIA, 1 US, 2 VC KIA, 1 SMG captured.

## Aug. 27, 1968

**1110H** (YD593387): 1/D found a base camp of 15 bunkers. Also found were 100 rounds of AK-47 ammo, 1 9mm SMG, and miscellaneous documents. Results: 1 IWC, ammo destroyed, documents evacuated.

**1310H** (YD593187): Co. D found and destroyed a 250 lb. bomb.

**1711H** (YD597185 - 7 KM southwest of FB T-Bone): While moving up a hill Co. D made contact with an estimated reinforced enemy platoon, receiving automatic weapons fire resulting in 2 US WIA. The company sighted 35 1-man bunkers freshly dug and camouflaged, 15m to their front. Employing TAC air, arty, gunships, and organic weapons, the company maneuvered against the enemy platoon. The company received a heavy volume of automatic weapons fire, 10-20 RPG rounds, 5-6 60mm mortar rounds, and a ground attack from their front by 30 to 40 enemy. The heavy contact continued until dark. At 1917H the medevac ship went in and picked up 7 WIAs and received RPG fire. An additional WIA resulted from the RPG fire leaving 2 WIAs on the ground. At this time ARA and the BN CO (LTC James A. Heiter) went in and picked up the 2 WIAs and received 6-10 rounds of RPG fire with negative hits. Results: 9 US WIA, 1 US WIA (M), 12 NVA KIA, 1 IWC.

## Aug. 28, 1968
**1639H** (YD590185 -7KM southwest of FB T-Bone): Co. D made contact with an estimated reinforced enemy squad located l00m west of their position. The company received small arms, automatic weapons, and RPG fire, and returned organic weapons fire and employed arty. Results: negative US casualties, enemy casualties unknown.

## Aug. 29, 1968
**1600H** (YD590185): A search by Co. D of the Aug. 28 contact area revealed 20 bunkers, 3 OPs, and 3 NVA KIA.

## Aug. 30, 1968
**0926H** Co. D moved by air from YD590184 to LZ Sally, closing at 1038H.

## Sept. 1, 1968
BN CP located on FB T-Bone.
**1150H** (OP Apache): Co. D reports sighting of red smoke at YD616234, where no friendlies were reported. Arty was directed on the location.

## Sept. 2, 1968
**0912H** 2/D moved by OH-47 from YD628223 to COL CO Beach.

## Sept. 3, 1968
**1805H** 2/D moved by OH-47 from COL CO Beach to OP Apache.

## Sept. 6, 1968
**1045H** 1/D moved by air from YD606247 to LZ Sally, and at 1700H 1/D departed LZ Sally to conduct a RIF and ambushes in the area of YD628237. 2/D conducted a RIF from OP Apache to LZ Sally, closing at 1245H. 3/D conducted a RIF around OP Apache.

## Sept. 7. 1968
**0805H** 2/D moved by air from YD646224 to YD617262, closed at 0905H.
**0930H** (Y0608263): 2/D picked up 10 detainees (7 females and 3 males) and the "snatch team" took them to LZ Sally.
**0957H** 1/D moved by air from YD612239 to YD623262, closed at 1000H.
**1130H** (YD621271): 1/D picked up 3 detainees and sent them to LZ Sally; detainees later classified IC.

## Sept. 8, 1968

**1425H** (YD607262): While moving northeast, the point man of 1/D observed 2 individuals on the trail wearing khakis. The point man fired warning shots and the individuals fled north into a village. The element checked the area with negative results.

## Sept. 10, 1968

**1055H** (YD628262): 2/D apprehended 3 detainees (2 males & 1 female), who were taken to LZ Sally by a log bird.
**1710H** 1/D CA'd from Y0628241 to YD614208, closing at 1735H.

## Sept. 12, 1968

**1700H** (YD589221): Co. D observed sampans. The sampans were sunk by artillery with negative assessment.

## Sept. 14, 1968

**2020H** 1/D reported seeing 5 mortar flashes at Y0594184. They couldn't hear the rounds impacting but called in arty on the location.

## Sept. 16, 1968

**1204H** 2/D apprehended 2 women detainees (with no IDs on their person), who were released at 1510H since they had IDs at home.

## Sept. 17, 1968

**0758H** 2/D moved by air from LZ Sally to YD659268, closed at 0810H.
**0800H-1200H** (YD662258): Co. D during operation Eagle Flight detained and screened 176 persons (most by 2/D) in cooperation with Huong Phu (V) personnel and Huong Tra (D) Pacification Forces. All detainees were later released as IC.
**1042H** (YD620213): 3/D requested a medevac for 1 man with a possible broken shoulder, medevac completed at 1122H.

## Sept. 18, 1968

**1125H** Co. D requested a medevac for 1 man with a cut hand.
**1511H** 1/D conducted a RIF from OP Apache to LZ Sally, and became the reaction force. 2/D conducted a RIF to YD624235, and then to YD644243 to secure a downed Huey until extraction, then continued to OP Apache.

## Sept. 20, 1968

**0643H** 3/D CA'd from YD614208 to YD639251, closing at 0656H. At 0704H 2/D CA'd from OP Apache to YD625258, closing at 0711H.

## Sept. 25, 1968

**0920H** (YD596187): 1/D received sporadic small arms fire resulting in the point man being wounded, medevac completed at 1002H. The medevac bird also received small arms fire from 8-10 VC west of 1/D's position. The crew aboard the medevac bird had trouble getting the basket up and one crew member somehow got hung up and was hanging on the skid of the chopper when it took off, so the chopper had to land on a nearby LZ to get the man back inside the Huey. 1/D pursued the VC firing on the medevac bird, but the enemy fled to the north. Results: 1 US WIA.

Co. D became OPCON to 1-501, and provided security for COL CO Beach.

## Sept. 28, 1968

**0805H** Co. D returned to OPCON of 2-501, and Co. D (-3/D) moved by CH-47 from COL CO Beach to FB T-Bone, closing at 0823H. At 0957H 3/D moved by CH-47 from COL CO Beach to LZ Sally, closing at 1009H. At 1228H 3/D CA'd from LZ Sally to YD615206 (LZ secured by 1/A and 3/A), closing at 1235H.

## Sept. 29, 1968

Co. D(-) provided security for FB T-Bone.

## Oct. 2, 1968

BN CP located at FB T-Bone.

Co. D continued to provide security for FB T-Bone; with 2/D pulling ambushes at YD626207 and YD631211, 3/D ambushing at YD616205 and YD612210, and 1/D conducted a RIF to YD644218 and returned to FB T-Bone. 2/D conducted a RIF to YD609213 and 3/D conducted a RIF to YD629201.

## Oct. 3, 1968

Co. D continued to provide security for FB T-Bone.

**1200H** (YD648198): While on a RIF near FB T-Bone 1/D found 5 graves containing 5 NVA KIA. Results: 5 NVA KIA.

## Oct. 7, 1968

**1004H** Co. D (- 1/D & 2/D) moved by CH-47 from FB T-Bone to YD792204 (complete at 1011H), and reverted to OPCON 2-17 Cav.

**1030H** 1/D moved by CH-47 from FB T-Bone to YD847232 (complete at 1038H), and reverted to OPCON 1-501.

**1201H** 2/D moved by air from YD609200 to LZ Sally; at 1343H 2/D moved by CH-47 from LZ Sally to YD792204 (complete at 1355H), and reverted to OPCON 2-17 Cav.

## Oct. 9, 1968

Co. D (- 1/D) continued OPCON 2-17 Cav.; with 1/D OPCON to 1-501.

**1315H** 1/D moved by OH-47 from YD833229 to LZ Sally (complete at 1325H), and returned to 2-501 OPCON.

## Oct. 10, 1968

**0825H** Co. D (- 1/D) returned to 2-501 OPCON. Co. D (- 1/D) moved by truck from YD786203 to LZ Sally (complete at 0925H) and linked up with 1/D.

**1456H** Co. D conducted RIF to YD649252, then Co. D (- 2/D) continued to YD650226 and 2/D continued to YD660237.

## Oct. 13, 1968

**0945H** (YD598128): 3/D spotted 1 NVA with weapons, wearing green khakis walking along a trail. The NVA spotted the element and evaded to the west just as he was engaged with small arms and M-79 fire. The platoon pursued the enemy, but could not regain contact.

## Oct. 15, 1968

**1720H** (YD595131): Co. D spotted and engaged 3 enemy moving to the north with small arms and automatic weapons fire, causing the enemy to flee to the southwest. The unit pursued but could not regain contact with the fleeing enemy.

**1835H** 1/D moved by air from YD595131 to LZ Sally.

## Oct. 16, 1968

**0728H** Co. D (- 1/D) moved by air from YD595131 to LZ Sally (complete at 0808H) and linked up with 1/D.

**1150H** BN CP moved by air from LZ Sally to ZD116014.

**1417H** Co. D moved by CH-47 from LZ Sally to YD116104, complete at 1457H.

**1457H** 2-501 reverted to OPCON of 1st BDE, with the BN CP moving to FB Tomahawk (45 kilometers southeast of Hue).

## Oct. 23, 1968

**1538H** (Z0128938): 3/D engaged 1 NVA moving southwest along a trail. Results: 1 NVA KIA, 1 AK47 captured.

**1600H** (Z0128938): 2/D and 3/D engaged 5 NVA receiving small arms and RPG fire. The platoon returned fire with arty, gunships, and TAC AIR. Results: 1 US WIA, 2 NVA KIA, 2 AK-5O captured.

**1755H** (ZC128938): A medevac was completed for 2/D man WIA; medevac aircraft received ground fire.

**1800H** (Z0128938): 3/D received additional small arms and RPG fire from the southeast and the platoon engaged 1 NVA coming from the southeast. Results: 1 NVA KIA, 1 SKS and 1 claymore captured.

### Oct. 24, 1968

**0906H** (Z0124940): 1/D, while moving northwest toward Co. A, received small arms and automatic weapons fire from an initial estimate of 2 NVA in an enemy bunker. With a Pink Team maneuvering in the area, 1/D maneuvered against the enemy which was now believed to be a NVA platoon. 2/D began moving to link up with 1/D, which had received an unknown number of grenades and by 1005H had received 4 WIA.

Contact continued for another two hours as Co. D received satchel charges and heavy automatic weapons and RPG fire from the dug in enemy element. Medevacs were urgently requested for the seriously wounded, which by 1150H had grown to 7 WIA. The medevacs were not completed until 1301H.

In what was turning out to be a bizarre day, Co. D at 1440H received 3 additional WIA with shrapnel from light fire team RIF #10 who had mistaken the Company for the enemy. All the wounded required a medevac, which was completed at 1530H. Results for the day: 10 WIA, unconfirmed number of NVA KIA.

At 1807H Helicopter #26 (call sign Black Widow) crashed due to mechanical failure at location ZC126936. Co. D was sent to secure the chopper. Two helicopter personnel were medevaced at 1910H and two more at 1932H, as Co. D continued to secure the chopper.

### Oct. 25, 1968

**1001H** Co. D CA'd from Z0118946 to LZ Tom, complete at 1036H.

### Oct. 29, 1968

**1900H** Co. D received 30-40 60mm mortar rounds resulting in 3 WIA (M). Suspected mortar sights at ZD121001 and ZD122991.

### Oct. 30, 1968

**1040H** (ZD119995): Co. D found 8 freshly dug fighting positions, 3 82mm mortar rounds, 1 VC entrenching tool, and 15 empty 75mm RR canisters. Arty had recently impacted in the area.

# 7.
# The Days of Blue Falcon Ridge

## Chuck Leshikar

In the middle of October 1968, the Delta Raiders were operating to the southwest of Fire Support Base T-Bone deep in the mountainous jungle west of Hue, South Vietnam. The weather had been very rainy, and moving through the mountains was very difficult because of the wet, cold and mud. On October 13, the Company was moving in that area and we had stopped for a break. I was serving as the 3rd Platoon Leader. When we stopped for the break, I was called up to the Company Headquarters. On that day, the 3rd Platoon was the rear element, and was responsible for providing rear security. Before going to Headquarters, I established security on a major trail that ran down off of a ridge. While I was up at the Company Headquarters, I heard firing and I ran back to my element and found that an NVA soldier had walked up the trail and the rear security had fired on him. At the time, I asked the men why they hadn't blown their claymores and they said that they had just forgotten about it and had gotten nervous and fired on the NVA soldier. He fled to the east of our location and was not seen again.

The next morning, as the Company was moving out, I was checking out the sections of the perimeter that the 3rd Platoon had occupied. As usual, I found a number if items left behind that needed to be taken care of such as empty C rations cans, full C rations cans, ammunition etc. At one position, I found a claymore mine which had been left in place. I called Platoon Sergeant, SFC James Deland, to get the three men from this position back to the position. When the three men came back, I asked to see their claymore mines. One of the men did not have his claymore with him. I told him to retrieve the claymore and bring it to me. As he handed the mine to me, I noticed that it was unusually light. I took a close look at the mine and then removed the back. There was no C-4 explosive in it. I asked him where the C-4 was and he told me that he had used it to heat his meals. We immediately engaged in a very strongly worded and intense counseling

## Ch. 7 / The Days of Blue Falcon Ridge

session on why we do not used the C-4 from a mine to heat our meals. It also immediately became apparent why he had not used his claymore mine on the NVA soldier the previous afternoon. At the first break that day, all squad leaders checked their men to ensure that all claymore mines were serviceable. Not surprisingly, SFC Deland received a number of requests for new claymores.

The Delta Raiders continued to recon in force in this mountainous area and on October 15 around 10:00, the Company was informed that we would be resupplied that day and that we needed to find an LZ (landing zone). The 3rd Platoon was the point element that day and we moved up to a little hilltop. The Company set out security and the 3rd Platoon began blowing an LZ. The Platoon that was on point for the day had the task for blowing the LZ, so we collected all the C4 that we could get and we proceeded to blow the LZ. There was a lot of timber on this hilltop, and we used up a lot of C4. We had the LZ cleared and started resupplying around noon. The log bird (helicopter) came in and dropped off a five-day supply of rations for each man and resupply of ammunition, clean clothes, and what appeared to be cold soft drinks and left. The Company Headquarters element began to distribute the resupply of food and ammunition and, about 30 minutes later, the Company commander CPT Michael H. Feurer was informed that we were to stay on the LZ until further notice.

It was around 16:30 in the afternoon that we got word that we were going to be extracted from the LZ and moved back to LZ Sally which was welcome news because we could look forward to a couple of days rest and being able to clean up. The first extraction lift came in and informed us that there was one tree on the perimeter of the LZ that was too large and we had to blow the tree in order to get the extraction, so we collected up as many claymores as we could, removed the C4, and proceeded to blow this tree. The tree was so large that three men could not reach totally around it. We packed about one pound of C4 in the front and about three pounds in the back, then we blew it. It was one hell of an explosion — we looked up and saw the tree and it was just shaking at the top and it wasn't going over. The tree shook for what appeared to be three or four minutes (I imagine it was 30 seconds), and then it finally fell over the side of the hill and took the whole side of the hill out. The first flight of helicopters came in and picked up the 1st Platoon and then proceeded back to LZ Sally.

While the rest of the Company waited to be picked up, one of the 3rd Platoon's security positions saw three NVA soldiers coming up the side of the hill and opened up on them. The NVA fled. There were no NVA soldiers wounded or hit and they didn't return fire on us. About the same time, the extraction birds (helicopters) came back to pick up the second group of people. They picked up some from Headquarters and some from the 2nd Platoon and flew them back to LZ Sally.

At this time (it was around 18:00), a severe storm moved in — a lot of rain and lightning — and because of the storm, they cancelled any other lifts out, so the remaining Headquarters element, the 3rd Platoon and part of the 2nd Platoon, had to stay on the LZ overnight with this heavy storm in progress. We pulled into a tight perimeter. We still had most of the resupply from that day and stayed up most of the night because of the contact we had had with the NVA coming up the side of the hill. The next morning it started out to be a beautiful day. The rain had quit about 04:30 in the morning, so we had only had about an hour sleep when the sun came up and they informed us that the birds would be in to pick us up around 07:00 in the morning. The first birds came in around 09:00 and picked the rest of the Company and flew us back to LZ Sally. When the we got back to LZ Sally, instead of being able to rest as we had anticipated, we were informed that the Company had been extracted so that we could be move to another area which was just north of Da Nang to a fire support base called Tomahawk. In short order, we changed clothes, took a shower, got cleaned up and around 16:00, helicopters came and picked us up andflew us what appeared to be 30 kilometers passed Hue, down towards Da Nang. We landed at fire support base Tomahawk where we thought we would be able to stay the night.

Once the Company was all present, the Platoon leaders received orders from CPT Feurer on what the operation was going to be. The Platoon leaders had assumed that the Company would stay overnight on fire support base Tomahawk, but we were told that the Company would be moving out after dark, heading towards the mountains. When we left Tomahawk, Alpha Company was on the right, Delta Company was in the middle, Charlie Company was going to be CA'd via helicopters over on the left. The mission of the Delta Raiders was to move off Tomahawk during the hours of darkness, walk about 6 to 8 kilometers across a rice patty to the base of the mountains and then proceed up into the mountains. A night move was hairy anyway, but a night move with no rest between redeployments was even more hairy.

After dark, the Delta Raiders proceeded to move off the fire support base and it started raining. Alpha Company moved off Tomahawk at approximately the same time. They were moving down a ridgeline which was about 1 kilometer to our right and about 20:00, they made contact. Charlie Company was combat assaulted on the left about 4 kilometers to our left front and immediately made contact. Here was Delta Company moving down the middle across this open rice patty in around two to three feet of water, in the dark, with flares going off over Alpha Company and Charlie Company which silhouetted us perfectly out in the middle of this rice patty.

## Ch. 7 / The Days of Blue Falcon Ridge

We continued to move all night, trying to maintain noise discipline, trying to maintain any semblance of a military move with all the confusion of Alpha Company and Charlie Company being in contact. It was an extremely scary move that the Company made that night across this open rice patty especially in light of the lack of sleep we've had. Around 04:30-05:00 in the morning, we had crossed the open rice patty and had started up into the mountains. Around first light, we took a break for breakfast to get everybody oriented to the situation and then we would continue to move up into the mountains that day. About 07:00 some of the men noticed someone down in the rice patty walking around. It looked like he had been following us. We called for the artillery forward observer 1LT David Jakes and his sergeant to come over to the Company Headquarter so that a fire mission (artillery fire) could be called in on the individual out in the rice patty. The artillery forward observer came over and he informed us that he couldn't find his sergeant. We were later to find out that his sergeant had fallen asleep at one of our stops out in the rice patty and had been left out there and was following us. He ultimately turned around and made his way back to fire support base Tomahawk.

We moved on up into the mountains. For a couple of days, the Delta Raiders proceeded up the mountains with no contact at all. Alpha Company continued to havecontact on our right. C Company had sporadic contact on our left, and we were moving up the middle going up the mountains.

On the third morning just before we moved out, all hell broke loose on the perimeter directly across from the 3rd Platoon. Everyone on the perimeter immediately went to 100% alert. I left SFC Deland in charge and moved to the Company Headquarters to find out what was happening. As I arrived, 1LT Ronald Phillips was talking to the Battalion Command LTC Heiter (call sign Blue Falcon). 1LT Ronald Phillips was Delta Company XO. and was in command of the Company because CPT Feurer had been medevaced along with a number of the Delta Raiders because of emersion foot. (This condition caused the skin on your feet to peel off leaving bloody raw feet which were very painful to walk on. Emersion foot was caused by feet being constantly wet.) 1LT Phillips told Blue Falcon that the NVA had probed the perimeter and that Delta Company had one man wounded in the leg. The man was Harry P. Longbottom. Harry P. Longbottom was a very unusual soldier. He was definitely one that you wanted on your side in a fire fight. He is a whole story in and of himself, and I will not go into detail on his wounding at this time, but I do have to say that at the time Harry was "wounded by the NVA probing the perimeter" that he was scheduled to be court martialed for having controlled substances and that I always wondered why at the time that all the hell broke loose I had not heard any incoming rounds but only outgoing rounds. 1LT Phillips asked Blue Falcon for instructions on what to do. Blue Falcon told 1LT Phillips that he had a "God-damn Airborne Rifle Company, so go out and get me some dicks." We immediately sent out patrols but found no sign of the enemy.

On October 23, 3rd Platoon had the point, we were moving up the side of the mountain and came to a minor hilltop that had a major trail crossing it. The steep mountains were very difficult to climb because we each had five days of rations and a large supply of ammunition, radio batteries, and food. We were only scheduled for resupply every five days and had to carry five days of supplies in our ruck sacks, a back-breaking burden. The ruck sack straps cut into our shoulders. Their weight caused frequent stops. Their weight also caused thigh searing, knee wrenching agony on the steep uphill climbs. So, I felt that a break was in order, and used the trail as a reason to take a break. This trail was probably three to four feet wide and had signs of recent heavy traffic. I stopped to put out security so that the point squad could recon down this trail both ways and decide which way to proceeded. The rest of the Company was in a file down the side of the mountain. We had looked down the trails and found out they were well-used trails with fresh signs of both bare feet and Ho Chi Minh sandals prints. The point squad had regrouped back at the security point. I was talking to my squad leaders about which way we needed to proceed when SP4 Thomas J. Eggles opened up full automatic. He had been guarding the trail that continued up the mountain. I ran over to see why he had fired and found a dead NVA soldier. The NVA soldier was carrying approximately 6 satchel charges, a brand new AK-47 with a folding stock. His uniform indicated he was from a Sapper Battalion. We immediately got on the radio and called back down to CPT Feurer and told him what had happened. He sent the 2nd Platoon up to help us secure the area. In the process of moving back down to guide 1LT Edward L. Hogenauer's Platoon up to the contact area, we encountered a group of five to six NVA coming up the trail from the opposite direction carrying a wounded man in a hammock slung from a pole. Several of us opened up on them. After a brief fire fight, we began to check the area out and found out that the NVA in the hammock was the Company Commander of an NVA Sapper Company. We recovered a notebook that contained a list of his men and other information which was sent to the S-2 (Battalion Intelligence Office).

After we regrouped, the Company set up a perimeter, then we got orders from Battalion that we were to move down the trail that the NVA had come up and try to connect up with Alpha Company. It was around 17:30 when we got our orders and it was starting to getting dark. The Delta Raiders were very nervous because of the enemy contact that we had that day.

## Ch. 7 / The Days of Blue Falcon Ridge

Third Platoon took point and we moved out down the ridge line. We walked maybe 25 to 30 meters down this ridgeline when we heard an explosion and called back to find out what had happened. It turns out that the 2nd Platoon was taking the satchel charges off of the dead NVA soldier and one of them had detonated and one of the 2nd Platoon squad leader's hand had been blown off, so we had to stop and medevac him. It took approximately 30 to 40 minutes to complete the medevac, after which the 3rd Platoon moved on down the ridgeline. The ridgeline was probably 20 to 25 meters wide and then dropped off on both sides into almost a sheer drop off, so we couldn't maneuver on this ridgeline at all. We moved until it was at least 30 minutes after dark. CPT Feurer got word from Battalion that we were to stop and establish a night defensive position on the ridgeline. The next morning we got up and 1st Platoon commanded by LT John E. Frick took point and headed out down the ridgeline. The Company had moved approximately an hour or so before the 1st Platoon made contact with an NVA unit that was dug in on the ridgeline. The lay of the terrain was that of a ridgeline that dropped down about 20 to 30 meters into a saddle and then rose up on the other side. The NVA were dug in on the top side of the saddle that the Company needed to cross.

1LT John Frick maneuvered his element against the dug-in NVA and came under extremely heavy fire. As so often occurred in the mountains, the NVA were just a short distance away when contact was made. The NVA was dug in maybe twenty meters away but you could not see them.

The 1st platoon tried to inch toward the enemy, but their fire just ate up the trees and rocks around them. It stared to rain RPG's and hand grenades into the 1st platoon area so they began to push forward again. Then the fire really stared pouring in, so heavy that I thought it sounded as if a company was dug in ahead of us. At this point CPT Feurer told the 1st platoon to pull back. As they began to withdraw, a lot...

A lot of RPG (rocket propelled grenades) were fired at his men along with a great deal of satchel charges which were thrown down into the saddle. LT Frick, along with a number of his men, were wounded in this initial firefight, and the 1st Platoon withdrew. The 1st Platoon pulled back up the ridgeline. All of the wounded were medevaced at this time, and CPT Feurer called in artillery on the enemy location. Because the ridgeline was so narrow, it was hard for artillery to hit the bunkers where they were dug in because it would either fall short or go over the ridgeline because of the narrowness of the ridgeline. So then CPT Feurer called in helicopter gunships and tried to soften up their position.

That afternoon, LT. Hogenauer's 2nd Platoon was told that they would be moving in on the NVA positions and when they started moving in they

The Days of Blue Falcon Ridge / Ch. 7

immediately came under heavy fire, mainly RPGs and satchel charges with some automatic weapons fire. They suffered probably 8 or 9 wounded men. Among them was Arthur Williams who later died of his wounds in December of 1968. Arthur Williams was a very happy young man from South Carolina. He was the type that had a very positive attitude and spread his happiness and good attitude around. The company missed him. The Company pulled back to a point to medevac the wounded and we got all the wounded medevaced. The Company was running very low on ammunition. CPT Feurer told me that the 3rd Platoon was going in next, so I went down and reconned the area with two of my squad leaders, SGT Roy L. Barber and SGT Ronald Scott. We looked at the situation, developed a plan and started to move in when the Company Commander called and said that we weren't going to be moving in that night; we were going to pull back into a night defensive position and we were to expect a resupply chopper any minute. So we pulled back into a tight perimeter. It was just right at dusk when the resupply chopper came and was hovering overhead because there was no place for it to land. The men on the helicopter were kicking out ammunition and food supplies for us…and I heard an AK47 fire three shots. After you hear the Soviet 7.62mm round cracking nearby you never forget the sound, and this was definitely an AK47. As soon as the AK47 quit firing, the Company started receiving mortar rounds which were going over us. We heard three more shots from the AK47; the mortar adjusted and then they were hitting short of us. We heard three more rounds and then they

Delta Raiders • **107**

were hitting all around us. But none of the mortar rounds hit in the Company area, however. The narrow ridgeline was protection for us just like it had been for the NVA. This was one of the heaviest mortar attacks that I experienced in Vietnam.

Just as the helicopter started to pull off and leave the area, there was an explosion and it fell over the side of the hill in flames. By this time, it was totally dark. The 2nd Platoon went down to secure the helicopter; the 3rd Platoon was setting up on the avenue of approach from the NVA bunkers and guarding that area. We were able to recover three of the people who were aboard the helicopter. The pilot and one of the door gunners were trapped inside the helicopter and burned inside of it. They broughtback the co-pilot and we prepared to medevac the people who were on the helicopter. The medevacs came out and we were trying to get the co-pilot on board. He had suffered a severe and very mangled right leg, it was just hanging on by threads. He had lost all of his finger tips and was burned over quite a bit of his body. I will never forget standing on that ridge line to hold a strobe light to guide the helicopter in with. I was a standing target for all to see. The helicopter hovered above us with its spot light shinning down on us, the wind from the blades whipping around us. It seem to be a dream. All the tragedies of that day were around us. I felt as if I were outside of my body watching this scene take place. It was if I was watching the twilight zone. I was immediately returned to reality when I heard an AK47 fire three rounds. I knew what was about to happen and it did. The mortar tube started firing again. Again, I had three shots and the mortar rounds shifted to the other side of the ridge line. The NVA was adjusting mortar fire on us as we tried to medivac of our wounded Delta Raiders.

The medevac lowered the basket and the pilot was placed in it and as it was going up one of the other men who had been on the helicopter walked up to me and asked me "Sir, am I very bad?" I looked at him and I said, "No, you're not hurt very bad at all. You'll be okay." And the young man looked at me and said, "Sir, do you know who I am?" And I looked at him and said, "No, I don't." The man was burned all over his face, had all of his hair gone and was burned pretty bad. I was trying to comfort him and tell him that he was not very bad when he informed me that he was SGT Frank Wingo, who I knew very well but I couldn't recognize because of the extent of the injuries and burns. It caught me totally off guard when he told me his name. That moment is something that I've thought about over the years. I can't forget how I felt or, more to the point, how I really didn't feel. I was surprised that I didn't seem to feel anything. But, I couldn't feel. I was trained not to have any emotions, and especially not to show any emotion to the men. So, part of me had no feelings at all, just numbness. Yet, in a distant place of my soul I did feel and did care. I can't keep from thinking about how he must have felt — that his injuries were so bad that I didn't recognize him. I wanted to do something, but was totally unable to. I felt helpless and that I should have been able to make it all right — all of it — the burns, my failure to recognize him — everything. This haunts me still.

We were in the process of medevacing him and one of my squad leaders who was on the helicopter, SGT Robert Dunn, who later died as a result of his burns. We were able to get all of the wounded men out that evening and the next morning the 3rd Platoon was on point. The Company had approximately 47 men in the field on this morning. The normal strength to the Company in the field was around 110 men.

The 3rd Platoon was to proceed across to where the NVA were dug in. We got up very early and went down and reconned the area. It appeared to be quiet. I went up about to where I thought the bunkers would start and didn't see any signs of theNVA. Then I went back and got the 3rd Platoon ready to go. I set up a machine gun to cover us on one side and we proceeded to shoot M79 rounds up in the trees to try to get airbursts down on the NVA. While doing this, Alpha Company Commander, CPT Robert Mayor, called and told us that we were hitting his unit with the M79 rounds, so we had to cease with that. We proceeded to move out and went up and found all the bunkers empty. They had been evacuated overnight and there was nothing left but a large number of heavy blood trails. The Delta Raiders had found the courage to go into the killing fields after the enemy and had caused a great deal of damage to the NVA. During these days I had experienced emotions that I had never even imagined before, and have seldom known since. I felt happy to be alive, and sad for all the men that had been wounded. I was happy that my platoon had not been in the rain storm of RPG's and hand grenades that the 1st and 2nd platoon had been through. I felt guilty that I had not done more to help the Delta Raiders in this battle. I learned how quickly that we can become separated from our friends in time of war. All of these things are still in my memories.

That was what happened on what a number of the men called Blue Falcon Ridge, named after the Battalion Commander's call sign, Blue Falcon. The reason that the men called this Blue Falcon ridge is because of the technique of the Battalion Commander exercising his leadership from three thousand feet up in his Command and Control helicopter (C&C bird). A C&C bird is a helicopter crammed with radios from which commanders at every level from battalion up were able to fly over their subordinate units and give orders to them from a safe vantage point high above. Up in the C&C bird it was very easy for a battalion commander to direct not only the company but also the platoons and even squads. "Take that ridge line" was

## Ch. 7 / The Days of Blue Falcon Ridge

easy to say from a position high above, where the air was cool, the fatigue of having humped a rucksack all day was nonexistent, and the sound of RPG's exploding was not heard.

My recollections of these days are filled with pride that these Raiders performed their jobs well and did what few others could have done. These men were subjected to not only the stress of combat, but also to physical hardships — heat, humidity, mud, leeches, biting insects, booby traps, mines, poor or no food, no sleep, wounds, fatigue, fear, loss of close friends and in some cases, death.

We all suffered, we sacrificed and some died. I will not forget these men, living and dead, with whom I shared so much — these men who hold their country so dear, and did their duty for their country.

Ch. 7 / The Days of Blue Falcon Ridge

# 8.
# Chronology
## October 31, 1968 – May 31, 1970

**Nov. 1, 1968**
BN CP located at LZ Sally.

**Nov. 3, 1968**
1146H 2-501 (-Co. D) returned to OPCON of 2nd BDE from 1st BDE. Co. D at FB Tomahawk, temporarily OPCON to 1-327.

**Nov. 4, 1968**
LTC Joseph O. Wilson took over as commander of the 2-501 from LTC James A. Heiter.
1433H Co. D arrived at LZ Sally by air from FB Tomahawk and returned to OPCON of 2-501 and 2nd BDE.

**Nov. 5, 1968**
BN CP located at FB Birmingham.
0847H Co. D moved by air from LZ Sally to FB Bastogne, complete at 0942H; this would be the first of many days scattered over the next three years in which Delta Company would operate in the FB Bastogne area. The Company conducted a RIF operation to YD606107 and set up a blocking position in support of the 3/3 ARVN REGT with 3/D at YD604095.

**Nov. 8, 1968**
1305H Co. D moved by air from Y0620095 to FB Birmingham, complete at 1325H. Co. D then CA'd from FB Birmingham to YD737032, following a combat assault by Recon Platoon. Following the combat assault Co. D conducted a RIF to YD7503 and YD7504. 1830H Co. D had 1 man medevaced because of high fever.

**Nov. 9, 1968**
Co. D provided security for FB Birmingham and remained on standby for CA until 1410H, when the CA was cancelled.

## Nov. 10, 1968

**1017H** Co. D CA'd from FB Birmingham to YD737083, complete at 1047H. The Company then conducted a RIF to YD739072.

## Nov. 11, 1968

Co. D (-2/D) occupied a NDP at YD739072, with 2/D at YD737069. The Company conducted a RIF to YD753065, conducted a BDA (bomb damage assessment) of a B-52 strike at that location; and then conducted a RIF to YD745060, with 3/D conducting a RIF to YD742063.

## Nov. 12, 1968

**1825H** Medevac completed for 1 man from Co. D who cut himself using a machete. Nov. 13, 1968 Co. D conducted a RIF to YD753065 and continued a BDA of a B52 strike at that location. The Company then conducted a RIF to YD747050, with 2/D conducting a RIF to YD749055.

## Nov. 14, 1968

B-52 bomb damage assessment at YD753065: 80% of the target area was covered, no LZs were created by the strike. No caves or tunnels were exposed, no trench lines were exposed and no bunkers were in the area of the strike.

## Nov. 15, 1968

**1407H** Co. D moved by air from YD735034 to FB Birmingham, complete at 1444H.

## Nov. 16, 1968

Co. D (-3/D) relieved Co. A (-) of security for FB Birmingham. At 0900H 3/D relieved a Co. A platoon of security at the POHL Bridge and became OPCON of Co. B.

## Nov. 17, 1968

BN CP at FB Birmingham. Co. D assumed the position of battalion reserve.
**1105H** 1/D moved by air to FB Panther II.
**1554H** 3/D CA'd from FB Birmingham to FB Panther III (complete at 1602H) and assumed firebase security.
**1610H** An arty survey team moved by air from FB Panther II to FB Panther III, and at 1615H a dozer engineer team moved by air from Camp Eagle to FB Panther III.

## Nov. 19. 1968
**1030H** 1/D moved by air from FB Panther II to FB Birmingham, complete at 1036H.

## Nov. 21, 1968
BN CP located at FB Brick.
**0900H** Co. D (-3/D) CA'd from FB Birmingham to Y0835897, complete at 0919H. At 0950H 3/D CA'd from FB Panther III to Y0835897, complete at 0956H. The Company conducted a RIF to Y0829900 and then moved west to Y0642178.
**1237H** (YD817887): 3/D found 4 hootches without overhead cover and 1 bunker (15'x15'x6') with no overhead cover. Also located were 4 bags of rice, 1 bag of corn, digging tools (shovels, etc.), and 2 pair of black pajamas. At YD823887 the platoon also located 4 collapsed hootches.
**1715H** (Y0825890): 2/D found 2 destroyed huts and 1 Battalion size mess hall, as well as the following: 2 AK-47, 1 US carbine, 5 SKS, 1 1903 Springfield rifle, 1 BN size mess hall, 1 canteen, 1 US first aid kit, 1 set knives, 2 fireplaces, 8 huts, pots and pans, shaving bag, oil drum, and 1 pair of woman's underwear. Results: 4 IWC, rest destroyed.

## Nov. 23, 1968
**1015H** A medevac was completed for 1 man from 1/D who had a high fever.
**1240H** (Y0838888): 1/D found 8 naked bodies on a trail (7 VC and 1 NVA) who were killed by 101st LRRP Team Nov. 20. Also found in the area: 20 lbs. of rice, 1 kettle, 4 pair of PJs, equipment left by LRRP Team on Nov. 20, grenades, shotgun, M-16 rounds, 1 bottle of whole blood, numerous LRRP rations, 3 poncho liners, 6 rucksacks, 1 sewing kit, and 5 claymore mines. Results: equipment and supplies destroyed.
**1345H** (Y0837891): 1/D found 2 huts and empty 32mm ammo boxes. Carving on a nearby tree read, "DA-DAO-BON, THIEU-KY". Results: huts and boxes destroyed.

## Nov. 24, 1968
**1550H** (YC89886): 2/D found 1 bunker 4'x6'x7' with 18' of overhead cover, 1 small hut for a trail watcher and a trail with a fresh trail marker place. Results: bunker and hut destroyed.

## Nov. 26, 1968
**0912H** Co. D moved by air from Y0838892 to FB Brick (complete at 1006H), and assumed security of the firebase.
**1216H** 3/D moved by CH-47 from FB Brick to FB Birmingham, complete at

1224H. 3/D assumed security mission at the firebase and became OPCON to Echo Company.

### Nov. 26-Dec. 4, 1968
Co. D responsible for the security of FB Brick.

### Dec. 1, 1968
BN CP located at FB Brick.

### Dec. 3, 1968
BN CP located at FB Birmingham.

Co. D (-3/D, OPCON E/2-501 at FB Birmingham) continued to provide security at FB Brick and improve defensive positions.

0245H (FB Brick): Co. D on perimeter guard spotted and engaged 2 individuals approximately 50-75m outside the perimeter with small arms and automatic weapons fire and grenades. FB Brick was placed on 100% alert, fired illumination and DT's.

0317H (FB Brick): Co. D on perimeter guard observed 1 individual outside perimeter wire, engaged with claymore and as the claymore went off the enemy threw a satchel charge which didn't result in friendly casualties.

0720H (FB Brick): A first light check of the perimeter area revealed blood stains but nothing else.

1352H 3/D moved by air from FB Birmingham to FB Brick (closed at 1405H), and returned to OPCON of Co. D.

1736H 2/D/1-501 became OPCON to Co. D/2-501 after moving by CH-47 from FB Boyd to FB Brick.

### Dec. 4, 1968
1744H Co. D (-1/D) moved by CH-47 from FB Brick to FB Birmingham, while 1/D moved by UH-1H from FB Brick to FB Birmingham.

### Dec. 6, 1968
1014H Co. D CA'd from FB Birmingham to YD693065 (completed at 1034H) and conducted a RIF operation to YD698060.

### Dec. 7, 1968
1325H (YD705057): Co. D discovered a hole 5' in diameter, 12-15 feet in the ground with soot inside, believed to be a ventilating system. A White Team from 2-17 Cav. called in to operate in the area.

## Dec. 8, 1968

**1337H** (YD708048): 3/D discovered 1 hut, 10'x12' with bunker underneath, which would hold 6 to 7 men. The bunker had not been used recently. A search of the area was made with negative results. Results: bunker destroyed.

**1609H** (YD706047): 3/D discovered 1 AK47 in a hold with 65 rounds of 9mm ammo. The area had not been occupied recently. A search of the area was made with negative results. Results: 1 IWC.

**1755H** (YD700047): 3/D found 4 huts which showed no signs of recent use. A search of the area also revealed cooking equipment and an empty wallet.

## Dec. 9, 1968

**1139H** (YD683039): 3/D discovered 4 huts, showing no signs of recent use, and 4 M-1 carbine in the area. The area looked like it had been hit by TAC Air at one time. Results: 1 IWC, huts destroyed.

## Dec. 11, 1968

**0844H** (YD675041): 1/D engaged with small arms fire 2 VC walking along a trail, resulting in 1 VC KIA, 1 VC WIA, and 1 M-2 carbine and 1 rucksack captured. The VC WIA fled to the west. Results: 1 VC KIA, 1 IWC, rucksack destroyed.

**1158H** 1/D reported hearing sniper fire in the vicinity of YD685035.

**1240H** (YD682049): 2/D sighted and engaged, with small arms fire, 2 VC carrying 2 105mm arty rounds. The enemy dropped the rounds and fled to the east. One of the enemy was also armed with a carbine. Results: the 105mm rounds were destroyed in place.

### Dec. 12, 1968
0851H (YD675041): Co. D found a grave containing 1 NVA killed by small arms fire 1-2 days earlier. Results: 1 NVA KIA.
1237H (YD684035): 1/D on a hill found 2 trails running south to north and east to west.

### Dec. 14, 1968
0802H Co. D moved by air from YD674040 to FB Birmingham, assuming security for the firebase. At 1554H 1/D moved by CH-47 from FB Birmingham to FB Panther II, assuming security for the firebase.

### Dec. 14-30, 1968
Co. D provided security and improved defensive positions at FB Birmingham and FB Panther II.

### Dec. 15, 1968
2105H (FB Panther II): 1/D received small arms fire from YD792105, with negative casualties, area was engaged with arty.

### Dec. 16, 1968
3/D conducted a RIF along Highway 547 with one tank and established a blocking position at YD746125. The platoon screened 60 Vietnamese woodcutters then returned to FB Birmingham.

### Dec. 18, 1968
1852H One squad from 1/D departed FB Panther II to provide security for a stalled 5- ton tractor trailer at YD803093. The driver of the trailer got on the wrong road although he was on the road to FB Boyd, the trailer was found with half of it off the road hanging in space.

### Dec. 19, 1968
A squad from 1/D continued to secure a stalled tractor trailer. A maintenance team arrived at 1322H and at 1419H the vehicle was moving on down the road to its unit (27th Engineers). The 1/D squad returned to FB Panther II at 1435H.

## Dec. 25, 1968
2243H 1/D at FB Panther II spotted a gook in the wire approximately 200m from their position. The area was fired up with M-79 and small arms fire. The area was checked at first light with negative results.

## Dec. 26, 1968
0925H (FB Birmingham): Co. D requested a medevac for 1 man (John Mejia) who had a lacerated arm as a result of his .45 pistol discharging while he was cleaning it, medevac complete at 0940H.

## Dec. 30, 1968
At 1742H 1/D moved by CH-47 from FB Panther II to LZ Sally, closing at 1755H. At 1654H Co. D (-1/D) moved from FB Birmingham to LZ Sally, closing at 1704H. Co. D was relieved of security for FB Birmingham by Alpha Co.

## Dec. 31, 1968
BN CP located at FB Birmingham.
Co. D spent the night at LZ Sally and at 0759H the Company moved by CH-47 from LZ Sally to FB Birmingham, closing at 0906H. At 1017H the Company CA'd from FB Birmingham to YD795008, closing at 1031H.

## Jan. 1, 1969
BN CP located at FB Birmingham.

## Jan. 2, 1969
1230H (YD792018): Co. D discovered a suspected VC rest area. There were 3 trails leading west, north, and southwest from the location. The rest area was used by approximately 8 individuals 15 minutes before the unit arrived. The enemy fled in an unknown direction. Results: negative.

## Jan. 4, 1969
1118H Co. D (-2/D) moved by air from YD793022 to FB Birmingham. At 1045H 2/D moved by air from YD800018 to FB Birmingham, closing at 1100H. At 1523H Co. D moved by CH-47 from FB Birmingham to YD820310, closing at 1557H (the LZ was secured by elements of Co. C 1-501). Upon closing the LZ Co. D became OPCON to 1- 501.

## Jan. 9, 1969
1448H 2/D moved to FB Panther II, assumed security for the firebase and improved defensive positions.

## Jan. 11, 1969
**1130H** Co. D (-2/D at FB Panther II) conducted a RIF to COL CO Beach, closing that location at 1236H.

## Jan. 12, 1969
**1315H** After occupying a night location at COL CO Beach, Co. D (-2/D) moved by CH-47 to FB Birmingham closing at 1352H. Upon closing the firebase, Co. D returned to the OPCON of the 2-501 and assumed security for the firebase.
**1855H** FB Birmingham received several 75mm mortar rounds from an undetermined location.

## Jan. 13, 1969
**0415H** Co. D (-2/D) departed FB Birmingham and conducted a RIF to YD708079. At 1002H 2/D moved by CH-47 from FB Panther II to YD706084 (LZ secured by Co. D(-).
**1415H** (YD709068) Co. D found 6 bunkers, 50 empty 75mm mortar rounds, and 6 unfired 75mm rounds. It was determined that the fire received by FB Birmingham at 1855H on Jan. 12 came from this location.
**1645H** Co. D (-2/D) moved by CH-47 from YD709069 to FB Birmingham and at 1650H 2/D moved by log ship from the same LZ to FB Panther II.

## Jan. 16, 1969
**1725H** (YD774066): Co. D spotted 6 to 10 VC. Arty and ARA were employed with negative results.
**1901H** 3/D engaged one 1 VC with small arms fire and directed ARA on the area with unknown results.

## Jan. 17, 1969
At 1000H Nam Hoa District Headquarters reported that an estimated platoon size enemy force was observed crossing the river from west to east on a bamboo raft in the vicinity of YD790114. At 1025H one squad from 2/D departed FB Panther II and conducted a RIF to YD790114. At 1048H Recon Platoon moved by CH-47 from FB Birmingham to FB Panther II, closing at 1104H. At 1147H 1 squad from 2/D observed and engaged 1 VC at YD792114 with unknown results. The squad heard movement of an unknown size enemy force. At 1228H ARA arrived at YD790114 and continued to engage suspected enemy locations until 1530H. At 1230H Troop B 2-17 Cav. conducted a RIF to YD790114 and established blocking positions.

At 1320H 1/D moved by CH-47 from FB Birmingham to FB Panther II and relieved 2/D of security mission for the firebase. Units with 2 tracker dog teams and Pathfinders continued to sweep the area of suspected enemy deployment, supported by ARA with negative results. A diesel drum drop and aerial PSYOPS broadcasts were conducted in support of the sweep operation. At 1703H 2/D and Recon Platoon returned to FB Panther II, and at 1738H 1/D returned by CH-47 from FB Panther II to FB Birmingham.

## Jan. 18, 1969

**0950H** Co. D (-2/D) CA'd from FB Birmingham to FB Normandy (YD690018), closing at 1010H. Co. D(-) provided security for the 155 Arty Battery at FB Normandy and improved defensive positions, while 2/D continued security at FB Panther II.

**2040H** (FB Panther II): 2/D sighted 4 VC with a starlight scope attempting to move equipment across the river at YD786117. Mortars and gunships were employed with negative results.

## Jan. 18-25, 1969

Co. D (-2/D) provided security for FB Normandy and 2/D provided security at FB Panther II, with defensive positions improved at both locations.

## Jan. 25, 1969

**1600H** Co. D (-2/D) moved by air from FB Normandy to FB Birmingham, assuming security of the firebase.

## Jan. 26, 1969

**0005H** (Y0791108): GSR at FB Panther II observed movement. 2/D fired 81mm illumination, and arty was employed with negative results.

## Jan. 27, 1969

**0848H** 3/D moved by log ship from FB Birmingham to Radio Relay site (YC767963), closing at 1035H. 3/D assisted Co. E in providing security for the Radio Relay site and improved defensive positions. At 0909H Recon Platoon became OPCON to Co. D and moved from Radio Relay site via log ship to FB Birmingham and assisted in providing security at FB Birmingham.

## Jan. 28, 1969

**1003H** 1/D conducted a CA from FB Birmingham to YD767081. At 1512H Co. D, at Y0762075, discovered and destroyed 24 empty 75mm containers and 6 bunkers (4'x4' with 1' overhead cover). At 1600H 1/D returned by air from YD761078 to FB Birmingham.

**Jan. 29, 1969**
1603H Co. D (-2/D and 3/D) at FB Birmingham requested a medevac for one man with a very high temperature, completed to 22nd Surg at 1617H.

**Jan, 30, 1969**
1103H (YD705105): Co. D discovered 60mm mortar fuses, and one 82mm fuse lying in the open that was not boobytrapped. Results: destroyed.

**Feb. 1, 1969**
BN CP located at FB Birmingham.
Co. D (-2/D and 3/D) continued to provide security for FB Birmingham, 2/D continued to provide security for FB Panther II and 3/D continued to assist Co. S in providing security for the Radio Relay site.
0040H (YD763129): Co. D and Co. C observed rockets being fired from YD762115 in the direction of Hue. Thua Thien TOC reported at 0045H that 5 incoming 122mm rockets impacted in Hue resulting in 11 civilian KIA and 6 civilians wounded and minor damage. US arty fired counterbattery on the suspected enemy location YD762115, resulting in 5 secondary explosions.
0050H (YD764127): Co. D and Co. C reported that Nam Hoa District Headquarters received 15 RPG rounds from a suspected enemy location at YD755110. There was 1 PF WHA from this attack. At 0130H an additional 7 RPG rounds were received from a suspected enemy location at YD760127. The 15 rounds landed outside the compound and 7 rounds landed inside. Results: 1 PF WHA (E).

## Feb. 3, 1969

**2024H** (YD800109): 2/D spotted lights 100-150m to the south of their position at FB Panther II, and four trip flares were activated but no movement was observed. The area was engaged with M-79 fire, and the area was checked at first light with negative results.

## Feb. 4, 1969

**0823H** 2/D moved by CH-47 from FB Panther II to FB Birmingham, closing at 0830H.

## Feb. 5, 1969

**0808H** Co. D (-2/D and 3/D), reinforced by OPCON of 2nd Platoon Co. A, conducted a CA from FB Birmingham to YD794005, closing at 1910H.

**1105H** (YD793005): Co. D discovered 8 boobytrapped 60mm rounds with pressure-type firing devices. The element also discovered 54 foxholes, 75 lean-to frames, 1 grave containing a skeleton, 3 bunkers (2'x4'x3') approximately 2 to 3 days old, and a well-used trail running east to west. The area had been used within the last week. Results: all destroyed.

**1400H** (YD795000): Co. D discovered a platoon-size NDP approximately 2 to 3 days old. The NDP consisted of 14 foxholes and 3 huts (4'x6'). At 1455H the Company engaged 1 VC with small arms fire at 100-150m. The enemy did not return fire and fled southeast. A search of the area revealed 1 pack with blood on it containing 2 khaki shirts, 2 khaki trousers, 10 lbs. of rice and 30 rounds of AK-47 ammo. Results: all destroyed.

**1531H** (YD794997): Co. D was engaged with automatic weapons fire by 4 to 5 enemy 150-200m south of their location. The element returned small arms fire and the area was checked with negative results. Feb. 6, 1969 1011H (YD766098): Co. D discovered 2 foxholes (1'x4'x4' ) approximately one month old, and one 82mm round not boobytrapped. Results: destroyed.

**1030H** (YD794986): Co. D discovered 60 empty boxes for Chicom 60mm mortars. The boxes were described as very old. Results: boxes destroyed.

**1123H** (YD793987): Co. D engaged 1 to 2 enemy with small arms fire at 300m. The enemy fled southwest. During the sweep of the area at 1315H, the unit received 2 bursts of automatic weapons fire from the west. The unit returned fire and swept the area with negative results.

**1637H** Co. D(-) released OPCON of 2nd Platoon Co. A.

## Feb. 7, 1969

**0520H** (YC779993): Co. D(-) observed an enemy camp fire and employed arty upon suspected enemy location with unknown results.

**1255H** (YC772962): Co. D received 1 Hoi Chanh, wearing a VC helmet and uniform, who was evacuated to LZ Sally. Results: 1 detainee (Hoi Chanh).

**1618H** After conducting RIF operations to YC779975 and YC776965 Co. D (-) closed at the Radio Relay site (YC768961) and assisted Co. E in providing security for the Radio Relay site.

### Feb. 9, 1969
**0600H** Co. D (-2/D) moved by CH-47 from the Radio Relay site to FB Birmingham, closing at 0735H.

### Feb. 10, 1969
**0809H** 2/D moved by CH-47 from FB Birmingham to COL CC Beach, closing at 0830H. At 1600H 2/D returned by CH-47 from COL CC Beach to FB Birmingham, closing at 1610H.

### Feb. 11, 1969
**1417H** Co. D conducted a CA from FB Birmingham to YD737082, closing at 1421H.

### Feb. 12, 1969
**0918H** (YD736090): 1/D found fresh foot tracks (non-US) on a trail. The platoon followed the tracks with negative results.

### Feb. 13, 1969
**0905H** (YD743103): 3/D discovered signs of 30 to 35 barefoot individuals who were resting in the elephant grass approximately 4 to 8 hours earlier. The platoon followed a small foot trail to the river with negative results.

### Feb. 15, 1969
**1110H** (YD761089): 2/D discovered 20 empty 75mm canister rounds and 10 sighting positions (3'x5'x3') approximately 1 month old. Results: all destroyed.

### Feb, 16, 1969
**1204H** (YD748118): 1/D found and destroyed 2 electric blasting caps with blue wires attached that were not US.

### Feb. 18, 1969
**0835H** (YD778088): Co. D discovered a recently used trail running southwest-northeast, large enough to accommodate a platoon. The trail had

been used in the last 24 hours. The area was checked with negative results.

## Feb. 28, 1969
Operation NEVADA EAGLE ended.

## March 1, 1969
Operation KENTUCKY JUMPER and the strategic operation MASSACHUSETTS STRIKER began.
BN CP located at FB Birmingham.
**1543H** Co. D, along with 1 Platoon + of Co. C/326 Engineers and 2 mortar squads (OPCON to Co. D), moved by air from FB Birmingham to FB Whip (YC590877), closing at 1700H. Co. D(-) provided security for the Engineer Platoon and 2 mortar squads and improved field fortifications.

## March 4, 1969
**1506H** (YC588885): 2/D observed 1 VC approximately 200m north of their position. The platoon engaged with organice weapons and the VC returned fire and fled to the north. 81mm mortar fire was employed upon the fleeing enemy. A sweep of the area revealed 3 empty VC LRRP ration packages and 29 - 30cal carbine rounds.

## March 6, 1969
**1306H** (YC587876): Co. D at FB Whip received sniper fire from the northwest from an estimated 2 enemy, resulting in 1 man from engineers slightly wounded in the shoulder. Due to inclement weather the man was not medevaced until 1640H the following day (March 7). The area was engaged with 81mm and arty. Two squads swept the area and discovered footprints leading northwest and several AK-47 shell cases. Results: 1 US WIA (E).

## March 8, 1969
**0705H** (YC589878-FB Whip): 2 VC with AK-47s fired on FB Whip. Co. D returned fire and the enemy fled in an unknown direction. Results: 1 US WIA (M: Ronald J. Taterman of 3/D).

## March 18, 1969
**1001H** Co. D moved by CH-47 from FB Whip to FB Boyd, closing at 1055H and became OPCON to 2-502.

## March 20, 1969

**0830H** Co. D was released OPCON of 2-502 and moved by 2.5 ton truck from FB Boyd to FB Birmingham, closing at 0944H. At 1021H Co. D CA'd from FB Birmingham to YC568830, closing at 1059H.

## March 21, 1969

**1112H** (YC565824): 2/D received small arms fire from 3 to 4 NVA west of their position, resulting in 1 Tracker Dog WIA. The unit returned fire and the enemy fled. Supported by Arty and ARA the platoon swept the area with negative results. While maneuvering against the enemy position, the platoon sustained 1 US WIA from a punji pit (medevac completed at 1120H). While conducting a detailed search of the contact area the platoon discovered 3 bunkers (4'x6' with 1' of overhead cover) interconnected with a trench line. Results: 1 US WIA (E) and 1 tracker dog WIA (E).

**1330H** (YC562824): 2/D discovered a diary belonging to a squad leader. The book contained the names of 6 platoon leaders, number of personnel (143), a political speech, a training schedule, number of weapons, ammo inventory, and a radio callsign. Results: document evacuated.

## March 22, 1969

**1130H** (YC579828): Co. D received a burst of automatic weapons fire. The area was engaged with M-79 and small arms fire. The area was swept with negative results.

## March 23, 1969

**0936H** (YC599836): 3/D received small arms fire from 1 NVA trailwatcher. The platoon returned small arms fire and the enemy fled. The platoon pursed the enemy with negative results.

**1240H** (YC590809): 2/D discovered a bunker complex containing 16 well constructed bunkers 3'x5' with overhead cover, a classroom 8'x10' with 8 desks, podium and bottle of red ink and a cloth with frame used as a blackboard. The unit also discovered a field hospital or dispensary (8mx8m) with 2 operating tables, litter poles and several bottles of medicine. A hole 1.5' in diameter and approximately 30' deep was discovered 200m south of the camp. The hole was covered with leaves. A kitchen with miscellaneous equipment was also discovered. The area showed signs of recent use by an estimated platoon. A detailed search of the area was conducted, and at 1755H the platoon reported finding an additional 12 bunkers (10'x12' with 3' of overhead cover) containing sleeping gear for a platoon. The area also had a wooden sidewalk with hand rails, water point, latrine, and cooked rice (4 to 8 hours old). Results: the medicine was evacuated and the remainder was destroyed.

**2130H** (YC593826): Co. D was engaged by an estimated NVA platoon. The enemy was very aggressive and employed 10 RPG rounds, several satchel charges, grenades and small arms fire. The enemy platoon attacked from the east and northeast of their NDP position. A 10-man NVA assault initially deployed under a barrage of RPG fire, closed within 10 to 15 feet of the Company's position, and attempted to breach the defensive perimeter with satchel charges. 1 satchel charge destroyed a M60 MG emplacement. 1 NVA sapper was killed and taken into the perimeter at 2214H. The enemy carried 1 AK-47 and a 3 day supply of rice. A second enemy element attempted to overrun the perimeter, but the Company, supported by a flare ship and 1 spooky gunship, continued to engage the enemy with organic weapons fire and forced him to withdraw. Contact was terminated at 2330H. The area was checked at first light and an additional 2 NVA KIA were found, along with 2 AK-47s, 6 satchel charges, 1 RPG round, and 180 AK-47 rounds. Results: 3 NVA KIA, 3 IWC, 1 US WIA (E: at 240942H), 5 US WIA (M).

## March 24, 1969

**0942H** A Medevac was completed to 22nd Surg for 1 man wounded the previous night.

## March 26, 1969

BN CP located at FB Whip along with the 2nd BDE CP.

**1021H** (YC581805): Co. D discovered 1 bolt action rifle, 1 Chicom grenade boobytrapped with an antipersonnel mine firing device. Results: boobytrap destroyed, 1 IWC.

## March 27, 1969

**0819H** (YC584794): Co. D had 2 individuals wounded when a boobytrapped M16 antipersonnel mine (Bouncing Betty) was detonated, medevac completed at 1000H. Results: 2 US WIA (E: James C. Camera and Richard S. Tomczuk).

**1314H** (YC576785): Co. D found and destroyed 1 SKS (stock had been burned off).

## March 29, 1969

Co. D occupied a night position with Co. B at YC600787.

## March 30, 1969

**1030H** (YC600797): Co. D received sniper fire from the west side of their LZ. The element returned fire and employed arty, with the sniper withdrawing to the southwest. A sweep of the area was made. Results: 2 US WIA (E: 1LT Stanford Bevis and Gordon H. Hoffman).

## April 2, 1969

BN CP located at FB Whip.

**1030H** (YC609801): 3/D had 1 man fall off a cliff striking his head and chest, becoming unconscious. Medevac was completed to 22nd Surg at 1145H.

## April 3, 1969

**0946H** Co. D, along with Recon Platoon (OPCON to Co. D), moved by air from YC610805 to FB Whip, closing at 1039H and becoming OPCON of 2nd BDE. At 1039H Recon Platoon was released from OPCON of Co. D. The Company occupied a night position at FB Fury.

## April 7, 1969

**0815H** 3/D moved by CH-47 from FB Whip to Eagle Beach, closing at 0843H. The platoon marshalled at Eagle Beach until 1600H when the platoon returned via CH-47 to FB Whip, closing at 1630H.

## April 9, 1969

**1535H** Co. D was released from OPCON of 2nd BDE and departed FB Whip, conducting a RIF operation to YC600873.

## April 11, 1969

**1140H** (YC607854): Co. D discovered and destroyed 1 hut (8'x10'), used in the last 72 hours.

**1230H** (YC604849): Co. D found a circular bamboo hut with one open side, which had been used as a sleeping quarters.

## April 14, 1969

**1045H** (YC607839): Co. D discovered fresh signs of the enemy digging up a sump in the Co. D NDP for April 13. A search of the area was made with negative results.

## April 15, 1969

**1000H** (YC598838): 2/D engaged 3-5 NVA receiving small arms fire. The platoon returned small arms fire and the enemy fled. TAC Air was em-

128 • *Delta Raiders*

ployed and 1 secondary explosion was observed. At 1025H the element discovered AK-47 brass on the ground and signs of 2 to 3 enemy fleeing north. A further search of the area was made with negative results.

**1330H** (YC592839): 2/D discovered an aid station and sleeping area consisting of 2 huts (12'x18') with bunkers underneath. Each of the bunkers would accommodate an estimated enemy squad. Also discovered were 1 Ml carbine, 1 NVA uniform, and miscellaneous medical supplies. The area had been used during the previous week. Results: 1 IWC, all else destroyed.

### April 16, 1969

**1400H** (YC597837): Co. D discovered 1 hut (8'x10') containing one 200 lb. bag of polished rice, approximately 4 months old in good condition. Results: all destroyed.

**1500H** (YC596837): Co. D discovered a NVA training area with several barbed wire entanglements. Area was very old and showed no signs of recent use. Results: destroyed.

### April 17, 1969

**1245H** (YC898844): Co. D discovered 5 huts (12'x12') with bunkers underneath (15'x20'). The area could accommodate an estimated platoon and had been used in the last 2 to 3 weeks. Results: all destroyed.

**1855H** (YC592837): Co. D discovered 1 grave, approximately 1 to 2 months old, containing 1 NVA body killed by small arms fire. Results: 1 NVA KIA.

### April 18, 1969

**1400H** (YC599842): Co. D discovered a suspected NVA ammo point consisting of a hole or storage bunker (10'x12') with a thatched cover over it. The hole contained 8 empty cases which had contained RPG rounds. Results: destroyed.

**1600H** (YC598847): Co. D discovered 23,100 AK-47 rounds packed in cases, lying in the open against tree trunks. Results: ammunition evacuated.

**1942H** (YC58942): Co. D heard movement approximately 200m northeast of their NDP. Illumination and arty were employed, and a check of the area was made at first light.

### April 19, 1969

**0824H** (YC599842): Co. D found a weapons and munitions cache in the open and uncamouflaged which contained the following: 103,950 AK-47 rounds, 22 75mm mortar rounds, 1 75mm armor-piercing mortar round, 459 60mm mortar rounds, 24 82mm mortar rounds, 46 RPG-2 rounds, 24 RPG-7 rounds, 30 SKS rifles, 5 AK-47 rifles, and 1 60mm mortar intact. Munitions were in excellent condition and all weapons were still coated with cosmoline and in excellent condition. The Company continued to search the area and found 2 empty caches 200 meters to the northeast. The enemy had emptied the caches during the past 12 hours.

**1200H** (YC600837): 3/D sighted and engaged 3 NVA with small arms fire. The enemy returned fire and fled west. The platoon swept the area with negative results.

### April 21, 1969

**1248H** (YC599842): 3/D received small arms and RPG fire from an estimated NVA squad. The element engaged the enemy with small arms fire and the enemy fled. A sweep of the area was made with negative results. Results: 1 US WIA (M).

### April 23, 1969

**1335H** (YC599830): 3/D found and destroyed 2 RPG boobytraps.

**1555H** (YC600835): Co. D discovered a heavy blood trail leading southeast. 3/D followed the bloodtrails and discovered a bandolier of M16 ammo and 3 US helmets at YC599830. Results: ammo evacuated.

### April 25, 1969

Co. D (OPCON of 2nd BDE) continued to provide security at FB Whip.

**1000H** 1/D moved by CH-47 from FB Whip to LZ Sally, closing at 1030H. The platoon marshalled at LZ Sally for impending operations.

### April 26, 1969

**1040H** 1/D moved by CH-47 from LZ Sally to FB Whip, closing at 1111H. At 1112H 2/D moved by CH-47 from FB Whip to LZ Sally, closing at 1127H.

## April 27, 1969

**0944H** 2/D moved by CH-47 from LZ Sally to FB Whip, closing at 1015H. At 1015H 3/D moved by CH-47 from FB Whip to LZ Sally, closing at 1042H.

## April 28, 1969

**0844H** 3/D moved by CH-47 from LZ Sally to FB Whip, closing at 0905H.

## April 29, 1969

**1130H** FB Whip received ineffective small arms from 2 NVA, located 100m southwest of the perimeter. Co. D returned fire with organic weapons and employed 81mm mortar fire on the suspected enemy locations. 3/D deployed and swept south and southwest of the perimeter and found 1 loaded RPG-2 launcher and heavy blood trails. The platoon followed the blood trails and found 1 NVA KIA by small arms fire. Results: 1 NVA KIA.

## April 30, 1969

**0937H** Co. D CA'd from FB Whip to YC697878, closing at 1025H.

## May 1, 1969

BN CP located at FB Whip.

**1210H** (YC696867): 3/D discovered 1 trail oriented north-south with boot tracks, approximately 12 hours old, of 4 to 5 individuals heading south. A search of the area was made with negative results.

## May 6, 1969

CPT Douglas Terrel took over as commander of Delta Company from CPT Robert E. Gates, Jr.

**0910H** Co. D moved by air from YC699893 to FB Whip, closing at 1028H. At 1028H the Company moved by CH-47 from FB Whip to LZ Sally, closing at 1150H.

    **1210H** BN CP moved by CH-47 from FB Whip to LZ Sally.

## May 8, 1969

Operation MASSACHUSETTS STRIKER and operation KENTUCKY JUMPER ended, and operation APACHE SNOW began.

LTC Robert L. German took over as commander of the 2-501 from LTC Joseph C. Wilson.

**0001H** 2-501 (incl. Co. D) became OPCON of the 3rd BDE.

## May 9, 1969

During the evening of May 9 the 2-501 (md. Co. D), along with the 1-506, and the 3-187, marshalled in the vicinity of FB Blaze (YD536020) for insertion the next morning into the area in and adjacent to the northern A Shau Valley. The elements had the mission, as part of Operation APACHE SNOW, to destroy enemy forces, bases, and lines of communication in the area.

## May 10, 1969

**0730H** The lead elements of the 1-506, 3-187, and 2-501 began moving to their respective landing zones with Companies B, C, D, and BN HQ of the 2-501 assaulting into a landing zone at YC288015, completed at 1047H, while Co. A secured and continued construction of FB Airborne.
BN CP located at FB Airborne (YD355070).

## May 12, 1969

**1210H** (YD288034): Co. D discovered 1 hut (20'x12') with 1 NVA gas mask inside. Results: hut destroyed and the gas mask evacuated.

## May 13, 1969

**0330H** FB Airborne (YD355070), defended by Co. A, was assaulted on three sides by two reinforced infantry and sapper companies supported by 82mm and 60mm mortars and RPG fire, with heavy casualties on both sides. Later in the day Companies B, C, and D were extracted from the field and reinserted into the FB Airborne area, and conducted reconnaissance in force operations to the north, south, and east of FB Airborne in search of the attacking force.

**1643H** (YD352074): Co. D received small arms fire from 2 to 3 enemy approximately 100m west of their location. The element returned fire and the enemy fled in an unknown direction. Results: 2 US WIA (E: Jose R. Estevez and Michael J. Larson).

## May 14, 1969

**1235H** (YD340076): Co. D engaged 3 trail watchers with small arms fire. The enemy returned small arms fire and fled in an unknown direction. A sweep of the area was made with negative results. Results: 1 US WIA (E: James T. Turman).

## May 15, 1969

**1128H** (YD342082): Co. D discovered 3 NVA khaki uniforms and 8 Chicom grenades, lying under a tree for approximately 1 to 2 days. Results: destroyed.

**1350H** (YD345086): Co. D discovered 1 cave with a small entrance, which would accommodate an estimated company size force. Frag grenades were thrown inside and a search was made revealing 1 NVA KIA, 1 SKS, 3 Mausers, 1 submachine gun drum, 3 shirts, 1 religious robe, a machete, and 1 first aid pouch. Results: 1 NVA KIA, 4 IWC, all else destroyed.

## May 18, 1969
**1455H** (YD355071-FB Airborne): Co. D on security at FB Airborne received six 60mm mortar rounds and six 82mm mortar rounds. CB was fired on the suspected enemy location YD356097. A sweep of the area was made. Results: 1 US WIA.

**1530H** (YD355071- FB Airborne): Co. D discovered 60 1/2 lb. satchel charges with fuses, and 3 RPG rounds lying near the firebase perimeter. Results: all destroyed.

## May 20, 1969
**1000H** While Co. D and Recon Platoon continued their security of FB Airborne, Companies A, B, and C assaulted Hill 937 (Dong Ap Bia, better known as "Hamburger Hill") from the northeast and east as part of a coordinated attack with 3 other battalions. Unlike the other 3 battalions, the three 2-501 companies encountered little enemy resistance.

**1055H** (YD354072-FB Airborne): Co. D and Recon Platoon at FB Airborne received ten 82mm mortar rounds from an estimated two mortar tubes. CB and ARA was fired on the suspected enemy location. A sweep of the area was made with negative results.

**May 21, 1969**

**0630H** (YD355072-FB Airborne): Co. D and Recon Platoon at FB Airborne received 4 to 6 rounds of 60mm mortar fire. CB was fired on the suspected enemy location YD357067. A sweep of the area was made with negative results.

**May 23, 1969**

**1048H** (YC321987): Co. D discovered 3 NVA bodies killed by small arms fire, lying in the open approximately 3 to 5 days old. Results: 3 NVA KIA.

**1120H** (YC320988): As Co. D began to move to high ground they received a heavy volume of small arms, RPG, satchel charges, and grenade fire from an estimated 2 NVA platoons north and northwest of their location. The Company maneuvered and employed organic weapons fire, ARA, TAC Air, and arty. The enemy was well dug in. Contact completed at 1500H. Results: 3 NVA KIA, 1 US KIA (Douglas Sommer); 8 US WIA (E) and 8 US WIA (H) including: William Des Jarden, William J. Englerth, Raymond Gagnon, Sylvester Grant, Charles Grebinger, Larry Lovell, Robert R. Martin, Clifford N. Masunaga, Bernard F. Miller, Edward E. Nichols, Gerald L. Nissen, Herman Sharp, Frank B. Thacher, Steven R. Walters, and Thomas L. White.

**May 30, 1969**

**1330H** (YC312992): Co. D observed and engaged 1 enemy carrying a 5-lb. claymore. A sweep of the area revealed 1 NVA KIA. While searching the area the element discovered 20 bunkers containing 1 spool of WD-2 commo wire, 1 AK-47 with 2 magazines, 21 82mm mortar rounds, 3 rounds of unknown type small arms ammo. The NVA had K3/9 insignia on the shoulder of his fatigue jacket. Results: 1 NVA KIA, 1 IWC, all rest destroyed.

**June 1, 1969**

**0925H** (YD333001 ): Co. D received 16 60mm mortar rounds from the southeast. CB was fired on the suspected enemy location YC338995. A sweep of the area was made with negative results.

**June 5, 1969**

**1213H** (YC405973): A loach with 3 personnel on board crashed due to failure of the rear tail rotor. It made a relatively safe landing and the only damage appeared to be the rotor failure. There were no injuries, and the ship was secured by Delta Company.

## June 6-10, 1969

Co. D provided security for construction of an airstrip at YC407975, in the northern A Shau Valley. The Company was OPCON to 3rd BDE and 2-502.

## June 7, 1969

Operation APACHE SNOW ended.

## June 9, 1969

**0930H** 2-501 (- Co. D) returned to OPCON of 2nd BDE from the 3rd BDE, with the BN CP located at FB Birmingham.

**1015H** (YC407975): Co. D engaged 3 to 5 enemy with small arms fire 150m to the west of the airfield. A sweep of the area was made with negative results.

## June 10, 1969

**0900H** Co. D moved by air from the Valley airstrip (YC407975) to Eagle Beach, complete at 0930H and returned to the OPCON of the 2-501.

**1820H** (YD755144): 1/D received 2 rounds of small arms fire from an azimuth of 190 degrees. The unit was unable to return fire due to the large number of innocent civilians in the area.

## June 11, 1969

**1009H** Co. D moved by air from Eagle Beach to FB Birmingham, complete at 1032H.

**1425H** Co. D CA'd from FB Birmingham to YD754026, complete at 1516H.

## June 12, 1969

Co. D constructed 1 ship LZs at YD772024 and YD772023.

## June 13, 1969

**0800H** (YD774024): Co. D found 8 60mm mortar rounds boobytrapped with pressure devices. The rounds were buried on a LZ site with the tips of their warheads exposed. The rounds appeared to be buried approximately 2 to 3 days ago. Results: destroyed in place 1649H (YD765015): Co. D spotted 2 to 3 NVA moving southeast. The unit was too far away to engage the enemy with small arms fire. Arty was employed and a cavalry team reconned the area with negative results.

## June 14, 1969

Co. D constructed a 1 ship LZ at YD770012.

**June 15, 1969**
Co. D constructed a 1 ship LZ at YD767014.
**June 16, 1969**
1019H Co. D CA'd from YD767014 to YD773033, closing at 1058H.

**June 17, 1969**
Co. D constructed a 1 ship LZ at YD721040.

**June 20, 1969**
0930H (YD713059): 1/D found fresh footprints and reconned the area by fire with negative results. At 1005H the platoon found 7 bunkers (4'x4') with overhead cover. The bunkers were along a trail running northwest-southeast. The area showed signs of recent use. Results: destroyed.

**June 21, 1969**
1150H Co. D moved by air to FB Birmingham and assumed security of the firebase with one squad at OP 56.

**June 24, 1969**
Co. D continued security of FB Birmingham with one squad and one 81mm squad at OP 56.

## June 27, 1969

**0712H** Co. D CA'd from FB Birmingham to YD822062, complete at 0820H.

**0910H** (YD826057 - 5 KM SE of OP Satan II): Co. D found 4 unknown type rubber plugs which had 2 round prongs 3/4' apart. The unit also found 2 yellow wires each 5" long similar to WD-1 wire, 6 plastic shipping plugs for 122mm rockets and 5 fuse plugs for 82mm mortar rounds. All the items appeared to be in the area for approximately 1 month. Results: destroyed.

**1714H** Co. D moved by air from YD821061 to FB Birmingham, complete at 1750H.

## June 30, 1969

**1607H** 1/D CA'd from FB Birmingham to YD 819109, complete at 1623H. The platoon conducted a detailed search operation with negative results.

**1806H** 1/D moved by air from YD817117 to FB Birmingham, complete at 1817H.

## July 1, 1969

BN CP located at FB Birmingham.

## July 1-5, 1969

Co. D on security at FB Birmingham.

## July 3, 1969

CPT John E. Kelly, Jr. took over as commander of Delta Company from CPT Douglas Terrel.

## July 6-12, 1969

Co. D at Eagle Beach on security. 1/D and 2/D rotated on security at the LCU Ramp.

## July 11, 1969

**1400H** (Eagle Beach): 2/D at the Pumping Station (south of Eagle Beach) received 6 to 8 rounds of small arms fire from an unknown direction (negative casualties). A sweep of the area was made with negative results.

## July 12, 1969

**1333H** Co. D (- 2/D) moved by air from Eagle Beach to FB Panther II (YD811080), complete at 1408H.

**1339H** 2/D moved by air from the LCU Ramp to the Pohl Bridge (YD756134), complete at 1405H.

## July 18, 1969
**1605H** (YD586086): Co. D spotted movement to the north. A sweep of the area was made with negative results.

## July 20, 1969
**1010H** (YD582096 - 4 KM W of FB Bastogne): Co. D found 1 new RPG round which was destroyed in place.

**1247H** (YD582096 - 4 KM W of FB Bastogne): Co. D received small arms fire from the northwest from 1 to 2 trailwatchers. The unit returned fire and the enemy fled north. A sweep of the area was made with negative results. Results: 1 US KIA (Alex Esequiel Martinez), 1 US WIA (E: Larry Banks).

## July 21, 1969
**1115H** (YD579099 - 4 KM W of FB Bastogne): 3/D engaged an unknown size enemy force with small arms fire and the enemy returned small arms fire. ARA and 1 airstrike were employed on the enemy location. A sweep of the area revealed 6 bunkers destroyed.

## July 22, 1969
**0930H** (YD581099 - 3 KM W of FB Bastogne): Co. D engaged 1 NVA, moving east on a trail, with small arms fire. The enemy returned small arms fire and fled to the southeast. A sweep of the area was made with negative results.

## July 23, 1969
**0830H** (YD580114 - 5 KM NW of FB Bastogne): Co. D discovered a grave containing 1 NVA killed by small arms fire 3 to 4 days previously. The unit searched the area and found signs written in the trees. One sign in Vietnamese read "Americans Keep Out". Results: 1 NVA KIA.

**1420H** (YD580114 - 5 KM NW of FB Bastogne): Co. D engaged and killed with small arms fire 1 NVA moving east. A sweep of the area revealed 1 NVA KIA and 1 AK-47. Results: 1 NVA KIA, 1 IWC.

## July 24, 1969
**0900H** (YD581119 - 4 KM NW of FB Bastogne): Co. D reported that the Cav. Team spotted 2 VC/NVA in the area. 2-17 Cav. employed arty and TAC Air. Delta Company moved in and at 1135H, reported 3 VC/NVA KIA, 1 NVA KIA by arty and 2 VC/NVA KIA by the Cav. Team. The enemy wore

blue uniforms and were well equipped with weapons in good condition. At 1200H the Company reported finding at the same location 3 AK-47 lying in the open. Results: 3 NVA KIA, 6 IWC.

## July 25, 1969

**0609H** (YD582117 - 3 KM NW of FB Bastogne): Co. D received 10 60mm mortar rounds from an unknown direction, with negative casualties or damage.

**0930H** (YD583123 - 3 KM NW of FB Bastogne): Co. D received small arms fire from 2 to 3 NVA. The unit returned small arms fire and a Pink Team engaged the enemy location; contact was broken at 0950H. Results: 1 US KIA (Jimmy Darrell Courtney).

**1120H** (YD583123 - 3 KM NW of FB Bastogne): Co. D had the 2-17 Cav. Pink Team accidentally fire on Co. D resulting in 1 US KIA (CPT John Edward Kelly, Jr., the CO of Delta Company) and 2 US WIA (medevaced to 85th Evac., medevac complete at 1215H). At 1230H LTC Robert L. German (the 2-501 CO) visited the Company's location and upon examining CPT Kelly's body believed that he was killed by enemy AK-47 fire rather than by 2-17 Cav. gunships. The record, therefore, officially lists CPT Kelly as a KIA by enemy fire; despite the fact that virtually everyone present at the time knew he was killed by friendly fire. Results: 1 US KIA (CPT John Edward Kelly, Jr.), 2 US WIA (E: William J. Englerth and Jose E. Mercado), and 1 US WIA (H: Earnest Hoof).

CPT Thomas M. Curtis took over as commander of Delta Company following the death of CPT John E. Kelly, Jr.

## July 30, 1969

**1200H** (YD875245 - 300m S of FB Sandy): 3/D discovered 800 lbs. of polished rice, in woven baskets (3'x4' and 6'x8') buried in the ground. The cache appeared to be new. The rice was turned over to the Vinh Loc district for distribution. Results: 800 lbs. of rice captured.

## July 31, 1969

**1300H** (YD896236 - 5 KM N of FB Saber): 3/D had 1 man step on a boobytrapped small arms round with pressure-type firing device. Medevac completed to 22nd Surg at 1320H. Results: 1 US WIA (E:).

**1350H** (YD873244 - 1 KM SW of FB Sandy): 3/D received small arms fire from an estimated 2 VC, resulting in negative casualties. The unit returned small arms fire and the enemy fled in an unknown direction. A sweep of the area was made with negative results.

## Aug. 1, 1969
BN CP located at FB Birmingham.

## Aug. 3, 1969
Co. D was responsible for the security of FB Birmingham.

## Aug. 6, 1969
Co. D (-2/D) remained at FB Birmingham with 2/D at FB Bastogne.

## Aug. 12, 1969
1020H (YD703030 - 2 KM NE of FB Normandy): Co. D spotted 30 fresh sets of footprints on a trail running south-north. A pink team reconned the area with negative results.

## Aug. 15, 1969
Operation CLAIBORNE CHUTE began.
FB Panther II (YD811080) redesignated FB Arsenal.

## Aug. 18, 1969
0800H (YD567130): A Kit Carson Scout working with Co. D (-1/D and 3/D) left his equipment at the Company's location and left the area. The unit left an ambush team behind in the area.

1110H (YD570124): Co. D found four strands of commo wire in the trees, running northwest-southeast. The unit sent a squad in each direction to check out the area with negative results.

## Aug. 19, 1969
1600H (YD572178 - 2 KM W of FB Helen): Co. C (3-187) captured a Kit Carson Scout who had deserted Delta Company on Aug. 18.

1645H (YD577134 - 3 KM S of FB Strike): Co. D exchanged small arms fire with an estimated squad of VC/NVA 75-100m from their position, while ARA worked the enemy location. A pink team screened the area as the enemy broke contact and fled in an unknown direction. A sweep of the area was conducted with negative results. Results: 1 US WIA (H: George L. Green).

## Aug. 20, 1969
Co. D (-1/D) on security at FB Arrow (YD799109) and 1/D on security at the Pohl Bridge (YD756134).

## Aug. 29, 1969
Co. D (-1/D) CA'd from FB Arrow and 1/D CA'd from the Pohl Bridge to YD805048 and FB Bastogne.

## Sept. 1, 1969
**1220H** (YD777033 - 2 KM SW of FB Satan II): Co. D discovered 1 bunker containing 6 82mm mortar rounds. The ordnance was old and the bunker showed no signs of recent use. Results: bunker and rounds destroyed.

## Sept. 3, 1969
**1024H** Co. D moved by air from YD775035 to LZ Sally, complete at 1038H.
**1313H** BN CP moved by vehicle from FB Birmingham to LZ Sally.

## Sept. 4-11, 1969
The 2-501 (incl. Co. D) conducted refresher training at LZ Sally.

## Sept. 11, 1969
Beginning at 0700H the 2-501 (incl. Co. D, fourth in order of movement) conducted a CA from LZ Sally to the vicinity of FB Helen (YD516219); Co. D CA'd to a LZ at YD554219.

## Sept. 19, 1969
**0020H** (YD569257): 3/D received 30 60mm mortar rounds, the closest of which landed 500m from one of their ambush elements. Arty was employed on the suspected enemy location and a sweep of the area was made at first light with negative results.

## Sept. 21, 1969
CPT John T. Thompson took over as commander of Delta Company from CPT Thomas M. Curtis.

## Sept. 25, 1969
**0400H** An explosion of unknown origin resulted in 10 US WIA from Companies D and C. 9 were medevaced to the BN aid station and 1 was medevaced to 85th Evac at Phu Bai; the medevac was completed at 0445H.
**1005H** Co. D CP located at YD638257: 1/D YD648248; 2/D YD618248; 3/D YD663243.

## Sept. 26, 1969
Co. D moved by air to LZ Sally, closing at 1700H.

## Sept. 27, 1969
Operation CLAIBORNE CHUTE ended.

**0055H** Co. D departed LZ Sally by truck (escorted by 3/D/2-17 Cav.), closing at the release point (YD715245) at 0110H, and arrived at YD714245 at 0135H; the Company was in position on the northeast perimeter for the cordon of Huong Tra.

**0400H-1600H** (YD677258 - 3 KM SE of LZ Sally): The 2-501 (including Co. D) conducted a cordon of Huong Tra, reporting 1387 personnel processed, 1349 classified as innocent civilians, 38 as civil defendants, and 11 as draft dodgers.

## Sept. 29, 1969

**0005H** (YD683263 - 4 KM SE of LZ Sally): A PF/RF Co. ambush observed 1 VC platoon. Gunship and arty were employed and Co. D set up a blocking force with negative results.

**1638H** Co. D moved by air from LZ Sally to FB Bastogne to assume security of the firebase, complete at 1749H.

## Sept. 29-Oct. 3, 1969
Co. D on security at FB Bastogne.

## Oct. 1, 1969
BN CP located at LZ Sally.

## Oct. 3, 1969
**0853H** Co. D moved by vehicle from FB Bastogne to Eagle Beach, complete at 1214H.

## Oct. 3-4, 1969
Co. D at Eagle Beach on standdown.

## Oct. 5-6, 1969
Co. D conducted RIPs in the vicinity of YD6008.

## Oct. 7, 1969

**1245H** (YD607074 - 2 KM W of FB Bastogne): 2/D discovered seven well-fortified bunkers (4'x4' with overhead cover) located in a semicircle. Three of the bunkers appeared to have been constructed within the past three weeks. A sweep of the area was made with negative results. Results: bunkers destroyed.

**1655H** (YD612071 - 3 KM SW of FB Bastogne): 2/D engaged 2 NVA with small arms fire 100m to the southwest. The enemy returned small arms fire and fled in an unknown direction. A sweep of the area was made with negative results.

**1735H** (YD614072 - 3 KH SW of FB Bastogne): 2/D received small arms fire from an unknown size enemy force firing from two bunkers (4'x5' with overhead cover). The element returned fire with organic weapons and employed arty on the enemy location. The enemy fled in an unknown direction. Darkness precluded a sweep of the area.

## Oct. 10, 1969

**1030H** (YD609068 - 3 KM SW of FB Bastogne): Co. D discovered 23 82mm mortar rounds concealed by a tree stump. A sweep of the area was made. Results: destroyed.

## Oct. 12, 1969

Co. D completed a 2-ship LZ at YD595063.

## Oct. 13-18, 1969

Co. D responsible for the security of FB Bastogne.

## Oct. 14, 1969

1 man (Randy Mergenthaler) from 1/D with an injured left leg required a medevac which was completed to 85th Evac. at 1040H.

## Oct. 18, 1969

**0030H** (YD628093 - FB Bastogne): 2/D engaged 1 VC at 5m. The enemy did not return fire and fled in an unknown direction. A first light check of the area was made with negative results.

**1403H** Co. D CA'd from FB Bastogne to YD654028, completed at 1437H.

## Oct. 20, 1969

Co. D completed a 2-ship LZ at YD666062, large enough to accommodate 1 CH-47.

## Oct. 22, 1969

LTC Bobby P. Brashears replaced LTC Robert L. German as CO of 2-501.

**1630H** (YD648071 - 1 KM SE of FB Bastogne): 2/D discovered 5 bunkers, all old and in poor condition. The platoon also discovered 2 bunkers (9'x9' with 2 overhead cover) which appeared to be fairly new. The area showed no signs of recent enemy activity. Results: bunkers destroyed.

## Oct. 28-Nov. 2, 1969
Co. D responsible for the security of FB Bastogne.

## Nov. 2, 1969
**1353H** Co. D CA'd from FB Bastogne to YD652027, completed at 1435H.

## Nov. 9, 1969
**1500H** 1/D had one man (Mike McCarthy) medevaced with a fever of 104; medevac completed to 85th Evac at 1559H.

## Nov. 10, 1969
**1126H** Co. D (-2/D and 3/D) moved by air from YD640011 to FB Bastogne, complete at 1234H.
**1459H** 2/D CA'd from FB Bastogne to YD615080, complete at 1510H.

## Nov. 11, 1969
The 2-501 (including Co. D) moved to LZ Sally for refresher training.

## Nov. 13, 1969
During the period of Nov. 11-13, the 1-61 (of the 5th Mech. Inf. Div.) received heavy contact near Quang Tri, resulting in 22 US KIA, 53 US WIA (E), and 122 NVA KIA. The 2-501, as the Division ready reaction force, was called upon to assist. In Operation FULTON SQUARE the battalion moved by air in 18 CH-47s from LZ Sally to Quang Tn and passed to the OPCON of the 1st BDE, 5th Mech. Infantry Division.
**1134H** The battalion, with Co. D in the lead, CA'd from Quang Tri to YD083635, complete at 1705H. The terrain consisted of rolling hills separated by thickly wooded draws, with the valleys covered by elephant grass with very few trees.

## Nov. 14, 1969
**0940H** (YD065622): Co. D engaged and killed 2 NVA in a bunker and captured 2 AK-47s. There were 8 bunkers located in the area. Results: 2 NVA KIA, 2 IWC.
**1205H** (YD054626): Co. D found leaflets, 3 NVA packs, US equipment, and 4 Chicom grenades. A sweep of the area was made with negative results.

## Nov. 15, 1969
**1147H** (YD064624): Co. D found a bunker complex consisting of 12 bunkers (6'x3'x4'), 2 with overhead cover. The bunkers were 4 to 6 months old with no signs of recent use. There was also a fighting position at each bunker.

**1237H** (YD067624): Co. D reported a "V" shaped trail marker with one stick perpendicular in the center and a metal can beneath. The Company also found 5 bunkers (4'x8'x3', with 2' overhead cover), and 1 Chicom mine.

### Nov. 16, 1969
**1233H** (YD064633): Co. D found fresh footprints of an individual moving in a northeast direction. A sweep was made of the area with negative results.
**1420H** (YD065623): Co. D found 1 dead NVA, 3 to 5 days old. A search of the area was made with negative results. Results: 1 NVA KIA.
**2135H** (YD066626): Co. D reports hearing people and drums.

### Nov. 17, 1969
Co. D (3rd Platoon in lead, followed by 1st and 2nd Platoons) CA'd into a Red LZ at YD085685, complete at 0915H. Although the LZ was 'hot", there were no casualties.
**0935H** (YD085685): Co. D received small arms fire from the southeast, with negative casualties. The element returned fire with negative results.
**1755H** (YD068639): Co. D saw lights and the firing of mortars.

### Nov. 18, 1969
**1212H** The 2-501 returned to LZ Sally from Quang Tri and resumed refresher training, arriving at 1239H. The 2-501 returned to OPCON of the 2nd BDE.

### Nov. 18-27, 1969
Co. D at LZ Sally for refresher training.

### Nov. 28, 1969
**0755H** Co. D(-) moved by air from LZ Sally to FB Birmingham, complete at 0807H.
The 2-501 CP moved to FB Bastogne.

### Nov. 30, 1969
**1409H** (YD621123 2.5 KM N of FB Bastogne): Co. D discovered 3 bunkers (4'x4'x6', with 1' overhead cover) about 3 to 4 months old that had been used within the past 48 hours. Also discovered in the same area were 2 Chicom grenades lying in the open. Results: destroyed.
**1500H** (YD623104 - 1 KM N of FB Bastogne): Co. D discovered a trail marker (3'x3' "V" cut in trail) pointing towards 1 bunker (10'x12' with 2' over-

head cover). The bunker was 2 to 3 weeks old, but showed no signs of recent use. A sweep of the area revealed indications of enemy activity within the past 3 weeks. Results: bunker destroyed.

## Dec. 1, 1969
SERTS (Screaming Eagle Replacement Training School ) was moved from Bien Hoa to Camp Evans.

## Dec. 2, 1969
1745H (YC571998 - 4 KM SE of FB Blaze): Co. C discovered seven 1-man sleeping positions which had been used within the past three days. A sweep of the area was made with negative results.

## Dec. 3, 1969
1/D had one man (John L. "Red" Keister) fall over a cliff and his M-60 hit him on the head, paralyzing his left arm. A dust off was requested at 1350H and completed to 85th Evac at 1438H.

## Dec. 7, 1969
LZ Sally redesignated Camp Sally.
Operation RANDOLPH GLEN began.

## Dec. 8-16, 1969
Co. D responsible for the security of FB Bastogne. The firebase at this time (the middle of the monsoon season) was covered with mud, knee deep in places.

## Dec. 11, 1969
1305H (YD582054 - 4 KM SW of FB Bastogne): Co. D discovered a partially destroyed bunker containing eleven 82mm mortar rounds and one Chicom claymore. A sweep of the area revealed no indications of recent enemy activity. Results: claymore evacuated, other items destroyed.

## Dec. 12, 1969
Former astronaut Frank Borman visited FB Bastogne and walked down the bunker line shaking hands with men of Delta Company.

## Dec. 13, 1969
1215H (YD582066 - 4.5 KM SW of FB Bastogne on HW 547): 1/D had a 5-ton truck detonate on an unknown-type mine with pressure-type firing

device. The truck was towed back to FB Bastogne. Results: negative casualties, minor damage to truck.

**1245H** (YD582066 - 3 KM SW of FB Bastogne): 2/D discovered one 81mm mortar round in poor condition lying in the brush. A sweep of the area revealed no indications of recent enemy activity. Results: destroyed.

## Dec. 18, 1969

**1302H** (YD587056 - 4 KM SW of FB Bastogne): Co. D discovered 50 bunkers (10'x5' with 2' overhead cover), 1 command bunker and 2 tunnels. The entrance to one bunker was boobytrapped with an unknown type of explosive and trip wire firing device. The complex contained one 82mm mortar round and miscellaneous equipment. An area sweep revealed no indications of recent enemy activity. Results: all destroyed.

## Dec. 20, 1969

**1525H** (YD556046 - 1 KM NE of FB Veghel): 1/D discovered 16 bunkers (4'x4'x4' with 1.5' overhead cover), containing miscellaneous gear and indications of enemy use within the past four days. Results: destroyed.

## Dec. 21, 1969

**1030H** (YD556046 - 1 KM NE of FB Veghel): 1/D discovered seven bunkers (4'x4' with 1 overhead cover), containing three cartons of US C-rations. Nearby, eight more bunkers were discovered (4'x4'x4' with 1' overhead cover), containing 65 AK-47 rounds and one empty wooden container with Russian markings and carrying handles (6'x8"x6"). The unit also found an observation platform in a tree. The area appeared to have been used by the enemy within the past two days. Results: container evacuated, other items and bunkers destroyed.

**1545H** (YD604075): 1/D found 5 bunkers (6'x12'x6' with no overhead cover), one of which had a wooden floor. The bunkers were 1 to 2 months old but showed signs of recent use. In the same area the unit found a tunnel 15' long which yielded nothing of intelligence value. Results: destroyed.

**1551H** (YD563063): 2/D found an observation platform 60' high, built about one month ago. Commo wire, both NVA and US, were found connecting the platform and an old fighting position. Area showed no signs of recent use. Results: destroyed.

**1725H** (YD556047 - 1 KM NE of FB Veghel): 1/D found six more bunkers 1 to 2 months old. The unit also found 20 RPG canisters, a pile of rope, a 55-gallon drum and one satchel charge with a pull-type firing device. Results: all destroyed.

**2300H** (YD557062 - 3 KM N of FB Veghel): 3/D discovered 17 bunkers (10'x12'x4' with 1.5' overhead cover), containing miscellaneous equipment and 2 hand grenades. There were no indications of enemy use within the past 6 to 8 months. Results: all destroyed.

### Dec. 22, 1969

**0920H** (YD556047 1 KM NE of FB Veghel): 1/D found 12 aiming stakes 16' long, 19 aiming stakes 20" long, 2 drums 12"x1.5" in diameter for 7.62 Soviet ammo, 2 empty 55 gallon drums, 20 6' long crowbars, 6 sledge hammer heads and 3 cases of 1' long metal spikes (72 spikes per case). There was also a road capable of handling truck traffic leading into the area. The entire area showed no signs of recent use. Results: all destroyed.

**1300H** (YD557062 - 3 KM N of FB Veghel): 2/D found 17 bunkers 2 to 3 months old. 1 bunker was 20'x5'x4' with 2' overhead cover and a smokestack on top; and 16 bunkers were 4'x4'x4' with 1.5' overhead cover. The unit also found a 10 gallon can, 1 US type WP grenade and 1 unknown type grenade. Results: all destroyed.

**1700H** (YD558062 - 3 KM N of FB Veghel): 3/D found 7 bunkers 6 to 7 months old, showing no signs of recent use. 5 of the bunkers were 12'x15'x6' with 1.5' overhead cover, and 1 was 10'x12'x6' with 1.5' overhead cover, and a CP bunker was 15'x20'x6' with 1.5' overhead cover. The unit also found 2 old ponchos, 1 NVA helmet, and 1 NVA boot. Results: all destroyed.

### Dec. 24, 1969

**1226H** 1/C CA'd from YD554046 to YD589060, complete at 1228H.

### Dec. 25, 1969

1/D spent Christmas Day at YD589060.

### Dec. 26, 1969

**1223H** 1/D CA'd from YD588057 to YD555037, complete at 1228H.

**1830H** (YD559052): 1/D found 8 bunkers (5'x4'x3.5' with 1.5' overhead cover). The unit also found 1 ammo drum, 1 protective mask, 1 steel helmet, 1 82mm mortar fuse, 2 Chicom grenades and miscellaneous medical supplies. The bunkers appeared to be over 1 year old and all equipment was rotted beyond salvaging. Results: all destroyed.

## Dec. 27, 1969
0917H (YD563044): 1/D found 8 82mm mortar rounds and 5 60mm mortar rounds in a small hole partially covered by leaves. The cache was located off the side of a trail, and appeared to be 6 months old. The area showed no signs of recent use. Results: all destroyed.

## Jan. 1, 1970
Operation RANDOLPH GLEN began.

## Jan. 4, 1970
0322H-0700H Co. D participated, along with other elements of the 2-501 and ARVN units, in a cordon operation near Eagle Beach.

## Jan. 4-7, 1970
Co. D on standdown at Eagle Beach.

## Jan. 7, 1970
0656H Co. D moved by air from Eagle Beach to FB Birmingham.

## Jan. 8, 1970
1107H Co. D CA'd from YD660093 to FB Blaze to provide security for two arty battalions on an artillery raid at FB Blaze.

## Jan. 10, 1970
1118H Co. D CA'd from FB Blaze to YD607124.

## Jan. 12, 1970
0955H (YD604137 - 4.5 KH SE of FB Strike): Co. D discovered a trail oriented northwest-southeast with fresh footprints of one individual moving northwest. While the element was conducting a sweep of the area they discovered one old campfire site. The Company estimated that the enemy had been in the area within the past 36 to 48 hours.

## Jan. 13, 1970
1037H (YD595138 - 3.5 KM SE of FB Strike): 2/1/D while following footprints on a trail received small arms fire from 1 to 2 NVA about l00m

away. The point man of the squad returned fire, and believed to have wounded one of the enemy. A blood trail was discovered and followed by 1st Platoon, which had reunited with 2nd Squad. At 1105H 1/D was put on 30-minute standby at FB Bastogne (27 men). At 1145H a Pink Team was employed that fired up the area. At 1457H the platoon reported finding 1 rucksack, 20 lbs. of rice, 1 cooking bowl, 2 AK-47 magazines with 60 rounds of ammo, 1 hammock, 1 entrenching tool, and 1 set of new NVA fatigues. Results: all destroyed.

### Jan. 14, 1970

**1420H** (YD587136 - 3 KM S of FB Strike): 1/D found 2 sets of footprints 24 to 48 hours old; 1 set heading north and the other southwest.

**1440H** (YD584134 - 3 KM S of FB Strike): 1/D discovered a bunker complex about 8 months old. Eleven bunkers were 4'x6'x4' with overhead cover, and 4 bunkers were 15'x12'x4' with ovethead cover. Also discovered were 15 fighting positions. There were no signs of recent use. Results: destroyed.

### Jan. 15, 1970

**1035H** (YD592137 - 3 KM S of FB Strike): 1/D reports one man WIA (hand) by shrapnel from an artillery short round. An urgent medevac was requested, which was completed to 85th Evac. at 1059H. The Co. D CO (CPT John Thompson) reported that it was the last round in a series that fell short (400m). Several rounds were fired, but apparently only 1 fell short. 1LT Chris Wall, the arty FO with Co. D, reported that the round went off at tree top level. Results: 1 US WIA (E: Eugene C. Alston).

### Jan. 16, 1970

**1245H** (YD583124 - 4.5 KM NW of FB Bastogne): 3/D discovered a tunnel complex consisting of three tunnels 28' long containing miscellaneous bottles, four 60mm mortar rounds, and three PRG rounds. Results: destroyed.

**1359H** (YD585125 - 4.5 KM NW of FB Bastogne): 3/D engaged 2 enemy at 20m with small arms fire. The enemy did not return fire and 1 fled in an unknown direction. A sweep of the area revealed 1 NVA KIA, and 1 AK-47 with 1 full magazine. Results: 1 NVA KIA, 1 IWC.

## Jan. 22, 1970

**1430H** (YD548148 - 3.5 KM SW of FB Strike): 1/2/D discovered 1 bunker (5'x6'x5') with a tunnel leading into a 5'x5' hut. The hut contained 1 9mm pistol, 4 AK-47s, 1 Chicom grenade, 1 machete, 1 AK-47 cleaning kit and some documents. The area showed no signs of recent use. Results: bunker and hut destroyed, documents evacuated.

## Jan. 23, 1970

**1015H** (YD558149 - 3 KM SW of FB Strike): 1/D discovered 3 blocks of TNT lying in the open on an east-west trail. A sweep of the area revealed no indications of recent activity. Results: destroyed.

## Jan. 26, 1970

**1354H** Co. D moved by air from YD563174 to FB Bastogne.

## Jan. 26-29, 1970

Co. D responsible for the security of FB Bastogne.

## Jan. 29, 1970

**0930H** (YD538072 - 4 KM NW of FB Veghel): Recon Platoon received seven 82mm mortar rounds and heavy small arms fire from an estimated two enemy platoons about 175m from their position. The element returned small arms fire and employed ARA. At 1058H 1/D was inserted to assist Recon Platoon and was engaged by the enemy with small arms fire. The element returned small arms fire and employed ARA and the enemy withdrew in an unknown direction.

At 1400H 2/D was engaged in the same area by an unknown size enemy force resulting in the death of the 2nd Platoon Leader, 1LT Joe Hearne Rufty. A sweep of the area by 1/D and 2/D revealed the following: 1 NVA KIA, 1 M-14 with 4 full magazines, 1 Chicom type 53 HHG and 10 bunkers containing 16 rucksacks, 100 lbs. of rice, 1000 rounds of 7.62 HG ammo, 4 RPG rockets1 3 RPG rocket boosters, 27 1/4 blocks of explosives, 1 Chicom claymore, 2 NVA gasmasks, miscellaneous documents, and miscellaneous clothing, equipment, cooking gear, and medical supplies. Results: 1 US KIA (1LT Joe Hearne Rufty), 1 NVA KIA, 1 IWC, 1 CSWC, documents evacuated to 2-501 HQ, rest destroyed.

## Jan. 30, 1970

**1025H** (YD541070 - 4.5 KM NW of FB Veghe) Co. D discovered 1 AK-47 and 1 NVA body killed by small arms fire during the previous days contact. Results: 1 NVA KIA, 1 IWC.

**1200H** (YD540060 - 2.5 KM NW of FB Veghel): 1/D discovered 6 bunkers (4'x4'x3' with 6' overhead cover). A sweep of the area revealed no indications of recent enemy activity. Results: destroyed.

**1635H** (YD539075 - 4.5 KM NW of FB Veghel): 3/D received AK-47 fire from an unknown size enemy force with negative casualties. The element returned fire and the enemy fled in an unknown direction. A sweep of the area revealed: 5 RPG rounds, 500 AK-47 rounds, 1 bipod for a Chicom type 53 HMG, and 5 rucksacks and miscellaneous clothing. Results: equipment evacuated, rest destroyed.

## Jan. 31, 1970

**1130H** (YD549082 - 4 KM N of FB Veghel): Co. D and Recon Platoon discovered one Chicom boobytrap with electrical detonator attached to one RPG round rigged with a mechanical detonator in the trees. The elements also discovered one Chicom claymore and one Chicom grenade boobytrap on a trail. Results: all destroyed.

**1153H** (YD551082 - 4.5 KM N of FB Veghel): Co. D discovered in a bunker three new RPG rounds still in their boxes with fuses and primers attached. There were no indications of recent enemy activity in the area. Results: destroyed.

## Feb. 1, 1970

**1221H** (YD541070 3.5 KM N of FB Vegnel): Co. D discovered one bunker containing 50 lbs. of rice, one rucksack, 6.5 lbs. of demolition, and some documents. Results: rucksack and documents evacuated, rest destroyed.

**1300H** (YD533073): Co. D found a trail 2' wide, hard packed and used within the past 48 hours by a possible battalion size element. The element checked the area with negative results.

**2009H** (YD543049): 1/D observed lights about 500m from their location, in the vicinity where Co. C 1-501 was extracted. Arty was employed and a shadow came on location. Co. C 2-17 Cav. made a first light check of the area with negative results.

## Feb. 2, 1970

**1040H** (YD542068): The area was saturated with a flame drop by CH-47s, and ARA spotted 12 NVA running out of the area. A Pink Team checked the area with negative results. Co. D moved into the area to check it out and conduct another flame drop. A second flame drop was executed at 1400H, with 15 sorties and 3 CH-47s. Co. D checked the area with negative results.

## Feb. 5-9, 1970
Co. D responsible for the security of FB Bastogne.

## Feb. 6, 1970
CPT Christopher C. Straub replaced CPT John T. Thompson as CO of Delta Co. (per Co. D Morning Report of Feb. 13, 1970). CPT Straub had been with BN S-5 (Sept. 13 - Oct. 9, 1969) and then with BN S-3 (Air BN HQ).
**1910H** FB Bastogne received 25 to 30 RPG rounds from the south.

## Feb. 15, 1970
**1416H** One of the Black Widow lift birds (believed to be Black Widow 34) working with the CA of 1/D crashed on LZ YD665061 with negative casualties. The pilot and crew were picked up by one of the other lift birds.
**1532H** Co. D CP moved by air from YD634084 to YD665061, location of 1/D and the downed Huey.
**1640H** The disabled Black Widow bird was extracted from YD665061 and taken to 5th Trans. at Camp Eagle.

## Feb. 17, 1970
**1205H** (YD644063): 1/D found 2 Chicom rifle rounds and 2 75mm rounds that were still in their casings. Results: 75mm rounds evacuated.

## Feb. 21, 1970
**1745H** (YD644114): 1/2/D discovered 15 foxholes (3'x3'x2' with no overhead cover), about 1 to 2 months old. The unit also found 2 graves with a marker 68. There were no signs of recent activity in the area. Results: foxholes destroyed.

## Feb. 22, 1970
**1030H** (YD620075 - 2.5 KM SW of FB Bastogne): 3/D found 4 RPG rounds and 1 M72 LAW in a hole along a trail. The vicinity was marked with pieces of bamboo tied to bushes pointing to the area. There were signs of recent enemy activity within the past 10 days. Results: destroyed.

**1430H** (YD644115): 1/2/D discovered 15 grave sites (including 2 found the previous day), 6 of which were closed and 3 of these had markers; the bodies appeared to be over a year old. The unit also found 2 bunkers (7'x4'x4' with 2' overhead cover). Everything appeared to be more than a year old. Results: bunkers destroyed, markers evacuated.

**1437H** (YD595085): The scout dog with 1/D alerted the element to movement to their front. A recon by fire was conducted and a Pink Team checked the area with negative results.

## March 3, 1970

**1312H** (YD634050 4.5 KH S of FB Bastogne): 2/D discovered 2 graves about 1 week old containing 2 NVA KBA. The bodies were wrapped in NVA ponchos. There was no ID discovered on the bodies. Results: 2 NVA KBA.

## March 4,1970

**1700H** (YD636058 - 3.5 KM S of FB Bastogne): 2/D discovered 3 graves about 1 week old containing 3 NVA KBA. There was no ID on the bodies. Results: 3 NVA KBA.

## March 5, 1970

**0900H** (YD633018 - 6 KM SW of FB Normandy): 1/D discovered an old enemy base camp containing the following items: 3 huts (12'x17'x60' ), 6 bunkers (2'x4'x4' ), 2 small fighting positions, 3 small latrines, 1 green NVA shirt (no markings), 21 82mm mortar rounds, 15 82mm mortar fuses, 4 60mm mortar rounds, 12 AK-47 rounds, 5 empty penicillin vials, and miscellaneous equipment. A sweep of the area revealed indications of enemy activity within the past month. Results: destroyed.

**0937H** (YD633030): 1/D had a man with a sprained ankle dusted off to the 326 Med.

**1059H** (YD628058): 2/D had a man (Larry Richardson) with a fever of unknown origin medevaced to 326 Med.

**1545H** (YD631021 - 6 KM W of FB Normandy): 1/D discovered 1 bunker (4'x6'x3') containing the following items: 1 damaged Chicom protective mask, 12 60mm mortar rounds, and 22 60mm mortar fuses. A sweep of the area revealed indications of enemy activity within the past 24 hours. Results: all destroyed.

## March 6, 1970

**1015H** (YD633016 - 6 KM W of FB Normandy): 1/D discovered 10 bunkers containing the following items: 1 damaged Chicom protective mask, 12

60mm mortar rounds, and 22 60mm mortar fuses. A sweep of the area revealed indications of enemy activity within the past 24 hours. Results: all destroyed.

**1725H** (YD635015 - 6 KM W of FB Normandy): 1/D heard movement about 30m from their location. A sweep of the area revealed fresh foodstuffs. Results: destroyed.

## March 7, 1970

**1000H** (YD635015 - 6 KM SW of FB Normandy): 1/D discovered 1 hootch (20'x40'x8'), probably used as a mess hall; under the hootch was a triangular bunker (8'xS'x6' with overhead cover). Also discovered were 10 large bunkers (10'x8'xlO' with 2' overhead cover) and 6 smaller bunkers (8'x4'x4' with 2' overhead cover).

The following items were found within the structures: 3 shovels, 1 pick, 7 baskets, 6 carrying cases (12"x4"x24), 1 old NVA rucksack, 2 new NVA ponchos, 2 pair of trousers and shirts that were starched and freshly laundered with labels "THE IN", 2 pair underwear, 1 7.62 machine gun (uses drum for ammo), 1 NVA helmet (written on front "THE", on back "BA THE"), 3 AK-47 magazines (1 full), 2 magazines unknown type, 1

M- 16 magazine, 1 US claymore bag, 1 9mm pistol magazine, 75 loose 7.62 rounds, 5 BA 30 magazines, 1 blasting cap, 2 NVA bayonets, 1 US bayonet, 1 bottle of LSA, 1 AK-47 (no bolt, rusty and inoperable), 3 ammo drums for machine gun, 8 medical bottles (no labels), 6 vitamin bottles, 4 syringe injectors, 22 1/2 lb. blocks of TNT, 12 1/2 lb. blocks wrapped in plastic and tied with vines for a satchel charge, 6 6 1/2 lb. blocks of TNT in sand bags, 3 1/2 lb. blocks of TNT in a closed metal container, 1 grave with skeleton, and 1 NVA letter or sketches. All items 1 year old except for the starched clothes. Results: all destroyed except for helmet and unidentifiable magazines.

**1535H** (YD634016 - 6 KM SW of FB Normandy): 1/D discovered 1 hut (12'x15'x6') and 1 bunker (2'x3'x3') containing 9 RPG shipping caps, 5 RPG booster charges, 1 RPG canister, and 1 NVA shovel. There were no indications of recent enemy activity in the area. Results: destroyed.

## March 8, 1970

**1640H** (YD636051 - 4 KM S of FB Bastogne): 1/D discovered 1 full AK-47 magazine and pieces of a letter. There were no indications of recent enemy activity in the area. Results: letter evacuated.

## March 9, 1970

**0815H** (YD635016 - 6 KM SW of FB Normandy): 1/D discovered 1 metal container hidden in the brush, containing 75' of Chicom detonator cord, 90 non-electric blasting caps, and 3 pull-type firing devices. There were no indications of recent enemy activity in the area. Results: destroyed.

## March 10-19, 1970
Co. D responsible for the security of FB Bastogne.

## March 13, 1970
1/1/D CA'd from FB Bastogne to YD607089 (hill overlooking FB Bastogne) to pull security for a mortar crew. 1/2/D also pulled security for a mortar crew on another hill overlooking the firebase.

**1854H** FB Bastogne received 10 60mm mortar rounds. 1/2/D, on a hill overlooking FB Bastogne, directed fire on suspected mortar location 200m northeast of their position.

## March 20, 1970
2-501 CP moved from FB Bastogne to FB Normandy.

## March 21, 1970
**1830H** (YD673988): 1/D discovered 3 sleeping positions (3'x3'x2'), 1 piece of paper with Vietnamese writing on it, and tracks of 9 personnel moving northwest in the last 3 days. Results: positions destroyed, paper evacuated.

## March 25, 1970
(YC673996): 2/D had 3 men with food poisoning dusted off; symptoms included cramps, vomiting, and temperature. 1 litter and 2 ambulatory cases taken from the location.

## March 31, 1970
**1136H** Co. D moved by air from FB Birmingham to Camp Evans, OPCON to 3rd BDE. Company stayed overnight at Camp Evans; during the evening part the Company watched the film 'Odd Couple'.
Operation RANDOLPH GLEN ended.

## April 1, 1970
Operation TEXAS STAR began. The operation called for continued extensive patrol, surveillance, and security operations in coordination with the 1st ARVN Regt. in the area southwest of Camp Evans from the lowlands west of the populated areas of Phong Dien District to the canopy area northwest of the A Shau Valley to locate and destroy enemy units, base areas and cache sites, and interdict enemy movement into the lowlands and to provide maximum protection for the population. Also, to conduct combined airmobile operations in reaction to hard intelligence, and provide combat support for combined operations and ARVN operations.
Co. D moved from Camp Evans to FB Jack.

## April 7, 1970
During the day 2 LZs were constructed by 2/D and 3/D at YD534186 and YD551192; approach east, exit west with negative obstruction (1 A/C).
Due to heavy 3rd BDE contact in AO Pear the 2-501 was given a new AO south and southeast of FB Ripcord in support of the 2-506 and the 1st ARVN Regt.

## April 9, 1970
**1038H** (YD332174 - 1.5 KM SW of FB Ripcord): 1/D engaged an unknown size enemy force with M-60 and small arms fire 30m from their position along a trail. The enemy returned small arms fire and withdrew in an unknown direction. A sweep of the area revealed 1 NVA KIA, 1 AK-47

with folding stock, and miscellaneous documents. Results: 1 NVA KIA, documents evacuated.

**1050H** (YD339173 - 1.5 KM S of FB Ripcord): 3/D received an unknown number of 60mm mortar rounds from an unknown size enemy force impacting 300m north of their position. At 1105H 3/D received another unknown number of 60mm mortar rounds impacting 150m south of their position. At 1130H artillery was employed on the suspected mortar location at YD359172, 1500m east of the 3/D position. A sweep of the area was made with negative results.

**1625H** (YD332174 - 1.5 KM SW of FB Ripcord): 1/D received heavy small arms and RPG fire from an unknown size enemy force 20m from their point man while moving down a trail. The platoon returned organic weapons fire and the enemy withdrew in an unknown direction. ARA was employed and a sweep of the area was made. Results:4 US WIA (E: Joseph Adams, Mike Cooksley, Garrett Stewart, and Charles West); 7 US WIA (H: Jose Alicia Torres, David Beyl, Martin Cirrincione, Mark Kelley, Terry Palm, Lee Savage, and Carl Shannon).

## April 10, 1970

**0945H** (YD338179 - 1 KM SW of FB Ripcord): 210 engaged 1 enemy with M-60 machine gun fire 10m from their position. The enemy returned small arms fire before being killed. A sweep of the area revealed 1 NVA KIA, 1 AK-47 with 3 full magazines, 1 Chicom grenade, and miscellaneous LBE. The NVA KIA had been wounded earlier, apparently by 1/D the previous day. Results: 1 US WIA (H), 1 NVA KIA, 1IWC, rest destroyed.

**1030H** (YD332176 - 1.5 KM SW of FB Ripcord): 1/D discovered a bunker complex consisting of 21 bunkers (20'x10'x8' with 2' overhead cover) and 24 fighting positions. There were indications of enemy activity in the area within the past 3 to 4 days. Results: destroyed.

**1056H** 1/D in the area of the previous days contact (1625H) found 1 AK-50 and 1 NVA KIA. Results: 1 NVA KIA.

**1100H** 1/D discovered 3 15 lb. bags of rice, 1 pair of sandals, 2 1 lb. satchel charges, 3 full AK-47 magazines, and 1 bamboo-type basket lying in the open. There were indications of enemy activity in the area within the past 3 or 4 days. Results: destroyed.

## April 11, 1970

**1700H** (YD375161 - 3 KM SE of FB Ripcord): 3/D received small arms fire from 1 enemy 100m north of their position. The platoon returned small arms fire and the enemy withdrew in an unknown direction. A sweep of the area was made with negative results.

## April 12, 1970

**1300H** (YD340181 - 1 KM S of FB Ripcord): 2/D discovered 7 to 8 caves used by 50 to 60 persons within the last 24 hours. The caves contained 2 fish traps, 1 AK-47 magazine (empty), 1 lb. of fish, 15 straw baskets, 1 bottle of penicillin, and a newspaper clipping. Signs in the area indicate the enemy moved east leaving barefoot and HCM sandal tracks. Results: clipping evacuated, rest destroyed.

The 2-501 CP moved from YD337171 to FB Granite and assumed control of the firebase, with B/1-506 (providing FB security) becoming OPCON to 2-501.

## April 13, 1970

**1150H** (YD365160 - 5 KM SE of FB Ripcord): 3/D, OPCON to B/2-501, engaged 3 enemy bathing in a stream with small arms fire 15m from their position. There was no return fire. While searching the bodies the element received small arms fire from 3 to 5 enemy 75m from their position. The platoon returned small arms fire and the enemy withdrew in an unknown direction. A search of the area revealed 3 NVA KIA and miscellaneous documents. Results: 3 NVA KIA, 3 US WIA (H), documents evacuated.

**1655H** 3/D received 56 60mm mortar rounds. Artillery was employed on the suspected enemy locations at YD363155 and YD353255.

## April 14, 1970
**1455H** (YD363171 - 3KM SE of FB Ripcord): 3/D received small arms fire and an unknown number of RPGs from an estimated enemy squad 50m from their position. The platoon returned organic weapons fire and the enemy withdrew in an unknown direction. Artillery was employed and a sweep of the area was made. Results: 5 US WIA (E: Albert Bolden, Richard Trujillo, 5 US WIA (H)).

## April 15, 1970
**1415H** (YD362164 - 3 kM SE of FB Ripcord): 1 person from 3/D (Lanny W. Spears), wounded in yesterday's contact, was medevaced to 0/326 Med., along with 2 men from Co. B wounded earlier in the day.

## April 17, 1970
**1910H** The 2-501 was granted an AO extension to 1100H on the 18th since 1/D is in the 2-506 area and wanted the area for a NDP.

## April 18, 1970
LTC Otis T. Livingston succeeded LT Bobby P. Brashears as the CO of 2-501.
**1650H** (YD377163 - 4 KM SE of FB Ripcord): 1/D discovered 1 grave containing 1 NVA killed by small arms fire about 1 week ago. The body was dressed in old fatigues and wrapped in a poncho. There were also miscellaneous documents in the grave. Results: 1 NVA KIA, documents evacuated.

## April 19, 1970
**1440H** 3/D moved by air along with B/2-501 from YD373162 to FB Granite.

## April 20, 1970
**1305H** 3/D moved by air from FB Granite to YD386174 and returned to OPCON of Co. D.

## April 23, 1970
LTC Livingston recommended to COL Bradley (3rd BDE CO) that since A/2-501 had been in 2 serious engagements they should go to Eagle Beach in the place of D/2-501, which had been scheduled, and Co. D should be sent to the Co. A area. The recommendation was approved.

## April 25, 1970
**1040H** (YD373154 - 4 KM SE of FB Ripcord): 2/D engaged 5 enemy with small arms fire 30m from their position. The enemy did not return fire, but withdrew to the south. ARA was employed and a sweep of the area

revealed 2 NVA rucksacks containing 110 lbs. of rice and 4 blood trails moving south. Results: rice destroyed.

**1400H** (YD392152): 2/D observed 3 enemy moving east along a trail that ran along a stream. The platoon set up an ambush in the area with negative results.

## April 26, 1970

**1535H** (YD368154 - 5 KM SE of FB Ripcord): 2/D engaged 5 enemy with small arms fire 40m from their position. The enemy did not return fire, but withdrew in an unknown direction. Artillery blocking fires were employed and a sweep of the area revealed 4 NVA KIA, 2 AK-47s and 1 rucksack. Results: 4 NVA KIA, 2 IWCs, rest destroyed.

## April 27, 1970

**1540H** (YD366155 - 4 KM SE of FB Ripcord): 1/D engaged 1 enemy at 75m across a stream with M-60 fire. The enemy hid behind a rock and the platoon re-engaged him with M-79 fire and advanced on his position, resulting in 1 NVA POW. The element also captured 1 AK-47 and 1 rucksack containing 10 lbs. of rice. Results: 1 NVA POW, 1 IWC, rest destroyed.

**1545H** (YD365165  3 KM SE of FB Ripcord): 2/D engaged 1 enemy with small arms fire across a stream 150m south of their position. The enemy did not return fire, but fell 20m down a steep incline into the stream bed. The sweep by the platoon was hindered due to rugged terrain, but 1 NVA KIA is assumed.  Results: 1 NVA KIA.

## April 29, 1970

**0838H** Medevac completed to C/326 Med for man from Co. D with a possible rupture.

**1300H** (YD359151 - 3.5 KM SE of FB Ripcord): A White Team (2 LOHs on visual reconnaissance) flew uninvited into Co. D's AO.  While CPT Chris Straub (the Delta Company CO) tried to contact them by radio, one of the loaches (LOH) received .50 cal machine gun fire and went down in flames resulting in 2 US KIA.  The crash was witnessed by Co. D at a distance of approximately 1000m.  Co. D immediately assaulted toward the crash site with 1st Platoon in the lead, maneuvering along a stream containing large boulders.  1st Platoon, under sporadic enemy fire, knocked out two bunkers along the way before arriving at the crash site at 1455H. At 1305H (YD365153) 2/D and 3/D received RPG, machine gun, and small arms fire from an estimated enemy squad to the west of their position. The element returned organic weapons fire along the assistance of ARA gunships and the enemy withdrew to the west. A sweep of the area revealed 3 NVA KBSA fire, 1 NVA KBARA, and 1 NVA POW (WIA). Results: 4 NVA KIA, 1 NVA POW-WIA (Evacuated to Camp Evans). At 1440H 2nd Platoon medevaced 1 person (Robert J. Sims), who had slipped on a rock in a non-hostile injury, to 18th Surg.

1st Platoon removed the two burned bodies from the downed loach, placed them in body bags, and evacuated them from the crash site along with the radios. At 1825H (YD36151 - 3.5 KM SE of FB Ripcord), while moving along the stream in a heavy rain to linkup with Co. D, 1st Platoon discovered and captured 1 Hoi Chanh (without a weapon) who was hideing behind a large boulder. The reunited company formed a tight NDP perimeter in tall grass on a ridge above the junction of two streams, with the POW in the center. The company was repeatedly probed through the night. Co. D had no direct commo with the battalion — relaying through Co. C, and the arty PC had no commo with artillery.

## April 30, 1970

**0645H** (YD360155 - 3.5 KM SE of FB Ripcord): While Co. D was still in a tight defensive perimeter, 2nd Platoon engaged enemy with small arms fire 20m from their position. The enemy did not return fire. A sweep of the area revealed 1 NVA KIA and 1 AK-47. Results: 1 NVA KIA, 1 IWC.

The POW was medevaced to Camp Evans. Although clearly observed by the enemy, the medevac did not receive hostile fire. At 1225H (YD360156 - 3.5 KM SE of FB Ripcord) CPT Straub engaged one NVA, spotted in a tree on a hill above Co. D's position, with a LAW at long range. In response, Co. D received 40 60mm mortar rounds from an unknown size enemy force. Artillery and ARA were employed on the suspected enemy location YD353153. Results: 1 US WIA (E: Gene H. Carlson of 1/D), 1 US WIA (M). Delta Company left the AO by marching up a long steep hill (known by 3rd Platoon as REUP Hill) and linked up with Co. C, where they set up their NDP.

## May 1, 1970

**0830H** (YD415210 - FB Gladiator): Shortly after Co. D CA'd to reopen the firebase, 2/D received 4 60mm mortar rounds which impacted 300- 400m from their position with negative results. A suspected enemy location was not determined. This was the first of many showers of mortar fire that the Company was to receive while on FB Gladiator.

**1020H** (YD415210 - FB Gladiator): 2/D received 8 to 10 82mm mortar rounds which impacted to one side of their perimeter and then 50m to the opposite side of their perimeter, all with negative casualties.

**1125H** (YD415210 - FB Gladiator): Co. D received 8 to 10 60mm mortar rounds impacting inside the perimeter resulting in 3 men medevaced to the 85th Evac. Suspected mortar position was YD398223. Results: 3 US WIA (E: Kenneth W. McCreight, Norman D. McGowans, and William G. Tompkins), 2 US WIA (M).

**1359H** (YD416212 - FB Gladiator): While a bird was landing bringing in engineers they received 3 60mm mortar rounds impacting inside the perimeter.

**1545H** (YD416212 - FB Gladiator): Co. D received 3 60mm mortar rounds which impacted outside the perimeter.

**1606H** (YD416212 - FB Gladiator): Co. D received 3 82mm mortar rounds impacting on the northeast helo-pad (1 was a dud). AF FAC "Bilk" was placed on station, with an air strike completed at 1646H. A pink team was also employed in the area.

**1643H** (YD416212 - FB Gladiator): Co. D received 5 82mm mortar rounds from an unknown location.

## May 2, 1970

**0300H** (YD419210 - 1/2 KM E of FB Gladiator): Co. D observed about 18 unknown type mortar rounds impact 500m to the north of FB Gladiator and 900m to the north of their position. A suspected enemy location was not determined.

**1840H** (YD419209 - 1/2 KM E of FB Gladiator): Co. D heard a mortar tube pop at YD411195. The rounds landed between FB Granite and Co. D. Artillery was employed on the suspected enemy mortar location with unknown results.

## May 4, 1970

**1750H** (YD416211 - FB Gladiator): Co. D received about 40 mixed 82mm and 60mm mortar rounds which impacted inside and outside of the firebase perimeter. Artillery and ARA were employed on the suspected enemy locations at YD416202 and YD396199. Air strikes were employed on the suspected enemy location YD413185 and a secondary explosion was observed. A first light check of the area was made with negative results.

**May 5, 1970**

0940H (YD416211 - FB Gladiator): Co. D received 4 82mm mortar rounds which impacted 50m to the south of the firebase perimeter. Artillery was employed on the suspected enemy location at YD396192. A sweep of the area was made with negative results.

1944H (YD416211 - FB Gladiator): Co. D received 1 60mm mortar round which impacted outside of the firebase perimeter to the northeast. Artillery and 81mm mortars were employed on the suspected enemy location at YD404209.

**May 7, 1970**

0920H 1/D CA'd from FB Gladiator (YD416212) to FB Granite (YD437190) to clean or police it up after its evacuation by Co. B/2-501.

1125H (YD437190 - FB Granite): 1/D observed 1 82mm mortar round detonate in the center of a 105mm pit with negative casualties or damage.

1407H (YD415210 - FB Gladiator): Co. D received about 20 82mm mortar rounds which impacted outside of the firebase perimeter. Artillery and 90mm Recoilless Rifle rounds were employed on the suspected enemy locations YD403185 and YD401195. Air strikes were employed on the suspected enemy location YD409195, resulting in secondary explosions and ammo fires. A sweep of the area was made.

**May 8, 1970**

2045H (YD416211 - FB Gladiator): Co. D observed flashlights in the area of YD420227, YD420190 and YD425189. 81mm mortars were employed on the suspected enemy locations and 2 secondary explosions were observed at YD425189.

**May 10, 1970**

2130H (YD416211 - FB Gladiator): Co. D observed 20 lights about 1200m to the northwest and northeast of their position. Artillery and 81mm mortars were employed and a first light visual reconnaissance of the area was made with negative results.

2315H (YD416211 - FB Gladiator): Co. D observed 50 to 60 lights about 1200m northwest of their position. Artillery and 81mm mortars were employed. The lights dispersed in different directions and disappeared.

**May 12, 1970**

Co. D moved by air (Hueys) from FB Gladiator to Phu Bai Airfield, and then from Phu Bai to Eagle Beach by CH-47s.

**May 12-14, 1970**

Co. D at Eagle Beach on standdown. While at Eagle Beach on May 13 the Company was visited by Joe R. Hooper, who had received the Congressional Medal of Honor on February 21, 1968, while a 3rd Platoon squad leader with Delta Company. Hooper was the most decorated U.S. soldier of the Vietnam War. He was introduced to the Company by LTC Otis T. Livingston and CPT Chris Straub.

**May 14, 1970**

1300H Co. D moved by air in CH-47s from Eagle Beach to Phu Bal.

**May 15-18, 1970**

Co. D at Phu Bai for refresher training.

**May 20, 1970**

0600H The 2/501 passed to the OPCON of 1st BDE.

2235H (YC837991 - 1 KM S of FB Brick): 3/D heard movement of an estimated 15 enemy 300m from their position. 81mm mortars were employed on the suspected enemy location. A first light check of the area was made with negative results.

**May 25, 1970**

0745H Co. D(-1/D and 3/D) moved by air from YC841973 to FB Brick, complete at 0750H. At 0754H 3/D moved by air from YC845983 to FB Brick, complete at 0757H: and at 0802H 1/D moved by air from YC841973 to FB Brick, complete at 0807H.

M.G. John J. Hennessey took over as commander of the 101st Abn. Div. from M.G. John H. Wright.

**May 26, 1970**

Co. D NDPs: CP and 1/D at FB Brick, 2/D at YC838991, and 3/D at YC836998.

**May 27, 1970**

1149H 1/D CA'd from FB Brick to YC806953, complete at 1203H; at l201H CP and 2/D CA'd from FB Brick to YC767962, complete at 1217H; and at 1219H 3/D CA'd from FB Brick to FB Blitz, complete at l225H.

## May 28, 1970

**0758H** (YC805946 - 4 KM SE of FB Blitz): 1/D received 1 satchel charge and small arms fire from 2 enemy 25m from their position. The platoon returned organic weapons fire and the enemy withdrew to the southwest. Air strikes and ARA were employed. Results: 1 US WIA (E: Carl Shannon), 1 US WIA (M).

**1321H** 1/D temporarily OPCON to Co. A 2-501 (hard luck Alpha).

**1635H** (YC803941 - 3.5 KM SE of FB Blitz): 1/D engaged 2 enemy with small arms fire 40mm from their position. The enemy returned fire and withdrew to the south. ARA, artillery, and a Pink Team were employed. A sweep of the area revealed 3 huts (20'x40'), and 1 bunker (8'xlO'x3' with overhead cover) containing 4 sets of starched fatigues (no markings), 1 60mm mortar round, 2 82mm mortar rounds, 2 1/2 lb. satchel charges, and 4 maps with Vietnamese writing. Results: 1 US WIA (E:), maps evacuated, rest destroyed.

## May 30, 1970

**0915H** (YC775943 - 2 KM SE of FB Blitz): Co. D discovered 1 grave containing 1 NVA KIA about 6 months earlier. Also discovered were 50 fighting positions. There were no indications of recent enemy activity in the area. Results: 1 NVA KIA.

**1658H** (YC801940 - 4 KM SE of FB Blitz): 1/D discovered 1 grave containing 1 NVA killed by small arms fire about 2 months earlier. No clothing or documents were found with the body. Results: 1 NVA KIA.

## May 31, 1970

**1550H** (YC781926 - 4 KM SE of FB Blitz): Co. D discovered 1 bunker (20'x4'x4' with 3' overhead cover), and 1 hut (20'x20' ) about 1 year old. There were no signs of recent enemy activity in the area. Results: destroyed.

# 9.
# The Introduction

## Raymond H. "Blackie" Blackman
### (3rd Platoon, 9 Apr 70 - 8 Feb 71)

*"Okay men, listen up! We're going on a real patrol today, outside the wire, to look for enemy activity in the area. This will be the real thing so stay alert. If you find anything out of the ordinary DO NOT — I say again — DO NOT touch it. If you see anything that looks out of place report it to me. I will be walking point. Keep your eyes on me at all times, walk where I walk, and don't bunch up. I won't have a bunch of cherries getting me killed."*

This is it. It's my last day of SERTS (Screaming Eagle Replacement Training School) and so far the only new thing I've learned is how spooky the bunker line is at night.

Bunker guard duty at Camp Evans sucks! Everything is black and quiet. You feel like you're out there all alone. Every noise sounds like an enemy soldier sneaking up to kill you. There's a dim flash far away, just bright enough to make you look. The faint shape of a mountain appears on the horizon, green and red streaks bounce around in the sky behind the mountain-mass, flares pop. Then you hear a muffled whooomph, kra-kra-kra-kraack, thdddd-thdddd, poo-poo-poo-poo poo-poo. The guy wrapped up in his faded poncho liner behind me stirs, "Those poor bastards are really hittin' the shit out there tonight, aren't they? Keep your eyes open man." Then it got black and quiet again, like nothing had ever happened.

"Listen up men. If I call your name get in that jeep over there. You're going to the 2-501 at Phu Bai. The rest of you will be assigned to a unit here at Evans. You can walk."

During the ride to Phu Bai my mind drifted back...back to Iowa. I didn't really have an opinion about Vietnam before being drafted. Things were going so fast that I hadn't had time to form one. After dropping out of High School I started my first job at a window and door factory, then got married. Most of my older friends were being drafted and going off to Nam. Some came home early, including one with both legs missing. They had all

Ch. 9 / The Introduction

changed. My draft classification was 1-A, and I wanted to know what to expect over there. None of my Nam Vet friends would volunteer any information and I was too scared to ask. Scared of my own friends! They really had changed.

Gary and I hadn't been friends before being drafted together. We lived worlds apart in the same town. He was single and wild, while I was married and quiet. We became buddies during basic and AIT at Fort Polk, Louisiana. Upon graduation he went to Vietnam and I went to NCOCS (Non Commissioned Officers Candidate School) at Fort Benning, Georgia.

After finishing NCO school, then OJT at Fort Ord in California, I found myself home again. My wife told me that she had seen Gary a few days earlier, but I didn't believe her. The next day we went to fill the car up with gas and there he was, sitting in his blue Malibu on the other side of the gas pumps. "Hey Gary, what are you doing here? You're supposed to be in Nam!" Gary got out of his car and limped over to me, "They got me man. They blew my foot off. I stepped on a booby-trap during my first mission. You on your way over?" "Yea, I leave tomorrow. How'd they get you fixed up so fast?" "Oh man, they aren't done yet," he replied, knocking on a wooden leg with his fist. "This one's only temporary so I could come home for a visit. I'll get the real thing after my stub gets hard." "How bad is it over there?" "It's bad man," he half whispered as he gave me a bear hug, "Whatever you do keep your head down and watch where you put your feet."

"Blackman...Sergeant Blackman!" The jeep stopped near a building where chest-high, cement-covered sand bags formed a half circle in front of the entrance. "I hope you know just how lucky you are, man. You'll be with Delta Company. A good outfit. The rest of you guys stay put. You're going to Alpha. Hard Luck Alpha." The driver went on to explain that Alpha had been hit hard on a firebase and lost a lot of men. The cherries in Alpha would out-number the old-timers. Not even a good situation to be in. "These guys in Delta, you listen to them. They know what they're talking about. You'll be all right man.

As the jeep drove off, leaving me standing in a cloud of dust, a large figure of a man came out the door of the building and headed toward me. With a huge smile on his face he reached out to shake my hand, "Sergeant Blackman? I've been expecting you. My name is John Schuelke. I'm the First Sergeant of Delta Company, 2nd of the 501st. Welcome. Come on in and I'll get you squared away.

As we walked around the cement-bags, I noticed a sign hanging to the right of the door. "BE PROUD YOU'RE A GRUNT. DELTA COMPANY HAS EIGHTY PERCENT FEWER CASUALTIES."

Top Schuelke explained that the company was in the field and I'd be joining it on its next log day. In the meantime there were a few guys in the rear for various reasons that he would introduce me to later. In fact a couple of them were in the 3rd platoon, the one I'd be assigned to. He went on to say that Captain Chris Straub was the CO of Delta Company. Top assured me that Straub was a fine leader who takes good care of his people.

After taking me to supply, Top escorted me to a hooch. "Hey…look at that!" "Looks like we got us a new man." "Come on over here and drop your stuff on this cot." "Where ya from man?" "How's things back in the World?" "What platoon ya goin to?" "He's gotta be goin ta third man. "Yea, we been short handed since Re-Up Hill!" "Ya goin ta third man?" "Want a beer?" "What's your name man?"

Upon entering the company hooch I was bombarded with questions as a small group of scruffy looking characters headed my way. They all looked genuinely happy to see me, as though we were old friends who hadn't seen each other for a long time. Three Vietnamese men, who looked very young, sat side by side on a cot in the far corner with puzzled looks on their faces. One had a stupid looking grin on his face, almost like it had been painted there. They seemed very much out of place.

"Hey man, don't worry 'bout those guys…they're on our side now." Huh??? "Yeah, they're captured NVA. They were given a choice: go to jail or let us pay you fifty bucks a month to be a scout." "They call 'em Kit Carson

Scouts." "They're supposed to walk point and find the booby traps for us. What a crock!" "Ain't no NVA gonna walk point for me man. "There it is!" "Oh well, they never stay around long anyway." "So, how's the World?" They didn't really want me to say anything. I think they were just happy to see a new face. A replacement. I was fresh from the World and they had almost forgotten what civilization had been like. I could talk later.

Top walked out of the hooch saying something about leaving me in good hands.

Jerry Bull introduced himself first, "You'll probably be going to 3rd platoon. Ask for 3rd squad. That's my squad. It's the best. Let me show you how to pack your ruck. You'll need a frame for this thing. It rides too low without one. Of course we're out of them right now but I'll snatch up the first one I can for ya."

As the huge pile of stuff on my cot started to dwindle and my rucksack looked like it would split at the seams, I asked a stupid question, "Do I really need all this stuff?" "Oh this ain't all of it! You'll need at least two more canteens of water, a Claymore, maybe six frags, a quarter pound of C-4, an ammo can for your personal stuff, and a hunting knife. Can you think of anything else guys?" No, please!! "Yea man, you gonna need some dry socks and foot powder, maybe a towel." "Better get him some bug juice!" "They'll probably give you some 60 ammo or a LAW to carry when you get out there too." Oh no!!

Bull, a big red-headed southerner, had decided to take me under his wing. He was in the rear for two reasons. He'd be leaving for R&R in a couple days, but first had to get the doctor's O.K. at Camp Eagle. He explained that Delta Company was operating in a nasty AO. Third platoon had been sent to re-enforce another company that was in trouble on a hill…a place they named Re-Up Hill, for obvious reasons. Guys from the other company were re-enlisting for an MOS change, just so they'd be taken off that hill, and to the rear to sign the papers. I was told that it had brought about a change in the rules. From now on you can't re-up unless you're already in the rear on stand-down.

Suddenly I don't feel so "Lucky to be with Delta." I'd be replacing a guy who had been wounded in a ambush not too long ago, and the company was still in the same AO, near Firebase Ripcord. This was really starting to get scary!

Early the next morning there was a company formation — for all four of us. We were a sorry looking bunch of guys trying not to wobble at attention. Top informed us that all was well in the field. Delta would move to an LZ in two days for supplies. That's when I'd go out. Bull was sent to Camp Eagle and the other guys were assigned various details within the confines of the Phu Bai wire. After all the shuffling around that I'd been through in the past two weeks it looked like the Army had found a place for me. I was told to write home, send my new address and tell 'em I'm okay. Take it easy today. You'll be pulling guard duty in our sector of the Phu Bai Bunker Line tonight.

Our jeep pulled up to the Raider supply pile near the control tower at the Camp Evans log pad. There were other piles there. They all looked the same. How they knew which one belonged to Delta Company had always been a mystery to me. A steady stream of helicopter traffic whirled in and out. They all seemed to be going to, or coming from, the same general direction, that is, the mountains to the west. A Crane would take off as a Chinook landed. Two Cobra Gunships sat waiting for a Loach to warm up. Slicks landed to pick up their cargo. An amazing sight! Organized chaos! Business as usual in The Nam.

A slick landed near our pile and I helped the supply Sergeant load the C's. A chill ran up my spine when I noticed the door gunner fiddling with his M-60 Machine Gun and ammo. Well Blackman, you really got yourself in a fine mess this time. These guys are serious. There's gonna be real shooting out there. The words of our Drill Instructor at Fort Polk popped into my mind: "and all you 11-Bravos will be going to the land of the two-way rifle range."

I had ridden in a helicopter before, at Benning, but it wasn't the same as this. That Chopper had soft seats and doors and had landed like a feather in a large open field at our bivouac site. No machine guns were hanging out the doors, and no men were hiding in the jungle wanting to kill you. Oh yes…this was different all right.

As our chopper started passing over the mountains I momentarily forgot about the war that I was rapidly approaching. The vastness and beauty of the jungle-covered mountains helped me overlook the ugly bomb craters and TDZ's scattered here and there along the way. The view was breathtaking, and made me feel insignificant. Why would anyone ever have a war in a place this beautiful? It was love at first sight. I instantly wanted to come back some day (under different circumstances, of course). I'd build a log cabin right down there, on that small hill facing the waterfall.

The slapping rotor blades pulled me out of the trance. Colored smoke was rising from a ridgeline with a small bald spot in the center. We started to circle and go down fast. I've never been in a falling elevator, but this must be the way it feels. The trees and mountains quickly grew to full size. The door gunner slowly moved his M-60 back and forth as he searched for the enemy in the jungle below. My heart pounded its way up into my throat. We're gonna die. They're gonna shoot us right out of the sky.

## Ch. 9 / The Introduction

Hey, wait a minute? I don't see anyone down there. I'm supposed to meet a whole company out here. You guys screwed up bad. We're landing on the wrong LZ. These guys are gonna leave me here all alone…

We touched down. By the time I opened my eyes two guys were running up to the chopper. They had appeared from nowhere. Two more were on the other side. Half the C-Rations were unloaded before the door gunner had a chance to tell me to get out. I rolled over on my hands and knees and slid out backwards. Damn this rucksack anyway!

As I stood there in the middle of the LZ, wondering what to do, I strained my eyes in the hopes of seeing the rest of Delta Company. There was a guy between two stumps with a radio. One kneeling down next to him. Another carrying a case of C's off the LZ and into the jungle. As the slick lifted off someone appeared before me. He was wearing a steel pot, had a bandolier of magazines around his shoulder and carried an M-16. He yelled in my ear, "My names Dotson. I'm the 3rd Platoon Sergeant. You'll be with us. We gotta get off the LZ now. Follow me." On the 3rd platoon sector of the perimeter Dotson introduced me to Lieutenant Bass, then the guys in 3rd squad. I was never referred to as a "cherry." In fact everyone seemed glad to get the extra help.

I was given a LAW and a couple smoke grenades to add to my already heavy rucksack. I only weighed about 115 pounds soaking wet, so I just knew that I could not possibly carry all this stuff up and down these mountains for a whole year. Conservatively speaking, humping a ruck was like strapping a 60-pound bag of redi- mix concrete over your shoulders and walking up and down the steps to the Washington Monument for 8 to 10 hours in August. Then imagine also carrying a rifle, fighting your way through thick jungles and swift mountain streams and doing it every single day from dawn to dusk.

We moved out to set up an NDP (Night Defensive Position) away from the LZ. I still hadn't seen all of Delta Company, but only part of 3rd platoon. It would be at our first stand-down in Phu Bai, about three weeks later, that I would see them all at once and in one place.

Humping in the middle of the column is boring. I had no idea what I was supposed to do except struggle to put one foot in front of the other. "Your left right…your left right."

My brother and I used to play Army and not so very long ago. We'd gather up all the able bodied kids in our neighborhood and choose sides. But this is no game, no "Bang bang, you're dead" here. I was always brave then, but wondered would I be brave now?

One time my brother went on a recon mission and hid in the rafters of an old garage being used as the neighborhood enemy Headquarters. He fell and broke his arm. I ran for help. My dad was furious, "Why the hell didn't you stop him?" I'd never been able to stop him before. He was my big brother and should know better. Now I'm an E-5 and in a real war. Why am I thinking about my brother now? He isn't here with me...or is he?

My brother had tried desperately to spare me from going to Nam. He was a Communications Technician in the Navy and put his first transfer in for Vietnam when I dropped out of High School. He would put three more in before I got my draft notice. The Navy refused his request. He was needed elsewhere. Ironically, my new First Sergeant, Top Schuelke, had taught ROTC to my brother when he was in High School. Maybe a little bit of my big brother is here with me.

In the morning, after I had learned what leeches were, we moved out, down the mountain toward the valley below. After only a few minutes the ruck had kicked my ass. At least we were heading down, which was the only thing that saved me. My squad was on point and I was last man. They would slowly work me toward the front as time went by so that within three months I could expect to walk point.

After reaching the bottom of the mountain we found a river. This wasn't a good place to cross so we turned upstream, trying to stay as near the huge rocks along the bank as possible. A Loach that was following the river passed over us.

CRACK! CRACK!! CRACK!!!

When I was 14 years old the neighbor man and my dad took my brother and me on a hunting trip for pheasants. Two flew up right in front of us. My knees went weak. Three shots fired. No birds. "I only heard three shots! Who didn't shoot?" I had instinctively aimed but was unable to pull the trigger. "I'll never take you hunting again!" The neighbor was true to his word and never took me hunting again. My dad had told me not to worry about it. "Lots of guys freeze up the first time."

I was worried now. Would I freeze up over here? There is no way of telling how a man will react in combat until it actually happens.

The guys in front and behind me disappeared behind the rocks along the river as the Loach exploded into a ball of fire. I dropped in place and became wedged between some small rocks and my ruck. I was urged by someone to "take cover man!" "Hey, get over here! Don't lay there in plain sight!" After collecting my wits I struggled to free myself and crawled behind a boulder where two others from my squad had taken refuge.

A squad of NVA was sitting on the rocks across the river from us eating dinner. They were just sitting there big as you please taking pot shots at the bird. They hadn't seen or heard us, and we didn't know they were there till it was too late. In fact our whole platoon had already passed them.

## Ch. 9 / The Introduction

Most of my platoon and all of the men in the platoon behind us opened up. The Loach had been the scout of a Pink Team, so two Cobras were already on station. It was over in hour/seconds. I didn't shoot, so I earned my CIB without firing a round.

A sweep of the area revealed three NVA killed by small arms fire and one killed by ARA (Aerial Rocket Artillery). A squad from one of the other platoons broke off and went around us to check for survivors from the Loach. We knew there wouldn't be any.

When the patrol came back, I got my first good look at the enemy. One of the men was carrying an NVA soldier on his shoulders. He had been wounded and was crying out in pain. The man carrying him was mad and not keeping it a secret. I later learned that they had found him hiding behind a rock, wounded in the leg. He had a small wooden medal pinned to his shirt. A medal given to him for shooting down a helicopter.

A couple hours later one of our platoons received a "Hoi Chanh" without a weapon.

After the wounded NVA prisoner and the Hoi Chanh were evacuated, we moved away from the river. The guys talked little about the firefight. I couldn't understand it. A Loach crew had died, we had killed four NVA soldiers, taken one prisoner and had another surrender to us, yet very little was said about it. It was as if it had been "all in a days work." Would I become this callous as time went by? Were their hearts made hard from combat, or was it a natural protection against insanity?

At first light the next morning, a quick burst from an M-60 interrupted my breakfast. A single NVA with an AK-47 had been bopping down the trail near our NDP site, until one of our machine gunners nailed him cold.

A little later, before moving out, one of the machine gunners test fired his M-60 after repairing it. Immediately after the test fire there was a loud Whoosh…WHOOMPH! as the first of about forty 60mm mortars started dropping on us. I had seen and heard mortars fired during training, but had never been right under them when they impacted. I scrambled to a tree no bigger around than my leg in an effort to avoid being killed.

The only time I can remember feeling this helpless was when I learned how to swim. The method my brother had used was common. He drug a screaming little brat out from the safety of the shallow water in the swimming area at Lake Mannawa and left me. Then, I would either sink or swim, die or live.

I survived the mortar barrage but was one scared puppy. Two Raiders had been wounded during the attack. Artillery and ARA were called in on the suspected NVA position. It's gonna be a long 10 months and 20 days. Yes, I was already counting my time left in this country.

When the smoke cleared, we moved out, but later doubled back and set up an ambush around the NVA that we had killed during breakfast. We would NDP around his body. I can't recall if it was a company or platoon size ambush, but do remember where I was to sleep…head to head with the dead gook. I avoided looking at him for awhile, but later decided that I'd better make sure he was really dead. I had this funny feeling that he wasn't and didn't want him to get up and slit my throat in the middle of the night.

First I took two quick glances at his body. The third glance turned into a long stare. While looking at him I wondered if he had a wife and family. I know we had been trained to think of the NVA as the enemy and not human beings, but I couldn't help it. I had seen dead people before at family funerals, but this was different. He was laying there all full of holes and his family didn't even know he was dead yet. In a strange sort of way I felt sorry for him. I got little or no sleep that night.

The next morning we started humping up a big hill. The jungle was thick and dark, hotter than hot, and I wasn't used to my ruck yet. The straps were digging into my shoulders deep and every time I tried lifting the weight, it felt like my skin was on fire where the straps had been. Everyone was drenched in sweat and you could hear muffled grunts and groans along the column. That's probably why they called us Grunts.

We were about half way up the hill when the whispering among the 3rd platoon guys began. They seemed nervous and much more alert. "This is it man. This is the trail to Re-Up Hill." "Are you sure?" "Yea, I'm sure. The ambush was right over there man. They're gonna make us go back up there. This is one bad place." "Keep your eyes open man, we're goin' back to Re-Up Hill." "They better not make us NDP up there." "There's dinks here. I can feel em!" "I don't need this crap at all. I'm gettin WAY too short!"

The weight of my ruck and tender shoulders were forgotten.

After reaching the top of Re-Up Hill, we circled the filled-in foxholes. Only an occasional whisper could be heard, "There's the place Bull got hit." "The RPG's came from there." "This hole took a direct hit." Re-Up was eerie. You could feel that men had died here. We NDP'd on the hill that night. Nobody in 3rd platoon slept.

The next morning we left Re-Up Hill and went to an LZ. We were to be CA'd to an abandoned firebase called Gladiator. Our job was to secure it so Artillery and Mortars could be installed. It would be my first Combat Assault and I was extremely apprehensive. None of the old-timers knew much about the new AO but we all hoped it would be more quiet than this one. After the last few days I just wanted to catch my breath.

Because of this move, and the fact that some of the guys had mentioned being in the Firebase Birmingham and Bastogne areas before going near Ripcord, I asked someone where our permanent AO was. We didn't have one. The 2nd of the 501st- had become the Swing Battalion and we could expect to be popped into any AO where extra help was needed, or where NVA presence was suspected. "Oh great!"

Being on a company size Combat Assault from one AO to another with it's long line of Slicks and Cobra escorts is impossible to describe. One has to experience it to know the many feelings involved. It would start with a sense of relief that you were leaving a bad area. You would think that anywhere has to be better than this or does it? Then you got terrible feeling that something bad would happen at the pickup zone, especially if we had to cut an LZ. Once in the air you could kick back and enjoy the ride, but in the back of your mind you knew we had to land sooner or later. When the Slicks approached the new LZ you felt a strange mixture of different emotions as the Artillery prep stopped and the Cobras dove into finish the job. Then you felt the bottom drop out of your bird as it took you into the blessedly cold LZ. Well, at least for a few precious moments.

As our bird touched down red smoke came billowing through the open doors making it difficult to see. The door gunner quickly started moving his M-60 from side to side frantically searching for something to shoot at. Then came the blood curdling cry, "INCOMING!" At the same time the door gunner was repeating, "Get out fast. It's a HOT LZ. It's a HOT LZ."

Now there's a job that I know I couldn't handle. Being a door gunner and going on CA's every day just wasn't my idea of an easy tour. Of course my tour hadn't seemed too easy so far either.

As I slid down the side of the hill where my squad was frantically trying to dig in, several mortar rounds impacted all around the hastily set up perimeter. Although digging a hole with explosions going off all around you is extremely difficult, you can do it very fast Six more separate mortar attacks rained on our position that day with four Raiders being wounded.

We stayed on or around Gladiator for the next twelve days while it was being built up, and were constantly being mortared. I've never really been much of a fighter but became frustrated that there was nothing for us to shoot back at. We were helpless against the mortar. We could watch for flashes from the tubes and Artillery in on the suspected locations, but of course the enemy had already moved by then.

During one of those days someone walked up behind me as I was digging 'just a little bit deeper.' "How's it going soldier?" As I turned to see who it was I replied, "Not worth a.. uh, darn, Chaplain." "What seems to be the problem son?" "Well, sir, we've been getting mortared every day since getting here and there isn't anything we can do about it." By now a

Sergeant Major had walked up beside the Chaplain and said, "Well Sergeant, I have to tell you that the report I have read so far about our activities in this AO have indicated that we are doing very well indeed. As long as we kill ten of the enemy for each of our own casualties, we feel that we are winning." I couldn't believe my ears. An acceptable value, or price, of 10 to 1 had been put on each American life. I turned around without responding and began digging again. I don't know how long they stood there behind me, but they must have figured out that our conversation was over because when I finally looked again they had gone.

As soon as Gladiator had been built up, we closed it back down and were flown to Phu Bai, then to Eagle Beach for my first up and down. We went to Eagle Beach in Chinooks and I didn't like it one little bit. Those big choppers had no open doors to hang my M-16 out of and we couldn't see what was going on.

Soon after arriving at Eagle Beach I learned just how much time line Company could blow off in a rear area, and why the REMF's would just as soon we never come back for a visit. We considered ourselves special and wouldn't comply with the rear area conduct.

I can't say I enjoyed my introduction into this special group of men called Raiders, but the experience gave me a feeling of confidence, pride, and belonging. They were — and are — the very best people I have ever met.

# 10.
# Chronology
## June 3, 1970 – June 26, 1970

**June 3, 1970**
**1400H** (YC801921 ): 2/D requested a Medevac for 1 man (Coy A. Broxton), which was completed to 55th Evac at 1435H.

**June 5-13, 1970**
Co. D operated in the Khe Le Moi River valley near FB Brick. This valley was recalled by CPT Straub (Co. D CO) as the "silent valley," since it had a geology that prevented FM radio communication.

**June 5, 1970**
**1103H** 1/D CA'd from YC800944 to YC822936, complete at 1115H.

**June 7, 1970**
**1401H** (YC837926): Co. D found 1 hooch (4'x6' ) about 6 months old. Results: destroyed.

**June 8,1970**
**1835H** (YC841932): 1/D found 1 hooch (4'x6') about 3-4 months old. There were no indications of recent enemy activity in the area. Results: destroyed.

**June 10, 1970**
**1015H** (YC857936): 2/D found 7 US smoke grenades, 4 M-79 (rounds, 6 M-16 magazines (full), 3 H-26 frag grenades, 3 US tripflares, 1 US strobe light, and 1 US map with markings found in the open. All estimated to have been in the area about 5 months. Results: map evacuated.

**June 13, 1970**
**1408H** Co. D (-1/D) moved by air from YC863957 to FB Brick, complete at 1423H. At 1423H 1/D moved by air from YC855960 to FB Brick, complete at 1430H.
**1435H** Co. D moved by CH-47s from FB Brick to Phu Bai, complete at 1523H. The Company stayed overnight in the battalion area at Phu Bai.

## June 14, 1970
**0912H** Co. D moved by truck (3 cattle cars) from Phu Bai to Camp Evans, complete at 1020H. Co. D passed from the relative quiet of the 1st BDE AO to the OPCON of 2-506 and 3rd BDE. After waiting in vain the remainder of the day for Hueys to take the Company to the field, the Company stayed overnight at Camp Evans.

## June 15, 1970
**0927H** Co. D CA'd from Camp Evans to YD334202.
**1530H** (YC327204 - 2 KM NW of FB Ripcord): 3/D found 1 cave (15'xlC'xlO' ) and 2 caves (10'x12'x15'). The caves contained 34 RPG rounds, 1 175mm arty round, cooking equipment and other miscellaneous equipment. 1 cave was boobytrapped at the entrance with a pressure firing device. The element also found 1 NVA AT mine with "MAT-NAY- HVONG-VEMOC-TIEU" written on it and some bottles of clear liquid. There were 4 trails leading from the area to the northwest, southeast, southwest, and north. There were no signs of enemy activity in the area within the last 2-3 days. The platoon set up an ambush in the area. Results: ammo, boobytrap, and other equipment destroyed: bottles of liquid evacuated to Camp Evans.

## June 16, 1970
**1130H** (YD329206 - 1 KM NW of FB Ripcord): 2/D discovered 1 bunker (6'xS'x3' with 10' overhead cover). The bunker contained 1 barrel and 1 bolt from an M-16 rifle. A sweep of the area revealed indications of enemy activity within the last 30 days. Results: rifle parts evacuated, bunker destroyed.
**1130H** (YD327204 - 2 KM NW of FB Ripcord): 3/D discovered a cave containing 13 separate rooms. Items found in the cave included 6 NVA shirts with an insignia consisting of a No. 26 with 2 horizontal lines underneath the number (S-2 comment: 6th Co., 2nd BN, 803rd NVA Regt.), numerous sleeping mats, 12 RPGs, 1 first aid bag with miscellaneous medical supplies, and 11 60mm mortar rounds. There were indications of enemy activity in the cave within the last 30 days. Results: medical supplies and shirts evacuated, rest destroyed.
**1240H** (YD327204 - 2 KM NW of FB Ripcord): 3/D discovered 3 graves containing 3 NVA KBA about 14 days earlier. Results: 3 NVA KIA.
**1555H** (YD327204 - 2 KM NW of FB Ripcord): 3/D discovered the following in a crevice covered by rocks: 51 RPGs, 30 82mm mortar rounds, 9 metal canisters, 32 82mm mortar charges, 10 cans of powder for 82mm mortar charges, and 180 loose AK-47 rounds. Results: 1 RPG round evacuated, rest destroyed.

## June 17, 1970

**1315H** (YD330203 - 2.5 KM NW of FB Ripcord): 3/D found a 1 lb. satchel charge with tripwire and a pull type firing device. There were indications of enemy activity in the area within the last 24-36 hours. Results: destroyed.

**1955H** (YC325243 - 1 KM S of FB O'Reilly): 1/D heard sounds like wood chopping 250m northeast of their position. 81mm mortars were employed on the suspected enemy location YD327249.

## June 20, 1970

**2305H** (YD303238 - 2 KM SW of FB O'Reilly): 3/D heard and observed the flash of a mortar tube firing in the vicinity of YD302244. 81mm mortars were employed on the suspected enemy mortar location.

## June 25, 1970

**1044H** Co. D moved by air from YC299255 to FB Record. The Company had a fresh change of clothes and stayed overnight on the firebase.

## June 26, 1970

**0910H** Co. D CA'd from FB Ripcord to YD299256.

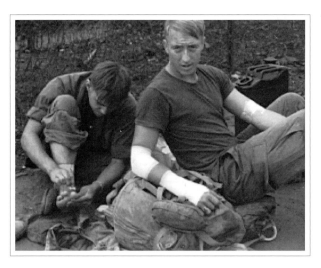

# 11.
# July 11, 1970

## Rod Soubers

On July 11 I got the word that I would be going back to the platoon the next day. The morning of the 12th (a Sunday) I left Phu Bai for Camp Evans by jeep with SGT Lusk (the Co. Supply SGT) and Carl Shannon, who was also returning to the Platoon after receiving medical attention in DaNang for his "delicate" wound received in early June. We arrived at Camp Evans shortly before noon. Sometime during the early part of the afternoon we learned that a chopper would not be going out to the Company until the next morning. At this point we did not know where the Company was located or what they were doing. As we were on our way to Camp Evans, the Company was in the process of moving onto Hill 805 near FB Ripcord, unbeknownst to the three of us. Most of the time, the three platoons of the Company operated separately in the field. This time, however, was one of the few occasions when the Company operated as a single unit.

For most of the afternoon Shannon and I walked around Camp Evans and spent a fair amount of time in one of the watering holes. Late in the afternoon or early evening of the 12th we were standing around the jeep shooting the breeze with Lusk when we picked up the radio commo of the Company and learned that they were in contact and had suffered some casualties, which were in that the process of being medevaced into the Camp Evans med-station. We had no idea at that point who was wounded or the details of the contact. We just ran down to the hospital to await the arrival of the medevacees. All I could think about at the time was whether Dave (Beyl) or someone else from 1st Platoon would be one of the wounded. The medevac chopper arrived shortly after we got there and we learned that all of the wounded were from 2nd Platoon.

We located some unoccupied cots for the night in one of the EM quarters. Early the next morning (the 13th), we loaded our rucks down with extra hand grenades, M-60 ammo, M-16 ammo and 2 claymores. Our rucks

Ch. 11 / July 11, 1970

had to weigh nearly 80 to 100 pounds. It was still early in the morning when Shannon and I left Evans by chopper for the Company, still not knowing where they were located. As we entered the mountains I marveled again at how beautiful they looked and how deceptively tranquil they appeared from above. On approaching the LZ I noticed Ripcord was off to our right and not all that far away. As the Huey slowed for its approach into the LZ the strong wind was making it difficult for the pilots to stabilize it for a smooth landing. When it reached the LZ, it hovered above for a brief period of time swinging left and right, and then took off and circled around for another approach. It came in a second time, but was not able to touch ground. As it hovered about six to eight feet above the LZ, Shannon and I dropped our rucks to the ground and jumped. We put our loaded rucks on our backs and humped to the Hill where the Company had set up a defensive perimeter. The LZ was about 200 yards from the Hill with a sloping dip or saddle in between. The area between the LZ and the Hill was fairly open except fora few small trees near the LZ and many felled trees scattered around. What few trees that were standing looked heavily shell scarred with most of the bark stripped off. As heavy as our rucks were, I was glad that the distance was relatively short. As we neared the 1st Platoon perimeter (directly facing the LZ) the Platoon seemed to be glad to see us. As I came into the 2nd Squad area, I recall Roger Miles greeting me with his friendly sarcasm. After getting directions from him on the location of 3rd Squad, I walked down the line to my left to the 3rd Squad position. The first person I came in contact with as I got to 3rd Squad was Dave, who said with a grin on his face, "Well, look what the wind blew in." It sure was good to be back with the platoon again.

With some relief I dropped my ruck, removed the claymores, unloaded the extra ammo and gave the carton of Winstons I had brought for him. I was not surprised when he told me that he had been out of cigarettes for two or three days. Shortly after arriving back in the Platoon, 3rd Squad went out on a recon in the area to the left of the LZ, circling around and coming back into the Company perimeter by way of the ridge line that ran into the 2nd Platoon position. As we were walking along the side of a slope, my right knee started giving me trouble again so I grabbed a branch from a large bush to help my balance, but the branch gave way and I went sprawling to the ground. Rat Guimond, who was behind me, said jokingly "Now what am I going to hold on to." Along the ridge line we found some blood trails, but I can't recall finding anything else.

For much of the, afternoon we helped put out consantina wire, mostly in front of the 1st Squad position to the left of the big rock that was close to the spot separating 1st and 2nd Platoons. Aside from that, there was very

little done to shore up our defensive position. Third Squad had dug out sleeping positions that sloped back into the hill, but no foxholes. I didn't detect any sense of urgency or expectation on the part of the platoon, despite the fact that the 2nd Platoon sector had been hit the previous night. No one at the time seemed to know how long we were going to be on the Hill, or for that matter why we were on the Hill. As usual, we were not informed about the nature of the mission. Presumably Palm and Cooksley were briefed about the details of the mission, but they did not share the information with the rest of the Platoon aside from the squad leaders, who also played it fairly close to the vest. After being in Nam for seven and a half months, I was used to being kept in the dark about why we were operating in a certain area, about why we were moving in a particular direction, or why we did just about anything, except for the primary purpose of survival. A grunt just did what he was told, went through the motions, and tried to stay alive. Since we were usually uninformed about the nature of our mission, our only sense of purpose was for survival.

*Delta Raiders* • **185**

During the hottest part of the afternoon most of 3rd Squad was crowded under a poncho liner that was set up as a makeshift tent or sunbreak. The wind was still fairlybrisk although not as strong as it had been earlier in the day. At this point, 3rd Squad had the following people on the Hill: William Jones, Denny Belt, Paul Morton, Dave Beyl, myself and the gun team of Rat Guimond, Drew Gaster, and Nose Collins. During this period, Rat Guimond was telling us about his new bride, a Thai girl he had met while on R&R in Bangkok. Rat was probably in the happiest most positive frame of mind he had ever been in since coming to Nam. Rat had a tendency to be critical and satirical about things (like many of us), but not that day. William Jones, a black E-5 who was acting squad leader while Benny was on an R&R, was telling us about his German wife that he had met while on tour in Germany. He proudly showed us a picture of her that he carried in his wallet. Jones was RA (regular Army), had been in the army a number of years, including a previous tour in Nam, and was five or six years older than the rest of us. He apparently had been with the Platoon only a few days, since Denny Belt indicated that he had been acting squad leader for a while after Benny went in for R&R.

During the early evening we set out about four or five claymores in front of 3rd Squad's position. Dave and I set up our sleeping position, chowed down and brought each other up to date on what we had been doing over the past few weeks. I had been in the rear 13 days (since June 30), which was almost as long as Dave's 15 days in February when he was in for his teeth. I talked about my experiences back in the rear and told Dave that BJ Thomas (Dave's favorite singer) had won a grammy for his song "Raindrops Keep Falling On My Head" — an appropriate song for Nam during the monsoon season. I also kidded Dave about turning 21 while I was gone (July 6). Dave's birthday was so close to July 4th that he said his dad referred to him as his "4th of July baby." Dave didn't have a whole lot to say about what the platoon had been doing since June 30, apparently it was the same old routine with nothing out of the ordinary. He was looking forward to going on R&R in Hawaii in a couple of weeks when he would be able to see Debbie again. Hawaii was the only R&R location where Nam GIs could meet with their wives, so it was understandably very popular with married men. Bangkok and Sydney were the most popular with single men. He was a bit worried or self-conscious about seeing Debbie again with the condition of his jungle rot. He felt better, however, when I told him that my jungle rot had pretty well cleared up in a weeks time back in the rear by taking a shower every day, and that he would probably have enough time back there for his to clear up as well. I kidded him about it, but knew that he was pretty sensitive about it.

July 11, 1970 / Ch. 11

Each squad had double guard that night with Dave and I scheduled to pull guard in the middle of the night around 2:00. Denny Belt and someone else (I can't recall who) were pulling the first or second guard, when I heard Denny yell, "They're moving down there." Dave and I were not yet asleep at the time, but just laying down in our sleeping position, located in back of and slightly above the perimeter line. Shortly after Denny yelled, this being sometime after midnight, everyone was on alert and laying down along the dugout area we had along the 3rd Squad perimeter. About the same time firing broke out all along the line, and within a brief period of time after contact (just a few minutes), SGT Jones was shot through the head, killing him instantly. The next morning we saw the path of the bullet through his helmet with a hole in front and a hole in back. At the time I was positioned to Jones' left and somewhat back. Nose Collins, who was to his immediate right, shook him after he was hit and was saying in a pleading tone of voice "Sarge, are you all right?", "Come on, Sarge, you're OK aren't ya." I recall at the time that Jones was crouched down near the edge of the dugout area looking over the edge when he just slumped forward. The wind was howling so much and there was so much fire from our side that a person couldn't be sure exactly where the incoming fire was coming from. This was a problem most of the night, all we could do was look for flashes or simply put a blanket of fire out all along our front. We had only a crescent moon that night, so we had very little natural light — which was improved from time to time by parachute flares. Shortly after Jones was hit, we blew our claymores and would periodically throw grenades down the hill during the course of the next hour or so (many of which were duds).

It is difficult to remember the exact sequence of events that followed, but sometime after Jones was hit Rat Guimond left his MG position and was running off to my left toward the 2nd Squad position and the next thing I knew, he fell down the hill, stopping about fifteen feet below and to the left of our position in an open area next to a small tree. My first split-second reaction was what the hell is he doing down there, when at just about the same time it dawned on me that he was hit. Denny and I, who were the nearest to him, instinctively decided that we had to go down and bring him up the hill above our position so that the medics could attend to him, since we had to assume he was still alive. Using common sense and not having the time to deliberate over all the options, we thought it would be best to go down after him when the flares were not up in order to avoid detection, thinking that the dark would give us some cover.

As soon as the flare that was up at the time went out, we went down after him. When we were only a couple of feet from Rat, Denny (who was on my left) froze in his tracks yelling "I'm hit, I can't move." At about the same time I felt my helmet jerk (the next morning I noticed that a round had made a crease along the side of my helmet strapping, the elastic band). Within seconds after he was hit, I grabbed Denny over my shoulder and somehow managed to get him back up the hill above our position so that medics could attend to him. He had been shot twice through the stomach and was cussing a blue streak as I carried him up the hill, since the pain was so intense. After I got him up to a level spot above our position, I wrapped a poncho liner around him while at the same time yelling for a medic.

I then went back to our position on the line, hesitant to go back after Rat given the intense fire we were getting in that location. About this time Mike Cooksley cameover to our side of the perimeter, and I and others filled him in on our situation telling him that Rat was still down below us but we needed heavy covering fire in order to go after him, given our previous experience. As we were talking, 3rd Platoon sent over two or three men to help reinforce our position. Mike said that he would have the whole position put out covering fire if I and another guy would go after Rat. He also said to be sure to go down when the flare was up and the whole area was fully illuminated, which was the proper time since the gooks would be laying low in order to avoid detection. When the next flare went up, a man from 3rd Platoon (I didn't know his name and vaguely remember what he looked like) and I went down and brought Rat back up the hill and laid him down near Denny's position. He was unconscious but still alive at the time. He appeared to have been hit in the head. Rat rarely wore a helmet and did not have one at the time he was hit, which may or may not have made a difference. I again went back to our position along the line. Sometime later, I can't recall how much later, I remember looking back and up toward the bright lights of a hovering medevac chopper as they lowered a basket apparently for Denny and Rat. It was the first time I had ever seen a medevac attempted at night! We didn't know until the next morning that Rat had died on the way into Camp Evans.

My primary emotion at the peak of the battle was not of fear, but of anger. I had little thought about being hit or dying. All I could think about was killing those goddamned gooks! It is difficult to explain, but in the heat of contact you are riding an emotional high with a mixture of anger and exhilaration as your adrenaline shifts into overdrive.

It is difficult to recall how long the period of contact lasted that night, but it seemed like most of the night. The Company would shoot up small parachute flares, but the strong wind would carry them across the 1st Platoon perimeter in a left to right direction in a matter of seconds, illuminating the area for a period of little more than five or six seconds. The larger flares that were shot over from Ripcord were much more effective, providing brighter illumination for a longer period of time (two or three times longer). During the course of the battle it became evident that the NVA was using the cover of darkness for movement. Whenever the flares were up the NVA were apparently crouched low and motionless.

During this period, we received fire support from Cobra gunships along the front of our perimeter as well as from Quad 50's on Ripcord. The Cobra support was very close to our positions, but it certainly did give our morale a boost — those gunships could really kick ass! It was fascinating to watch the tracer rounds of the Quad 50's heading for our hill in an arc landing just below our positions between the LZ and the Hill. As they were firing I recall Dave saying "I sure hope they have the right range coordinates!" We may also have had artillery support, but I can't remember it.

During the darkness Dave would fire M-79 rounds at occasional flashes that appeared along the tree line to our left across the open area, as well as spot rounds in an arc facing our perimeter. After Rat was hit I believe Drew Gaster took over his M-60, assisted by Nose Collins. Drew also took over as squad leader after Jones' death. I don't recall Paul Morton being in the area along the line at all during the period of contact. Denny told me later (in 1971 when I saw him again in the states) that Paul was behind a rock above our position complaining about having something in his eyes and not being able to see. Denny still remembers, with considerable bitterness, seeing Morton being behind that rock while he was laying on the ground severely wounded. With Belt, Guimond, Jones, and Morton out of action, all we had left in 3rd squad was Dave and I and the gun team (Gaster and Collins), so the reinforcements from 3rd Platoon were certainly welcome. 3rd Platoon was fortunate in that their perimeter was along the steepest slope or side of the Hill. As a result, I don't believe their perimeter was hit the entire time we occupied the Hill.

Sometime during the course of the night the wind carried a strong teargas down the perimeter in our direction and everybody grabbed their gasmasks. We learned sometime later that a round had apparently hit a tear-gas shell that one of the M-79 men carried in the area of the "big rock."

We didn't get any sleep that whole night and by the time daylight rolled around we were physically and emotionally drained. The Hill now had an eerie stillness about it. We walked around almost in a daze, as smoke from the many small fires ignited by the firefight was whipped around by the wind. Shortly after daylight Dave walked down the perimeter to 2nd and 1st squads and learned the full extent of how badly we had been hit. During the course of the night we were unaware of what was happening along the remainder of the 1st Platoon perimeter, since most of the time we were preoccupied with our own situation. He came back with tears in his eyes to tell me that Red Keister and Terry Palm had been killed. He said that Red had most of his head blown off and that he was told Palm had died in Doc. Grubidt's arms after having been shot in the chest. Jack Godwin had part of his foot blown off and Tony Chandler, Adams, and possibly Cooper, had burst eardrums. The physical and emotional toll of the night had reached the point that we both just sat on the side of the Hill and cried. After a period of silence in which we just looked out toward the dense foliage between the Hill and Ripcord, Dave said, "Well Rod, at least we made it through." The collective morale of 1st Platoon was lower at that point than at any time since I joined the platoon in early December. We also learned that two men from 2nd Platoon had been killed while helping 1st Platoon (SGT James Hembree and Keith Utter).

During the course of the night, I do recall looking over toward the 2nd Squad position and seeing a man down in front of their perimeter. Within a few seconds I saw another man with glasses walking down toward him, but before he reached the manon the ground, he was hit and also went down. I didn't know who these two were at the time, but surmised later that they must have been Hembree and Utter (with glasses).

The small fires burning in the open area below our position would occasionally set off one of the unexploded hand grenades during the early morning. Fragments from one of these grenades wounded Nose Collins, who was medevaced back to Camp Evans that morning along with the other walking wounded from the previous night. It was only then that we made any attempt to put the fires out.

A couple of hours after daylight 3rd Squad (what was left of it) and parts of the other two squads went on a recon of the area to the left-front of the 1st Platoon perimeter. We found about seven or eight NVA bodies, including one that was badly dismembered (apparently the result of Cobra gunfire) and one big body that looked like it could have been Chinese. We also noticed signs that bodies had been dragged away. A body was also located not more than twenty feet from where we found Guimond and where Belt was hit. His right hand was blown off, probably indicating that he tried to throw back a grenade that was tossed in his area. It was our first realization that the gooks had managed to get that close to our perimeter. This gook was probably the one who had fired at Denny and I and possibly the same who that had hit Rat. At least one other body was found in front and fairly close to the 2nd Squad position.

After returning from the recon patrol, I was picked as part of a detail, consisting of men from all three platoons, to carry the KIA bodies over to the LZ for transport back to Graves Registration. The bodies had been placed behind a big rock separating the 2nd and 3rd squad sectors of 1st Platoon (not to be confused with the other big rock that separated 1st and 2nd platoons). The bodies of Terry Palm, William Jones, Red Keister, SGT Hembree, and Keith Utter were placed in "body bags" which were similar to large heavy duty plastic garbage bags. I was one of four men to carry Terry Palm, and I was somewhat surprised at how heavy he was.

The balance of the day was spent digging in and improving our defensive positions. The sense of urgency was in marked contrast to the previous day. All along the 1st Platoon perimeter men were digging foxholes deep enough to stand in and still have cover. The strong wind didn't make the job any easier. A man was likely to get dirt blown back into his face from the guy digging next to him, or even from his own digging. I recall looking over to the 2nd Squad area and seeing the comical sight of George Corts wearing a gasmask to provide some protection from the blowing dirt. Not only did we in the 3rd Squad dig a deep foxhole, but we also built a covered bunker consisting of logs above one end of our foxhole, a couple of ponchos on top and rocks and dirt above that. This position would afford us protection from shell fragments from RPG hits against the rock above our position.

Sometime during the day of the 14th or 15th we were reinforced with about twelve or fifteen new guys or "cherries." What a time for a new guy to get broken into life in the field. Lt. Ralph Selvaggi (Co. Executive Officer and former 3rd Platoon leader) came out with the new men from the rear to replace Palm as 1st Platoon leader. One of the new guys was assigned to 3rd Squad. His name was Greg Hudson and I recall that he was from Williston, ND.

On the 15th we experienced another strange incident. A Huey was in the process of coming in for a landing on the LZ front of us when it started making a stuttering noise, apparently experiencing mechanical problems. It did manage to make it to the LZ before crashing on the side of the LZ facing the Hill. Some men from our platoon ran over to the LZ to secure the chopper. A Chinook came out sometime later to take the Huey out but was unable to lift it, so it was left on the LZ with the intention of blowing it after we left the Hill. Apparently none of the chopper crew were injured in the crash, but the gun crew spent the night with us on the Hill while the pilots were flown back to Camp Evans.

The Hill was hit again during the next three nights (14th, 15th and 16th), but it was not nearly as bad as the night of the 13th. There is not much that I remember about the events of the next three days and nights on the Hill. A few items at random. On the third or fourth night I recall Mike Cooksley firing a 90 recoilless from a position above and to the left of our position. The M-67 90mm recoilless was used on the Hill to fire fleshette rounds (containing tiny darts that sprayed the target area). We were resupplied with ammo, hand grenades and some C's. I can't recall ever running short of ammo at any time on the Hill. During the night of the 13th I ran out of my own M-16 ammo, but was able to use the ammo that Jones had left.

On the morning of the 17th, I went out with Billy Gibson (and his radio) on LP duty about 200 yards down the ridgeline leading into the 2nd Platoon position. The Company had LPs down that ridgeline during the day the entire time we were on the Hill. The morning was uneventful and we were relieved by another pair around noon. When I got back to the 3rd Squad, I found out that we had been resupplied with clean clothes. Everyone in our squad had changed and left one set of pants and shirt for me, with the pants a bit on the small side. It was at this time that I learned we would be leaving the Hill toward the end of the day. Shortly after I had changed, Lt. Selvaggi came around to our position and was upset that our area had not been policed up — as if we didn't have enough to worry about. Since I was the only one at our position at the time I naturally received the full brunt of his verbal barrage. Clearly upset, I looked around for someone to help me out. Dave was above our position talking to Doc. Grubidt, and appeared to be the nearest, so I yelled up to him to get down here and give me a hand. Dave's temper reacted in kind as he yelled back that he was not a dog to be yelled at. But he did come down to help and the two of us managed to get the area cleaned up, piling most of the garbage in adumping area on top of the Hill. We both realized that our nerves were on edge and tempers were short. It was definitely time to get the hell off Hill 805!

Late in the afternoon we got the word to get ready to move out. We were happy at the thought, but too tired and somewhat numb from the events of the previous four or five days to be overjoyed. We were not yet out of trouble. 1st and 3rd Platoons, along with the Company CP, moved off the Hill just long enough to blow everything that had been left. Many of us were still wearing the flack jackets that we wore during much of the time on the Hill.

When we crossed the LZ the downed Huey was still there — it had not yet been blown up, and I'm not sure if it ever was. After we had gone a short distance beyond the LZ, we were told to move off the trail and set up a temporary perimeter as we usually do when we are taking a brief rest along a trail. We were apparently waiting for 2nd Platoon to rejoin the Company. 3rd Squad was off to the left side of the trail down a small slope about 15-2' feet from the middle of the trail. We sat there for a few minutes facing away from the trail (SOP), with Dave to my right and Hudson (the new guy) to my left. Then for some reason, I'm not sure why, the three of us stood up and turned to face the trail — maybe we thought the Company was getting ready to move out again.

Within a few seconds after we turned to face the trail, there was a loud explosion. The concussion effect knocked me off my feet. I didn't notice until the next morning that a piece of shrapnel had nearly penetrated through the front of my helmet — the second time in less than a week that my helmet may have saved my life. My first reaction after the explosion was that we had taken an incoming mortar round.

Within seconds I was out of my ruck, back on my feet, and instinctively firing into the bush on automatic and yelling at a stunned Hudson to do likewise. I then looked to my right and saw Dave about six to eight feet away, sitting down against his ruck facing away from the trail. As I moved toward him to see if he was alright, he said, in a calm conversational tone of voice, "Rod, I'm hit — get a medic." I rushed over to him and immediately noticed that he had been hit with a piece of shrapnel in the middle of his upper chest, in an exposed area not covered by his flack jacket. When I got to him he was just staring straight ahead with a blank expression, apparently in shock and slipping into unconsciousness. It was the scariest moment I ever experienced in Nam, more so than any time on the Hill. I was so scared at seeing Dave in this condition that I was literally shaking.

## Ch. 11 / July 11, 1970

I worked fast to get his ruck off, get his flack jacket off, tore his shirt open, and tore part of my shirt off to cover the hole in chest all the while screaming for a medic. As I was getting his flack jacket and shirt off, bubbly blood was starting to come out of his mouth and the hole in his chest. I got the hole in his chest covered and tilted hishead back, continuing to yell for a medic. As I looked up to the trail wondering where in the hell the medics were, I saw two or three different colored smoke grenades filling the air with smoke (apparently touched off by the explosion). I continued to hold my torn shirt over Dave's wound and continued to yell for a medic until I was nearly hoarse. The minutes went by — but still no medic! I don't know how much time went by before a medic finally came, it was probably 5-10 but it seemed like an eternity. I learned later that Ron Grubidt (1st Platoon medic) had his legs blasted by the blast putting him out of action, and the other Company medics were attending to other wounded men at the time.

A medic finally came, a skinny guy with glasses who I learned within the past year (1983) was the CP medic with the last name of Fowler. He patched Dave up and told me to get some guys to carry him up to the trail so that he could be medevaced out. He left to attend to someone else while I yelled for help to carry Dave up to the trail. At first, I couldn't raise anyone besides Hudson, but finally Cooksley (with a wounded leg) and Dinky (Shannon's scout) came down to help. Dinky, the only Chieu Hoi scout in 1st Platoon at the time, was on the Hill when Shannon and I rejoined the Platoon on the 13th. For the most part, Chieu Hoi scouts were worthless, but Dinky was clearly an exception. The four of us carried Dave up to the clearing along the trail. Along the way, I saw what was left of the 3rd Platoon scout. Shortly after someone told me that the scout had pulled a hand grenade on himself.

I guess we will never know for sure whether the "scout blowup" was an accident or suicide. Carl Shannon recently indicated that the scout had been apparently wounded in the leg and walked with a noticeable limp. According to Carl, Warner had warned him that if he couldn't keep up with everyone else he was going to leave him behind for NVA. Whether this scared the scout into a state of suicide is difficult for anyone to say, but it does provide a possible motive.

After we got Dave up to the clearing along the trail we tried to make him as comfortable as possible. He was having trouble breathing, was still unconscious, and Hudson and I (who stayed with him) had a feeling of helplessness. Shortly after we arrived at the clearing, a badly wounded black guy was brought up next to us. He had severe wounds on his head and much of his body. Until recently, I thought this man was Warner, but I learned that Warner was white, so I don't know the identity of the black man. When the medevac chopper finally came, it lowered a basket. The black guy was placed on the bottom and Dave was placed on top of him. As the basket was going up images flashed through my mind of the many experiences Dave and I shared. Somehow I knew it would be the last time I would ever see him. I said a silent prayer, pleading with God to help pull him through.

A short time later the Company moved on down the trail and set up a NDP around a small hill just as it was beginning to get dark. Before moving out, I had tied Dave's ruck to the back of mine to carry back to the rear. Fortunately neither ruck had all that much in it at the time, mostly personal items. Despite being wounded, CPT Straub stayed with the Company that night. Nearly all of us felt we were going to get hit sometime during the night, but our morale was so low I'm not sure we would have been able to adequately defend ourselves. I thought our morale had hit a low point after the night of the 13/14th, but it was even lower the night after the "scout blowup." Fortunately, we did not have any contact that night — the NVA missed a golden opportunity, but they may have been satisfied enough just to get Hill 805 back.

Shortly after daylight on the morning of the 18th we moved further down the trail to another LZ a relatively short distance from our NDP position. We didn't have to wait long before the line of choppers arrived to take us back to Camp Evans. We never were so happy to see a Huey as we were that morning. A few of the guys in the Platoon indicated later that some of the choppers received fire from the ground (or from the direction of 805) as they were coming in or leaving, but I don't recall it.

After landing at Camp Evans, I went over to a water truck located at the end of the landing strip to have a drink and to fill up some of my canteens. As I and a few others were filling our canteens, Paul Morton (who was taken off the Hill a few days earlier) came running over to tell me that Top (SGT Schuelke) had just told him and others that Dave had died earlier that morning. I immediately went over to Top, who was talking to some other men in the Company, to confirm what Paul had said. Top told me that Beyl had died while being flown to the DaNang hospital. My first reaction was one of disbelief and shock, despite the seriousness of his wound I was not prepared for or would not accept the possibility that he might die.

Later that morning the company traveled back to Phu Bai by truck. While riding in the back of the cattle truck to Phu Bai, I was in somewhat of a daze. My initial reaction of disbelief to Dave's death turned to numbness. I had lost the best friend I ever had — I suddenly felt all alone. The words of advice that one of Dave's uncles (a veteran of WWII) gave him before he left for Nam went through my mind. "Don't get very close to anyone Dave, because if something happens to him it will haunt you for the rest of your life." But as Dave once told me, you can't help but get close to someone while trying to get through this insane war.

When we arrived in the Company area at Phu Bai, I turned over Dave's personal effects to Top. Shortly after, I saw Benny (who had recently returned from R&R) and he told me that he had seen Denny at 85th Evac. and that he was in stable condition and was being flown to Tokyo. Later that afternoon the Company went to Eagle Beach for standdown. Most of the guys had a good time, apparently trying to put the past week out of their minds. But there was no way I could enjoy myself! Eagle Beach reminded me of Dave more than anything. It was during our first visit to Eagle Beach in early January that Dave and I really became close friends, and as related earlier, we probably had the best time of our tour in Nam during the May standdown at Eagle Beach.

Instead of joining the rest of the guys, I would spend much of my time sitting on the beach just staring out to the South China sea. I kept asking myself why? Why did Dave have to die? Dave had so much to live for. If anyone deserved to live it was Dave. Why couldn't I have been the one to take that piece of shrapnel? I felt there must have been something I could have done after he was hit to help him survive. We had depended on each other to help get us through the year, so for the longest time I felt that I had somehow let him down. It would take a period of over three years before I would be able to put this feeling of guilt behind me, but the pain of his death will stay with me the rest of my life.

July 11, 1970 / Ch. 11

Delta Raiders • **197**

# 12.
# Chronology
## July 1, 1970 – July 15, 1970

### July 1-11, 1970
For the first 11 days of July, Delta Company operated in the vicinity of FB O'Reilly without any contact or notable incidents.

### July 12, 1970
**0755H** Co. D CA'd from YD344270 to YD357196, complete at 0835H. The Company moved by land to Hill 805 (YD362188) which they assaulted without opposition and established a defensive perimeter around the crown of the hill. This would be the beginning of what would be known as the Battle of Hill 805, one of the many July engagements by units of the 3rd Brigade in the area around FB Ripcord.

**2122H** (YD362188 - Hill 805, 1.5-2 KM SE of FB Ripcord): Co. D received 30-40 RPG and small arms fire from an unknown size enemy force 250m northeast of their position. The Company returned organic weapons fire and the enemy withdrew in an unknown direction. The brunt of the attack was received by the 2nd Platoon sector of the perimeter, which faced a trail along a ridgeline leading up to the hill. In all, 81mm mortars, ARA, air strikes, and a flareship were employed. A first light check of the area was made. Results: 13 US WIA (E: 3 medevaced to Camp Evans shortly after contact and 10 evacuated to Camp Evans the following morning; including Barry L. Barnes, Jackie M. Brumbelow, Keith A. Cluff, Larry Ertel, Willie J. Lewis, James L. Poullard, and Carl E. Robinson), 3 US WIA (M).

### July 13, 1970
**0815H** (YD362188 - Hill 805): During a sweep of yesterdays contact area, Co. D discovered 4 RPGs with boosters lying in the open and indications of enemy activity in the area within the last 24 hours. Results: destroyed.

### July 14, 1970
**0102H** (Y0362188 - Hill 805): Co. D received a heavy volume of RPGs, satchel charges, and small arms fire from an unknown size enemy force 20m northwest of their position. The brunt of the attack was received by the 1st Platoon sector of the perimeter which faced an LZ with a saddle in

between. The element returned organic weapons fire and the enemy withdrew in an unknown direction (0203H) approximately one hour after initial contact, but not before heavy casualties were inflicted upon 1st Platoon. Men from both 2nd and 3rd Platoons were moved around the perimeter to assist the embattled 1st Platoon.

A medevac was completed for 2 men (Paul "Rat" Guimond and Denny Belt) at 0353H, Guimond was dead on arrival at Camp Evans. A medevac was also completed at 0426H for 1 man (Jack L. Godwin) who had a foot blown off by a satchel charge, for 1 man (Rodney "Nose" Collins) at 0753H, and for 6 men (Joseph A. Adams, Bruce "Tony" Chandler, Terry Cooper, Warren R. Hanrahan, David L. Weaver, and Bobby G. Hill) at 0945H. Airstrikes, flareship, ARA, artillery, Quad 50 (on FB Ripcord), and 81mm mortars were employed.

A first light check of the area revealed 5 NVA KIA, 1 RPG launcher, 4 RPGs, 1 AK-47, and 1 bag containing 10 1/2 lb. satchel charges. There were no indications of the enemy unit on the KIA clothing. There were also numerous signs of blood trails leading from the area. Results: 6 US KIA (Paul C. "Rat" Guimond, William F. Jones, John L. "Red" Keister, James T. Hembree (2nd Platoon SGT), 1LT Terry A. Palm (1st Platoon Leader, and Keith E. Utter); 9 US WIA (E: Denny Belt, Jack L. Godwin, Rodney Collins, Joseph A. Adams, Bruce Chandler, Terry Cooper, Warren P. Hanrahan, David L. Weaver, and Bobby G. Hill); 6 US WIA (M).

**1330H** 1LT Ralph Selvaggi (Co. D XO), along with 12 men (including 7 "cherries" or new men), reinforced Delta Company which had 30 men extracted from the field during the previous two days; with 1LT Selvaggi assigned as the new Platoon Leader of 1st Platoon, succeeding 1LT Terry Palm (KIA).

**1438H** An airstrike was completed for Co. D at YD363180 and YD363176.

**1525H** An airstrike was completed for Co. D at YD348177.

**2253H** (YD362188 - Hill 805): Co. D received an unknown number of RPGs, satchel charges, and small arms fire from an unknown size enemy force 20m to the south and southeast of their position. The element returned organic weapons fire and the enemy withdrew in an unknown direction. 81mm mortars, artillery (105 & 155), ARA, Quad 50, and flareships were employed.

## July 15, 1970

**0159H** (Y0362188 - Hill 805): Co. D received 37 82mm mortar rounds which impacted all around their position. 81mm mortars and artillery were employed on suspected enemy locations YD348190 and YD355221.

**0357H** (YD362188 - Hill 805): Co. D observed 3 trip flares ignite 15m west

of their position. The element employed organic weapons fire and artillery was employed to the west of their position. A first light check of the area revealed indications that numerous bodies had been dragged through the area. Also located were a wallet containing miscellaneous documents and photos, miscellaneous clothing with no indication of enemy unit, 2 first aid packs, and a bloody trail leading southwest. The element followed the blood trail until it ran out. Results: 1 US KIA (Gary Lee Schneider), 1 US WIA (E), documents evacuated, rest destroyed.

**1208H** Co. D requested medevac for 1 man (James Plenderleith) wounded previous night, believed to have collapsed lung; medevac completed at 1245H.

**1525H** A log bird resupplying Co. D had a power failure on LZ YD360188 (directly facing the 1st Platoon sector on Hill 805). The bird was secured by 1st Platoon of Co. D. At 1545H, while attempting to extract the log bird, a CH-47 (varsity 549) received a heavy volume of fire; but the extraction failed because the strap broke. All radios were removed from the aircraft. The pilot crew was evacuated, but the door gunners spent the night with Co. D on Hill 805.

**1845H** (YD362188 - Hill 805): Co. D received 3 82mm mortar rounds from an unknown enemy location impacting 40m west of their position with negative results.

# 13.
# A Combat Assault!

## Terry Moore

Huddled under the poncho, listening to the rain pelting through the very thick trees and my knees still shaking from the combat assault we had made earlier that day, I suddenly realized that a year was a very long time to stay alive in a hostile environment such as this. I had never seen a darker night in my life.

Only a year earlier, I was minding my own business and my new wife and I were busy starting our life together when suddenly this notice came from Washington informing me I had been drafted to the service of my country. It was a rude awakening. I had never entertained the vaguest thought of joining the military. The next year was very fast: Fort Bragg for basic, Fort Polk for infantry training, Fort Benning for Non-Commissioned Officer training, then on to Fort Jackson to work in a training company for the experience. My next assignment, as I knew it would be, was Viet-Nam. "A combat assault," the instructor was saying, "commonly called a 'CA', is when you, as a squad, platoon, company or larger are picked up by a sortie of helicopters and are moved from area a to area b." Now area b is a destination supposed to be occupied by the enemy. When you touch down on an LZ (landing zone), you must clear the bird as soon as possible to allow the helicopter to clear the danger zone and to allow the next bird to make his approach and exit in quick order. As soon as your feet touch, move off the LZ, form a platoon or company defense position around the LZ to protect the incoming birds and yourself. At the same time as all this is happening you must watch for booby traps and the enemy who may be waiting to make you welcome with a HOT LZ.

As I sat at Camp Eagle for orientation, in the distance I could hear the pounding of B-52 ordnance and could feel it rocking the ground I stood on. The building in which I sat vibrated and shook at its metal joints. Little did I know that the Delta Raiders were at that moment defending with their very lives a hilltop called only by the numbers "805."

## Ch. 13 / A Combat Assault!

The next day I was sent to the Company area of Alpha, second of the five o first, to report for duty. The first sergeant said for me to report to Delta Company Headquarters to help fill a void created by sixty percent killed and wounded defending Hill 805. I was stunned, without words, other than a simple, "yes Top", I proceeded to this new Company thinking, damn, what have I walked into now? It was the last week in July 1970.

I drew my gear, the Company came in for replacements. Besides myself there was Eugene Evans, Jerry Stearns, and Steve Kirkland who went to 2nd Platoon that day. We would make this first CA together and a lot more to come.

It was time for my first of 32 combat assaults. I had my rucksack on my back on my way to the chopper pad . I felt like I could hardly move. I don't remember how I got on my feet to walk in the first place. Three days supply of c-rats., four frags, two smokes, two claymores, four canteens, eight mags, M-16, 500 rounds M-60, a law, and my M-16 rifle. Damn, I needed a wheelbarrow.

I finally got to the pad. I don't remember an orientation of any kind about mission, area of operation, or anything. There was speculation and guessing among the men about where we were going and what we were going to do, but being the new guy, the cherry, no one told me anything. I was along for the ride and I had damn well better keep up and do as the others if I wanted to survive. We were spread out according to platoon and in order of which platoon was to lead. I think I was more numb than scared. I could see smoke in the distant hills as the F-4s were pounding the area into which we were going. I could feel the vibrations to my very core of existence. The old guys around me were talking and joking as if they were about to drive to Shoney's for a burger. I couldn't believe they weren't taking this seriously. As it turned out, they were. It was just another day on the job.

I didn't know the army had so many choppers. They came in a formation, sat down on the pad, I strained to get the heavy load off the ground and we rushed for the bird we were assigned. Almost instantly we were airborne. There were no seat belts, Hell there were no seats, not to mention no doors on this damn thing. I'm trying just to make room to keep my feet inside. I look to the guy on my right, Kenny Holgerson. He's sitting there with his feet hanging out as if he is on his back porch at home. I look down; it must be at least a couple thousand feet if it's a foot. We're crossing the first ridgeline now and I feel the bird start to circle. I could see a pair of cobras pacing back and forth around the area of insertion looking for a target and covering the slicks as they delivered their cargo of troops. I can see on a distant hill top where smoke is still billowing. The first bird makes its descent, the door gunners on both sides are laying down heavy defensive fire, and I'm thinking, "Please, let my first one at least be a cold landing." He's up and away. They're securing the area, appears to be no hostile action, another bird lands, and another. Suddenly my chopper almost falls from its lofty course to the ground below. A foot from the ground they almost throw us off. "Get Out! Get Out!" they yell. We go. My knees, will they carry me? Watch out for booby traps, get off the LZ, form your platoon position around the area. What has just happened to me?

I just survived my first aerial combat assault. It was a cold one. They would not all be that way. Thank God my first one was. I now at least know what to expect. We moved off the LZ into the jungle, into the night, into the Viet-Nam war. I was a Delta Raider. Geronimo!

Terry Moore  70-71

# 14.
# Chronology
## October 31, 1968 – May 31, 1970

**July 16, 1970**

**0246H** (YD362188 - Hill 805): Co. D observed a trip flare ignite to the east of their position and heard their mechanical ambush detonate to the west of their position. The Company engaged the area with organic weapons fire and immediately received 30 RPGs, an unknown number of satchel charges and small arms fire from an unknown size enemy force 50m west, south, southeast, and southwest of their position. The main direction of attack was from the west and southeast. The element returned fire with organic weapons, artillery, 81mm mortars, ARA, Stinger and Skyspots. Flareships and basketball were also employed throughout the period of contact. The contact terminated at 0304H with negative US casualties.

**0317H** (YD362188 - Hill 805): Co. D observed an unknown size enemy force 250m north of their position moving toward their location. The element engaged the enemy with organic weapons fire and ARA. The enemy did not return fire and withdrew in an unknown direction.

**0413H** (YD362188 - Hill 805): Co. D heard a mechanical ambush detonate to the north of their position and engaged the area with organic weapons fire. There was no return fire and at first light a check of the area was made revealing 2 NVA KIA by mortars, 2 AK47s, 5 full AK-47 magazines, 2 pouches containing 5 1/2 lb. satchel charges each, 50 AK-47 rounds in a leather pouch, 1 knife, 5 Chicom grenades, and 4 bottles of unknown type liquid. Results: 2 NVA KIA.

**0710H** (YD360188 - LZ facing 1/D sector of Hill 805): 1/D secured the downed log bird from a distance because it appeared that the aircraft had been tampered with overnight, a rope previously put to secure the rotor blade had been removed and a small compartment in the bird had been opened.

**0715H** A Pink Team was put on station for Co. D.

**2031H** (YD362188 - Hill 805): Co. D engaged suspected enemy movement with organic weapons fire 100m southeast of their position. ARA was employed and a first light check of the area was made with negative results.

**2055H** Col. Lucas (CO of 2-506 on FB Ripcord) reported that they had intercepted a NVA radio transmission. A Kit Carson Scout translated saying the NVA were massing for an attack on Hill 805 (location of Co. D).

**2358H** (YD362188 - Hill 805): Co. D observed their mechanical ambush detonate 150m to the west of their position. Artillery and 81mm mortars were employed on the suspected enemy position. A first light check of the area was made with negative results.

Weather note for July 16 in the 101st AO:

Temperature: Max. 105 min. 80 Humidity: Max. 85% Min. 45%

Winds gusting to 40 knots in the mountains.

## July 17, 1970

**0006H** (YD362188 - Hill 805): Co. D observed suspected enemy movement to the west and north of their position. ARA, artillery, and 81mm mortars were employed. A first light check of the area was made with negative results.

**0230H** (YD362188 - Hill 805): Co. D observed their mechanical ambush and trip flare detonate on the west side of their perimeter. The element engaged the area with organic weapons fire. The enemy returned satchel charges and small arms fire and withdrew in an unknown direction. ARA and artillery was employed. A first light check of the area was made with negative results.

**1630H** Co. D (- 2/D) moved off of Hill 805 to the north, crossing LZ360188 (facing the hill), after the Company consolidated all that was left on the hill and piled it on top of the hill. 2/D was temporarily left on the hill to destroy what was left, while the remainder of Co. D waited for the platoon 30m northwest of LZ360188. While Co. D was waiting for 2/D to rejoin the Company a Kit Carson Scout (attached to 3/D), sitting near the center of the Co. D perimeter, either killed himself by pulling the pin on a hand grenade or accidentally discharged a hand grenade. The Company engaged their perimeter with organic weapons fire thinking they had received an enemy mortar round.

Two men were medevaced (David Bey) and Wilfred Warner, who later died of their wounds from the grenade) and 3 other wounded men (Mike Cooksley, 1st Platoon SGT, Drew Gaster, and Ron Grubidt) were taken out by a loach from the nearby LZ. At approximately 1830H the Company moved to YD358190, where they established their NDP. Results: 2 US KIA (David R. Beyl and Wilfred W. Warner), 3 US WIA (E: Mike Cooksley, Drew Gaster, Ron Grubidt), 4 US WIA (M).

**1700H** (Y0360188 - LZ facing Hill 805): While descending a ladder over the LZ facing Hill 805, a sensor team and the aircraft took fire. The sensor and equipment were dropped in, but 1 man fell from the ladder breaking a foot. Permission was requested to abort the mission due to the time required in moving them to a NDP site. The injured man was evacuated. The pilot did not have commo with Co. D, the ground unit nearby, and did not ask for smoke.

## July 18, 1970

0700H After moving from YD358190, Co. D moved by air from YD353192 to Camp Evans, with the last 3 or 4 birds taking enemy fire on leaving the LZ. The Company was then moved by truck from Camp Evans to Phu Bai, and during the afternoon by truck from Phu Bai to Eagle Beach for standdown.

Later in the day during the afternoon, FB Ripcord suffered a crippling blow when a CH-47 (Chinook), in logistic support of the firebase, was shot down by enemy ground fire and crashed on the 105mm ammunition storage areas, causing a major fire and extensive damage. All six 105mm Howitzers of Btry B/2-319 Arty were destroyed. There was 1 US KIA (William D. Rollason, formerly of Co. D) and 4 US WIA.

## July 18-20, 1970

Co. D on standdown at Eagle Beach.

## July 20-23, 1970

Co. D at Phu Bai for refresher training.

## July 23, 1970

FB Ripcord was evacuated by the 2-506 and 3rd BDE.

## July 24, 1970

Co. D moved by air from Phu Bai to Camp Evans, where they stayed overnight.

## July 25, 1970

Co. D CA'd from Camp Evans to YD405234.

## Aug. 1, 1970

1130H (YDSOO2OO - 1 KM E of FB Rakkasan): Co. D found 8 old bunkers (4' x5 'x4' with 1.5' overhead cover). The bunkers were about 7-8 months old. There was no indication of recent enemy activity in the area. Results: bunkers destroyed.

## Aug. 4, 1970

**1607H** (Y0387185 - 2.5 KM SW of FB Gladiator): Co. D observed 1 enemy, in green fatigues with a rucksack, moving northeast 150m southeast of their position. Artillery was employed and an airstrike requested. When the airstrike came on station, Co. A observed 2 enemy in the open at YD387192, so the airstrike was diverted to that location. Results: 2 NVA/VC KBAF.

## Aug. 9, 1970

Co. D moved by air to Camp Evans where the Company spent the night.

## Aug. 10, 1970

Co. D CA'd from Camp Evans to YD413147.

## Aug. 16, 1970

Co. D CA'd from Camp Evans to YD362206.

## Aug. 19, 1970

**1030H** (YD348210 - 3 KM N of FB Ripcord): While leaving a LZ Co. D's first lift received one 82mm mortar round impacting 200m west of their position with negative casualties or damage. The second lift received three 82mm mortar rounds impacting 60m to the west of their position with negative casualties or damage. ARA was employed on the suspected enemy location Y0335223, and two secondary explosions were observed.

## Aug. 24, 1970

**0818** (YD37426D - 3 KM NNW of FB Mexico): Co. D observed Ho Chi Minh sandal prints on the trail. It appeared that 2-3 enemy had attempted to get close to their position during the night.

**0939H** (YD373259): Co. D received small arms fire from an unknown size enemy force in a cave. A White Team performing a search reported 10 huts (8'x8' with thatch roofs), about 12 natural caves, 1 apparent campfire, and 1 enemy in the entrance to one of the caves. An airstrike was employed. Results: White Team reported 4 huts and 4 caves destroyed.

**1200H** (YD374259 - 3 KM NW of FB Mexico): Co. D observed 2-3 enemy traveling west 200m southwest of their location. The enemy wore no shirts, wore rolled up trousers and straw hats. The element engaged the enemy with organic weapons. The enemy did not return fire and fled west.

**2140H** (YD373257 - 5 KM E of FB O'Reilly): Co. D observed a flashlight in the vicinity of YD371262. The element employed artillery and the light went out. The area was checked by a White Team at first light with negative results.

## Aug. 25, 1970
Co. D moved by air from Y0368254 to Camp Evans for an overnight standdown.

## Aug. 26, 1970
Co. D CA'd from Camp Evans to YD372200.

## Aug. 27, 1970
**0805H** (YD366187 - 2 KM E of FB Ripcord): Co. D engaged suspected enemy movement with organic weapons fire. The enemy did not return fire. A sweep of the area was made with negative results.

## Aug. 28, 1970
**1420H** (YD374181 - 3 KM SE of FB Ripcord): Co. D found 1 enemy KIA, dead about 1 day, believed killed by ARA. The enemy was wearing a green shirt and brown trousers. On one knee of the trousers the enemy had sewn a 1st Cav. Div. patch and on the other knee an 101st Abn. Div. patch. While the element was searching the KIA and surrounding area they observed 1 enemy about 200m southeast of their position. The element did not have time to engage the enemy. The Company searched the area with negative results. Results: 1 NVA KBAFA.

**1638H** (YD373180 - 3 KM SE of FB Ripcord): Co. D received a heavy volume of small arms fire, hand grenades, and an unknown type of mortar round from an unknown size enemy force. The element assaulted the enemy position employing ARA. After searching the initial enemy location at YD372180, the element found 7 bunkers (3'x3' with 3' overhead cover). The Company threw hand grenades into the bunkers and received 3 secondary explosions. The element also found 5 graves each containing 1 NVA KIA (undetermined date of death). The element also employed 2 airstrikes on YD370183. Results: 1 US KIA (Jay Allan Muncey), 2 US WIA (F: Roger Miles and Alto Griffin), 5 NVA KIA.

## Aug. 29, 1970
**1113H** (YD377518 - 3.5 KM ESE of FB Ripcord): Co. D discovered they were being followed by an estimated enemy platoon. The element employed artillery and ARA. The element search the area and found a blood trail

which they followed for 75m until it ended in a stream. The element continued to search the area with negative results.

**2200H** (YD375176 - 3.5 KM ESE of FB Ripcord): Co. D observed the flashlights of an estimated enemy platoon at YD372176. The element employed artillery with unknown results.

### Sept. 1, 1970

**1345H** (YD390186 - 3 KM SW of FB Gladiator): Co. D discovered 1 bunker (5'x5'x4' with 1' overhead cover), 1 mortar position (5'x7'), and a 2' wide northeast-southwest trail. The trail was well hidden from overhead observation and had been traveled within the last 5-7 days. Results: bunker destroyed.

**1420H** (YD416176 - 2 KM SSW of FB Granite): Co. D found two bunkers (20'x20'x5') containing one broken telegraph key, one NVA gas mask, three pair HCM sandals, one large wash basin, four 1-gallon metal fuel containers, four empty medicine bottles, three baskets, miscellaneous cooking equipment, two NVA canteens with cups, and one NVA steel helmet. The element also found in the same location two fighting positions (5'x9'), estimated to be about six months old. There were no indications of recent enemy activity in the area. Results: everything destroyed except medicine bottles which were evacuated to Camp Evans.

### Sept. 2, 1970

The 2-501 passed to OPCON of 1st BDE from 3rd BDE.

### Sept. 3, 1970

2-501 moved by CH-47 to LZ Ann and began assaulting into the FB Tennessee area by UH-H. Co. D secured FB Tennessee for the insertion of Btry A, 1st BN, 321st Arty.

## Sept. 5, 1970

**1800H** The Division terminated Operation TEXAS STAR and initiated Operation JEFFERSON GLEN/MONSOON PLAN 70 (OPORD 13-70). Operation JEFFERSON GLEN would be the last major offensive operation in Vietnam in which U.S. ground troops were involved.

During Operation TEXAS STAR the Division killed 2053 enemy, captured over 600 individual and crew-served weapons and over 200,000 rounds of ammo of all types, and destroyed or captured over 59 tons of rice.

## Sept. 6, 1970

The 2-501 closed FB Tennessee and moved to FB Birmingham.

## Sept. 12, 1970

The 2-501 moved to Phu Bai for refresher training and passed OPCON to 2nd BDE from the 1st BDE.

## Sept. 13-14, 1970

Co. D on standdown at Eagle Beach.

## Sept. 14-17, 1970

Co. D at Phu Bai for refresher training.

## Sept. 17, 1970

2-501 passed to OPCON of 3rd BDE, assuming control of the AO in the FB Rakkasan and FB Gladiator area vacated by the 1-506, with the battalion CP located at FB Rakkasan.

## Sept. 20, 1970

**1015H** (YD405243 - 3 KM NW of FB Gladiator & 1 KM N of FB Mexico): 2/D discovered 4 bunkers (8'x8'x6' with 3' overhead cover) and 3 fighting positions (3'x2'x3'). The last enemy use of the area estimated to be 6-12 months. Results: destroyed.

## Sept. 21, 1970

**1415H** (YD412247 - 1.5 KM NE of FB Mexico): Co. D discovered 1 grave (2' deep) containing 1 NVA KBA about 2 months earlier. The body was dressed in a black pajama shirt wrapped in a poncho. The body contained no documents or markings. Results: bunkers and fighting positions destroyed.

## Oct. 1, 1970

2-501 returned to OPCON of the 2nd BDE from the 3rd BDE, and assumed the mission of the Division ready reaction force. The 2-501 CP moved by vehicle from FB Rakkasan to Camp Evans, and from Camp Evans to Phu Bai by air (closing at 1930H).

Co. D continued operations in the area of YD5018 (OPCON of 1-506).

**Oct. 2, 1970**
Co. D humped overland to FB Rakkasan where they spent the night.

**Oct. 3, 1970**
Co. D moved by vehicle from FB Rakkasan to Phu Bai and returned to OPCON 2-501.

**Oct. 4, 1970**
Co. D moved by air from Phu Bai to FB Brick and assumed security of the firebase.

**Oct. 13, 1970**
**1840H** (YC835997 - near FB Brick): 2/D observed 1 enemy 600m to the north of their position. Artillery was employed.

**Oct. 15-17, 1970**
The Division implemented OPLAN 10-70, Typhoon Tropical Storm Contingency Plan at 15110H in response to weather reports that Typhoon JOAN would dominate the entire AO causing severe weather conditions for 4-5 days. Typhoon readiness conditions were terminated on Oct. 17 as weather conditions improved.

**Oct. , 1970**
Co. D continued operations to search for enemy forces, cache sites and staging areas.

**1019H** Co. D (- 1/D & 3/D) CA'd from FB Brick to YC945989 (closing at 1030H). At 1037H 1/D CA'd from FB Brick to YC954983 (closing at 1101H). At 11DDH 3/D CA'd from FB Brick to YC937985 (closing at 1112H). NDPs: CP & 2/D YC940990, 1/D YC941987, 3/D YC950981.

**Oct. 20, 1970**
LtC Michael A. Boos succeeded LtC Otis W. Livingston as the CO of the 2-501.

## Oct. 22, 1970
1505H Co. D (- 3/D) CA'd from YC945980 to YC844924 (closing at 1525H). At 1535H 3/D CA'd from YC953982 to YC845929 (closing at 01555H). NDPs: CP & 2/D YC843924, 1/D YC847924, 3/D YC847900.

## Oct. 23, 1970
1230H (YC851924 - 5 KM NW of FB Pistol): 1/D engaged 1 enemy with organic weapons fire 10m to the east of their position. The enemy did not return fire but withdrew to the east. Artillery was employed and a search of the area revealed 1 blood trail.

## Nov. 3, 1970
2020H (YC864943 - 3.5 KM S of FB Rifle): 2/D observed their PSID activate at YC861940. Artillery was employed and a search of the area made with negative results.

## Nov. 4, 1970
1055H (YC866944 - 4 KM S of FB Rifle): 3/D employing organic weapons fire, engaged 1 enemy on a raft moving northeast-southwest down a river 150m to the east of their position. The enemy returned small arms fire, swam to shore and withdrew to the east. Artillery and ARA were employed. A search of the area revealed 1 rucksack containing 25 lbs. of rice, 6 cans of food seasoning, miscellaneous cooking utensils, 30 yards of black material, 1 hammock, 1 sewing kit, 20 unknown type batteries, and miscellaneous documents. Results: rucksack and documents evacuated.

## Nov. 8, 1970
The 2-501 CP remained at FB Brick.
Co. D moved by air to FB Brick (closing at 1515H), and assumed security of the firebase.

## Nov. 8-19, 1970
Co. D responsible for the security of FB Brick.

## Nov. 19, 1970
Co. D CA'd from FB Brick to YC817953 (closing at 1045H).

## Dec. 1, 1970
Co. D moved by air from their field location to the Old Widow Web Pad at Phu Bai, closing at 1643H.

## Dec. 1-7, 1970
The 2-501 (including Co. D) conducted refresher training at Phu Bai.

## Dec. 7, 1970
The 2-501 moved by truck from Phu Bai to the Phu Loc District, with the 2-501 CP moving to FB Tomahawk.
The 2-501 became OPCON to the 1st BDE.
Co. D in the area of ZC1498 and ZC1396 continued search and ambush operations.

## Dec. 10, 1970
Co. D moved by truck to FB Tomahawk with 1/D moving to FB Los Banos, with firebase security assumed at both locations.

## Dec. 10-16, 1970
Co. D (-1/D) responsible for perimeter security at FB Tomahawk, and 1/D responsible or perimeter security at FB Los Banos.

## Dec. 14, 1970
While on security at FB Tomahawk, Co. D had one individual walk outside of the wire and trip a mechanical ambush, receiving fatal multiple frag wounds. Results: 1 US KIA (Richard L. Maynard).

## Dec. 16, 1970
**1545H** 3/D CA'd from FB Tomahawk to AT883941 (closing at 1555H).

## Dec. 17, 1970
**0916H** Co. D CP and 2/D CA'd from FB Tomahawk and 1/D at 1016H from FB Los Banos to 20156953. NDPs: CP & 1/D 20153957, 2/D 20150950, 3/D AT886938.

## Dec. 21, 1970
**1405H** 2-501 requested a total of 7 combat essential log sorties be flown for the 3/D, which has no meals.

## Dec. 25, 1970
Elements of Co. D and 2/Recon Platoon moved to FB Tomahawk for Christmas dinner. Co. D then returned to field locations.

# 15.
# Going Out On An Ambush Vietnam:
## July 7, 1970 - July 7, 1971

## Michael (Allen) B. Allen

Ambush! That was the ultimate of surprise, when they caught us napping, or better yet, when we could catch the enemy when they were not expecting us. That would be less painful for us, but still just as hell raising, enough to make a Grunt scared shitless. But we still did what we had to do and that was to do our job and get back to the world. When someone said, "Get back to the world," that meant home — the United States. That's where everybody was — your family, your friends, and your car!

When we were sent out for an ambush, we had to consider everything that was going on in the Area of Operation (AO). Sometimes the Company was pretty small, when many Grunts were absent because they were wounded, on Rest and Recuperation (R&R), killed in action (KIA), ill, or ghosting (hanging back). There it is! Then we often would work Company size, instead of the typical practice of operating in platoon size in the 3rd Brigade AO.

The 2nd 501st Infantry, 101st Airborne Division (Airmobile) was the swing Battalion OPCON at that time. Wherever the shit hit the fan, we hit the air and were air lifted to that area. Although an ambush would occasionally employ a platoon (invariably under strength) or a half platoon, normally setting an ambush meant going out with only a squad-size group of men. With the small number of Grunts in a group, usually referred to as an element, it became very dangerous. If contact should occur, your chances of making it would be drastically reduced. That's just great! I would think about what a Nam Vet told me back in the world, that your chances of being in a bad auto accident or killed in one were greater than getting messed up in the Nam. "Well," I thought "how the hell can that be! We're out here and this is the real shit! We're pushing our luck 24 hours a day, every day."

## Ch. 15 / Going Out on an Ambush

No matter how you look at it, an ambush in the lowlands, or rice paddies, or up in the mountains was the same. We were out there, kind of like a first alert. Ah, there's nothing like it, hunting and being hunted down on a continuous basis until we left the bush. Well, here we go again. Fight our way through the wait-a-minute vines and other jungle growth to get to the nearest Landing Zone (LZ) on some hill top, to be extracted and whisked off on another Combat Assault (CA). We would be flown to another hill or mountain top where there was an LZ close to where the enemy might be located.

The CA is over and the last helicopter drops off the last load of Grunts. The drowning sound of the engines and the slapping sound of the rotor blades are soon forgotten as everyone prepares to leave the LZ fully resupplied. A sheet of cardboard from the empty cases of C-rations is placed into the framework of the ruck sack to keep the cans of C-rations from digging into your back. Ruck up! Slowly we disappear into the hot, steamy jungle in search of the enemy, each one with M-16 bandoleers, and M-60 machine gun ammo wrapped around our waists, and crisscrossed over our chests. Our heavy ruck sacks on our backs, with the straps digging into our chest and shoulders, pulled us backwards. We had to lean forward to maintain our balance, gasping for air, while trying to wipe the sweat off our faces with the OD green towel that smelled like the rotting stockings on our feet.

Downward we descend into some no-name valley searching for signs of the enemy. With no signs of recent activity, the fear of enemy contact slowly disappears, and we begin the hard, steep climb back up to another mountain ridge where we would set up our Night Defensive Position (NDP). We were fully loaded with supplies for three or four days, anywhere from 70-100 pounds of ammo, explosives, and whatever type of weapon or weapons we were assigned to carry, plus water and C- rations. Each squad in the platoon had to have all of these weapons: M-16 rifles, M- 60 machine gun, M-79 grenade launcher, or the over-and-under M-16 rifle, M-79 grenade launcher combination, as well as the shoulder-launched rockets (LAWS), and machetes for busting trail. The RTO had the 25-pound radio and extra batteries to carry and an M-16 with ammo.

The point man and the man walking slack had it the roughest because they had to break trail. Busting trail through the thick jungle was always rough. The wait-a- minute vines would hook and grab you, a lot of times so bad that you could not pull yourself free. Then you needed help from your Grunt buddy to you get free because it's pretty hard to deal with them when you're fully loaded.

Before darkness sets in, we're into the NDP site. Being on higher ground was best, but a lot of times that did not happen. The artillery (Arty) is called, our position is given, the white phosphorus round is on its way and explodes over head. Adjustments as to the best place for the rounds to hit are made by the First Lieutenant (Platoon Leader), Platoon Sergeant, the Squad Leader, or by a Forward Observer (FO), whoever was in charge of the group at the time. When the artillery is notified and the needed adjustments are made, the live rounds start coming in, breaking through the air and the jungle: Whooo! Whoomp! Boom! Whoomp Boom! Whoomp Boom! They explode on the jungle floor or in the trees all around our Night Defensive Position. Then we are ready if the gooks sneak up on us.

Soon the smell of explosives and blown up vegetation overcome the silence of the jungle floor. Everyone is getting into their positions around the Command Post (CP). We get busy clearing the ground area as much as possible, and then chopping down or cutting other vegetation or ferns to make a mat on the ground. Then we would string up our ponchos on a branch or bush over our heads to get some protection from the rain, and also collect drinking water.

When everyone is in place, the ruck sacks are undone and broken into, digging in, looking for your favorite C-rations. Once in control of that situation it's time to make your little stove, pop in your heat tab or C-4, and heat-em up. While that's happening you get your cocoa or coffee set to roll, as long as you have water. Once the monsoon season started we also received lurps, dried meals in sealed pouches.

The rotation of pulling guard in your position is chosen. Hey man! No crashing on guard tonight or changing the watch. Yeh! No crashing on guard! Crash, crashed, or crashing meant falling asleep or going to sleep. All is taken in some what of a cool stride, it's a life and death situation 24 hours everyday.

After humping through the jungle all day long you often tried to figure out "What are we doing here, besides trying to keep ourselves alive? Are we fighting for a people that want to be free or is it just politics?"

We're out here like a bunch of nomads, soaking wet from sweat and rain, slowly rotting like the dead vegetation of the jungle. Almost every day it would rain in the mountains up in I Corps. It always seemed to rain between 1600 hours and 1800 hours until the monsoon season would set in and then it poured almost continuously. No clean uniforms were available, not once a week or even once a month. When we did get clean uniforms it was a free-for-all from grab-bags on standdown, or they might have brought the resupply out to a fire base. The jungle was our home with no comforts, no roof over our heads, no home-cooked meals, or beds. There was nothing. We were the property of the government; they owned us, we were their pawns. But what we did have was the respect of each other. We treated

## Ch. 15 / Going Out on an Ambush

each other like brothers, and we enjoyed playing Spades. That card game kept us from going insane.

There were also those pesky leeches to deal with, especially in the low, wet valleys as you humped through them. The leeches would fall onto you and try to crawl inside your fatigues. We had to wrap straps around our legs, or tie boot laces crisscross up to our knees to keep the leeches from crawling up inside. They would head for the warmest part of your body, under your arms, inside your eyelids, or wherever they could get in. The best way to get them off was to burn them off with matches or a lighter, or use the bug juice we used for the mosquitoes and those little black biting flies. The cool thing to do was stretch them, tie them in a knot, and say "take that, you damn leech!" While you were crashing at night there was always the chance some damn leech would have found its way inside your fatigues and filled itself with your blood until it burst, or until you rolled over during the night and crushed it. Then you would have a big, old blood stain and another damn sore to get infected. That was when you found out that you had been wounded during the night by a leech!

There also was the possibility of meeting a big cluster of ants tucked into the vegetation, thousands of them, and if you didn't see them above you and bumped into them, it would be too late. They would be all over you and your gear. Then you would have to strip down and clean the ants off your fatigues and gear. You had all those distractions to deal with besides watching for booby traps and gooks.

First platoon is going out on ambush about 300 meters away. There is nothing worse than going out on an ambush in an area where the enemy is suspected to be, and being in a smaller element, away from the rest of Company. We were always under strength and that made it worse: the anxiety, the agony, and the fear that tonight may be the last night that you will ever see the sunset. The thought of having your body blown apart and splattered about the jungle floor was not cool, but it did happen from time to time. We knew we were not invincible.

It's time to proceed and set up our trip flares, claymore mines, and battery operated mechanical ambushes with a trip wire. We would place this stuff around our NDP site, and also where the gooks would probably come down a high speed trail or a stream bed. We might spend one to three days there and then off again, maybe two to three clicks away.

Two types of ambushes were employed, manned and mechanical. Manned was when squad size elements were sent out away from the NDP site to intercept the enemy as they moved during the night. The trip flares helped for early detection. Once the enemy made contact the fire fight began. M-16s, M-60 machine guns, and also M-79 grenade launchers were in high demand. Arty and the Cobra Gun ships were also employed. This is how the Raiders pulled ambushes in the early months of 1968. Manned ambushes were used throughout the Raiders' tour but not as often later on.

Mechanical ambush was when battery operated detonation devices were used. Trip wire was hooked to a plastic spoon handle to separate the metallic material on the firing device. The battery was hooked up to the claymore mine. Detcord and blasting caps were used in a daisy chain effect

in which the detonation device was taken out of the grenades and a blasting cap fastened to detcord was used in its place. When all this worked, it was awesome. It was like strafing ducks with shotguns while they swim on the water in a pond. There it is!

We're all set up, and as darkness sets in we could hear the famous Re-Up Bird and the Uck-You Lizard. They would start "re-up uck-you, re-up uck-you, re-up uck- you!" It was humorous because it was like asking us to re-enlist in the army! Get my drift, like I might re-enlist! By then it was so damn dark you couldn't see your hand in front of your face. Your eyes were as big as dinner plates straining to see in front of your position, wondering where Charlie was until your watch was over and you fell asleep or crashed. Hopefully no one crashed on guard and the rotation made it through the night.

The thing that I thought about on and off was what if someone started coughing and couldn't stop, because that would certainly give our position away, putting us in deep danger. That never happened though. I don't recall anyone having any problems at all. It must have been all that outstanding

## Ch. 15 / Going Out on an Ambush

moisture in the air, or else God was on our side. When you would pull last guard it would always seem like the dawn would never come, and you were doomed to darkness forever. At last it would finally happen! First light!

Ah! How great it was to be alive and in one piece for another day, or maybe the day would be so damn bad that you wished you had died. There were times you might even wish for the million-dollar wound so you would be sent back to the world, and not have to put up with another day of insanity.

Here it is another day. Everyone has finished chow. LT Baker, who is the platoon leader, has gotten the word from higher-higher to move out. He passes the word to cool George (Rob) Robinson, our third Platoon Sergeant, "gather up your gear and ruck up, it's time to move out." Cool Rob would say, "move out 2nd squad, its your turn to walk point." At that time, someone would ask him "Hey Rob, what pit are we headed for today?" Sometimes no one knew, we were often breaking a new trail, chopping through double canopy, triple canopy, or moving on a high speed trail hopefully to hook up with the rest of the Company.

Another time, we are working the AO of Firebase Los Banos and Firebase Tomahawk. We are platoon size, off in another direction working the lowlands at the bottom of the mountains. Robinson has left the field today and is going on R&R. Douglas Fisher (Manny), our other cool Platoon Sergeant, is filling in. It is January 5, 1971. We are in sector ZC 167980. Some of the village people who live close by have told us that the NVA came down the mountains at night and raided the village taking food and supplies. Another night is upon us, an ambush site is chosen, a rocky dried out stream bed coming down out of the mountains. That's where the mechanical ambush will be set up. First and second squads will NDP close by. Arty is notified as to where their position is. Third squad is to go out on a manned ambush. We are headed about 200 meters north of the NDP along the bottom of the mountain. Around 1800 hours we start to prepare our ambush site. There is a small amount of brush, not much cover at all, and nothing to hide behind. We start placing our trip flares and claymore mines around our ambush site.

A few moments later Wayne Evers approaches Bob Gervasi (Big Man), Richard Padilla, and myself with blood running down his face. I ask "what the hell happened, man?" He said, "I don't know, there's something in my eye." So Big Man, Padilla, and I look into his eye as the rest of the squad came to assist. Squad leader Giles Shilling, Stephen Kirk, Francis Schaaf, and Rodofo Aguirre were at hand. A big leech had crawled into the backside of his eye. We tilt Evers head backwards as Big Man grabs the bug juice and squirts it into his eye. The leech does not come out. The decision is made that Evers is to be escorted back to the NDP site where the third platoon medic was. They got back to our ambush site about 2000 hours.

It is almost dark. Our ponchos are strung up and clear poly is draped on the sides. All seems cool as it begins to rain. The rotation of guard is chosen and we begin to settle in for a quiet night. About 2100 hours flashlights are spotted coming down the mountains. We are still somewhat relaxed and a short time after that Boom! One huge explosion goes off as the mechanical ambush at the NDP site detonated. Firebase Los Banos and Firebase Tomahawk start firing illumination overhead. The bright flares are reflecting light off our ponchos and poly because they are wet from the falling rain. Swiftly we begin to rip everything down, staying low to the ground so we are not discovered by the enemy, because they may be running in our direction. We could hear grenades exploding and automatic small arms fire from the NDP site.

There we sat in our ambush site on full alert trying to make ourselves invisible while cursing at those damn flares as they danced in the night sky turning darkness into day as they made the rain look like falling crystals from the sky. We waited for first light to come. As the new day came, we proceeded with caution to pick up our trip flares and claymore mines. Once that was done we headed back to the NDP site to rejoin the platoon. When we got back, there was already one dead NVA soldier lying in the clearing, another is up in the rocks surrounded by thick brush. A gaf and a long rope is brought in by helicopter. The gaf was thrown and hooked into the other dead NVA soldier's body and pulled to assure the body was not booby trapped with explosives. Once it was pulled down, he was dragged next to the other one. While all this was going on, I was taking pictures of the whole scenario, which included loading the two dead NVA on the helicopter, with two rucksacks and an AK-47 rifle that had also been captured.

Later, I learned that one of the NVA soldiers had been found alive after the mechanical ambush went off. Before we got back, LT Baker had asked for a volunteer to finish him off because he was so badly torn apart there was no way to save him. Eugene Clark volunteered to finish him off and that's when some of the small arms fire took place that we had heard while we were out on our own ambush.

Delta Company used the mechanical ambushes every day, if possible, once their effectiveness was known. Delta was always super quiet in the bush. Your life depended on it. When you were busting trail it was hard to be quiet, or when you had to make an LZ to get birds in and out to get logged or extracted. Every day that we were out there we always faced that uncertainty: "Where the hell are they? Who's going to ambush first?" Sometimes the rain or something else would trip the mechanical ambush, but when it did go off it would be like, now what? If it happened at night you would sit and stare into the darkness waiting for the next move. Arty would also fire flares for your assistance. The worst was when the NVA would come at us with flashlights during the night. They hung them on a tree or bush with a long string attached. Then from a distance they could move them from side to side but be far away from the point of light. They were trying to get one of us to fire a weapon because the flash would give us away. We were told there were always three or four gooks to a flashlight. Arty had our position, and hopefully the Cobra gun ships would be available, too. The thing we had to remember was not to give our position away to the gooks.

A couple of days later, we were on our way to Firebase Brick where signs of enemy activity were starting to surface. That was a nasty area of operation to be in, not cool at all. Once again we were to be tested. No rest for the weary.

To Delta Company: Our reunions, get togethers, and friendships prove that we will always be together. There it is! Geronimo!

## Going Out on an Ambush / Ch. 15

**UNCLASSIFIED**

DEPARTMENT OF THE ARMY
Headquarters 2d Brigade, 101st Airborne Division (Airmobile)
APO San Francisco 96383

AVDG-BA-C                                                                 22 February 1971

SUBJECT: After Action Report - Mechanical Ambush (U)

Commanding General
101st Airborne Division (Airmobile)
ATTN: AVDG-GC
APO 96383

Classified By: _____ 2d Bde 101 Abn Div
Subject to General Declassification
Schedule of Executive Order 11652
Automatically downgraded at two year
Intervals - Declassified on 31 Dec 77

1. (C) The following example of a successful combat action is indicative of the results that can be obtained from a well-planned and emplaced mechanical ambush. The unit involved was the 3rd Platoon, D Company, 2nd Battalion, 501st Infantry, 101st Airborne Division (Airmobile).

  a. On 21 January, the platoon discovered an east-west, high speed trail and established the platoon night defensive position (NDP) along the trail. The 2nd Squad was deployed to a pre-selected ambush location along the trail approximately 100 meters northwest of the platoon. At 1815 hours the platoon leader and two men moved from the NDP to the ambush site and emplaced the mechanical ambush as shown in Sketch 1. The ambush consisted of 4 claymores and 2 PSID transmitters. The claymore mines were sighted so as to place personnel moving along the trail in the center of the killing zone. After emplacing the claymores, the personnel moved back to a pre-selected position and attached the claymore battery and emplaced another PSID transmitter and two trip flares on the friendly side of the ambush (Sketch 1).

  b. At approximately 0700 hours on 22 January, the mechanical ambush was detonated. The platoon leader called for artillery blocking fires and deployed the 3d Squad to the ambush location while the 2d Squad provided supporting fires. When the maneuver element reached the ambush site the unit discovered 2 NVA KIA and an AK47 from another enemy soldier. At this time the 3d Squad received small arms fire from the southeast at a range of 25 meters. The squad returned fire and killed a 3d enemy soldier who had been wounded by the mechanical ambush.

  c. A subsequent search of the ambush area revealed foot prints of 4-6 enemy soldiers and a blood trail leading to the southwest. The platoon

**UNCLASSIFIED**

Delta Raiders • 227

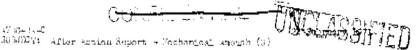

AVGA-DC-C
30 MAY 71: After Action Report - Mechanical Ambush (U)

leader began moving the platoon to the southwest in an effort to regain contact with the enemy. Another platoon from the company which was searching to the northeast found fresh bandages, morphine dispensers, and other signs of recent activity.

    d. A complete search of the ambush site revealed 3 enemy KIA, one arm, 3x AK-47 rifles, assorted clothing, a medical bag, a rucksack with additional medical supplies, and miscellaneous documents.

2. (C) When properly employed, the mechanical ambush is an effective weapon which can greatly assist the infantryman in accomplishing his mission. The most common form of mechanical ambush now in use by the 2-501 consists of three components:

    a. The explosive device - usually a series of four or more M18A1 Claymore Mines.

    b. The trip wire firing device - fabricated of easily obtainable materials and meeting the criteria of simplicity, reliability and safety (Sketch 2).

    c. The power source - most often a battery from a PRC-25 or an AN/PRC-25 radio.

3. (C) The degree of success of a mechanical ambush depends upon adherence to three basic fundamentals:

    a. Careful selection of the ambush site.

    b. Proper emplacement of the device.

    c. Rapid reaction by the ground unit upon detonation of the device.

4. (C) The site must be selected as a result of a thorough ground reconnaissance by the emplacing unit. The 3d Platoon of Company D was careful to select an ambush site far enough from their NDP to prevent detection of the NDP by the enemy prior to triggering the ambush. In addition, the platoon leader chose a site that tended to canalize the enemy's approach to the ambush site and his subsequent routes of withdrawal (Sketch 1).

5. (C) Once the ambush site has been selected the next step is the proper emplacement of the mechanical ambush. The claymores should be carefully aimed and positioned to effectively cover the entire killing zone. Special precaution should be taken to insure that the trip wire is firmly anchored. The trigger device should be pre-tested to insure that it will function properly and the power source must be located far enough from the claymores to preclude injury to friendly troops in the event of an accidental detonation.

2

AVDD-JA-C  22 February 1971
SUBJECT: After Action Report - Mechanical Ambush (U)

All components of the mechanical ambush should be camouflaged to prevent detection by the enemy. As an additional safety factor, trip flares should be employed on the friendly side of the ambush site to warn friendly personnel who might move into the ambush area.

6. (C) Upon detonation of the ambush, the friendly element must react immediately to fully exploit the effectiveness of the claymore firepower. Preplanned blocking fires, to include M-79's, mortars and artillery, should be employed to prevent enemy withdrawal and evacuation of personnel and equipment from the killing zone. Friendly elements must immediately sweep the ambush area in search of enemy dead, weapons, documents and equipment. All personnel must be alerted for wounded enemy soldiers and make every effort to capture these individuals as prisoners.

FOR THE COMMANDER:

2 Incl
as

ROBERT A. PRIEST
CPT, Infantry
Adjutant

Editors note: Delta Company began relying more heavily on mechanical ambushes during July, 1970 and our stay on Hill 805. We learned just how effective they could be there. They would definitely get your attention better than just using a trip flare, and slow the enemy down in the process.

## Ch. 15 / Going Out on an Ambush

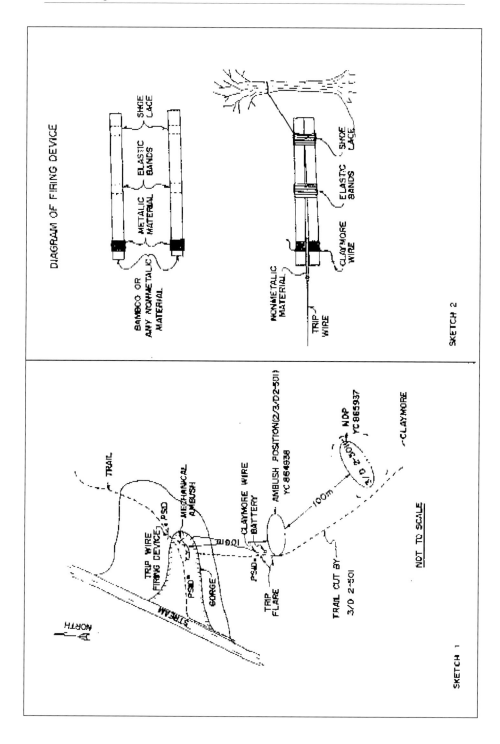

# 16.
# Chronology
## October 31, 1968 – May 31, 1970

**Jan. 5, 1971**
1855H (20167980 - 7 KM E of FB Tomahawk): 3/D observed their mechanical ambush detonate 80m to the south of their position. A search under arty illumination revealed 2 NVA KIA, 1 AK-47, and 2 rucksacks. The NVA KIAs were wearing green uniforms and rucksacks. The enemy was moving north-south. The weapon was in good condition. A further search of the area was conducted at 060700H. Results: 2 NVA KIA, 1 IWC.

**Jan. 8, 1971**
The 2-501 OP moved to FB Brick (replacing the 3/505).
Co. D moved by air from 201499 to FB Brick and assumed firebase security.

**Jan. 11, 1971**
0615H (YC835995 - near FB Brick): Co. D observed their mechanical ambush detonate 75m to the front of their position. A search of the area was made with negative results.

**Jan. 14, 1971**
1338H Co. D CP and 1/D CA'd from FB Brick to YD821004, 2/D CA'd from FB Brick to YD820014, and 3/D CA'd from FB Brick to YD810005 (complete at 1438H).

**Jan. 20, 1971**
1330H (YC865923 - 4 KM NW of FB Pistol): Co. D discovered numerous 2' wide trails oriented north-south. There were indications of enemy activity in the area within the last 3 days.
1620H (YC868915 - 4 KM NW of FB Pistol): 2/D discovered and destroyed 1 bunker (10'x12'x6' with 1' overhead cover). In the same area the platoon also discovered 5-7 sets of footprints on numerous 2' wide trails oriented northeast-southwest. There were indications of enemy activity within the last 6-12 hours.

## Jan. 22, 1971

**0708H** (YC864940 - 4 KM S of FB Rifle): 3/D observed their mechanical ambush detonate 600m to the north of their position. While searching the area the platoon received small arms fire from 4-6 enemy 200m to the west of their position. The element returned organic weapons fire and the enemy withdrew to the west. A Pink Team was employed and a search of the area revealed 3 NVA KIA, 3 AK-47s, and 2 rucksacks containing miscellaneous documents. Results: 3 NVA KIA, 3 IWO, documents evacuated

## Jan. 23, 1971

**0105** (Y0867933 - 5 KM NW of FB Pistol): 3/D employed arty and engaged a suspected enemy movement 75m to the north of their position. A search of the area was conducted with negative results.

**1800H** (YC863927 - 6 KM S of FB Rifle): 1/D discovered a 2' wide trail oriented northeast-southwest with footprints of an unknown number of individuals moving southwest. There were indications of enemy activity within the last 24 hours.

## Jan. 24, 1971

**1500H** (YC870924 - 5 KM S of FB Rifle): 3/D discovered 2-4 sets of sandal prints located on a 1' wide trail oriented east-west. There were indications of enemy activity within the last 2-4 hours.

## Jan. 25, 1971

**1500H** (YC844923 - 7 KM S of FB Brick): 1/D discovered a trail watchers position, a sleeping position (5'x8'x2' ), empty C-rations and a rice bag next to a 2' wide trail oriented east-west. 50m to the west of this position was a blood trail oriented east. There were indications of enemy activity within the last 2 days.

## Jan. 26, 1971

**1150H** (YC841921 - 8 KM S of FB Brick): 2/D discovered a grave containing 1 body estimated KBA 1 day earlier. There were indications of enemy activity within the last 24- 48 hours. Results: 1 NVA KIA.

## Jan. 28, 1971

**1317H** (YC834914 - 6 KM W of FB Pistol): 2/D received small arms fire from 5-7 enemy 15m to the southwest of their position. The platoon returned organic weapons fire and the enemy withdrew to the southwest. A Pink

Team was employed and a search of the area was made with negative results. Results: 1 US WIA (E).

### Jan. 29, 1971
**1037H** (YC823906 - 9 KM NE of FB Nuts): 3/D employing organic weapons fire engaged 3 enemy 35m to the southwest of their position. The enemy did not return fire but withdrew to the southwest. A search of the area was conducted with negative results.

**1430H** (YC826904 - 9 KM NE of FB Nuts): Co. D discovered 4 bunkers (l0'x20'x6') located 35m to the west of a 5' wide trail oriented northeast-southwest. There were indications of enemy activity within the last 4-6 months. Results: destroyed.

### Feb. 1, 1971
M.G. Thomas M. Tarpley succeeded M.G. John J. Hennessey as commander of the 101st Abn. Div.

**1130H** (YC825906 - 7 KM W of FB Pistol): Co. D received 2 RPG rounds from an unknown size enemy force 200m to the south of their position, resulting in 3 WIAs. Arty was employed. While searching the area at 1328H the element received small arms fire from an unknown size enemy force 35m to the northeast of their position, resulting in 1 WIA. The Company returned organic weapons fire and arty was again employed. A search of the area revealed several B-40 casings and signs that the enemy had fled to the southeast. Results: 4 US WIA (E to 85th Evac), enemy casualties unknown.

### Feb. 5, 1971
Co. D at FB Brick providing firebase security.

### Feb. 7, 1971
Co. D moved by air to FB Brick from field location.

### Feb. 9, 1971
**1316H** Co. D moved by air from FB Brick to Phu Bai to join BN for refresher training (closed at 1400H).

**1400H** The 2-501 at Phu Bai assumes mission as the Division Reaction Force.

### Feb. 10, 1971
**0835H** Co. D moved by CH-47 to Eagle Beach for standdown (complete at 0900H).

## Feb. 11, 1971
**0837H** Co. D moved by air from Eagle Beach to Phu Bai (complete at 1045H).

## Feb. 12-17, 1971
Co. D received refresher training at Phu Bai.

## Feb. 18, 1971
The 2-501 moved by air from Phu Bai to YD911046 for assembly in preparation for future operations. Co. D secured the north section of the BN assembly area.

## Feb. 22, 1971
**1326H** (YC951936 - 3 KM S of FB Boise): 3/D discovered 2-3 sets of footprints and a campfire site on a 2' wide trail oriented north-south. There were indications of enemy activity within the last 24 hours.

## Feb. 25, 1971
The 2-501 CP located at FB Bastogne (relieving 1-327). The Battalion passed to OPCON of 1st BDE at 1200H.
**0742H** Co. D moved by truck from YD914050 to FB Bastogne, complete at 0925H. Co. D later CA'd to YD5610 and YD5609 to conduct search and attack operations.

## Feb. 26, 1971
**2147H** (YD568107 - 5 KM SE of FB ZuLu): 4/D observed lights 300m to the northwest of their position. Artillery was employed and the lights went out.

## Feb. 27, 1971
**0955H** (YD559106 - 4.5 KM SE of FB Zulu): 4/D discovered a 1/5' wide trail oriented northwest-southeast, used by an unknown number of enemy. There were indications of enemy activity within the last 30 minutes.
**1000H** (YD559107 - 4.5 KM SE of FB Zulu): 4/D discovered 7 bunkers

(8'x12'x4' with 6" overhead cover), 20 bunkers (6'x8'x4') and 2 blood trails. All but 8 bunkers were under construction. There were indications of enemy activity within the last 24-48 hours. Results: bunkers destroyed.

**1605H** (YDSS61OS - 4.5 KM SE of FB Zulu): 4/D discovered 5 huts (20'x30'x6') containing several morphine bottles, bunks, empty pill bottles, gauze with blood on it, a fishtrap and commo wire. There was also a small stream in the area. There were indications of enemy activity in the area within the last 24 hours. Results: medicine evacuated.

**1950H** (YD5561D5 - 4.5 KM SE of FB Zulu): 4/D observed suspected enemy movement all around their position. A Nighthawk and flareship were employed. At 2040H the element observed 6 lights 15m west of their position and engaged the area with fragmentation grenades and claymore mines. A search of the area was conducted at 0700 the next morning with negative results.

## Feb. 28, 1971

**0400H** (YD567110 - 4.5 KM SE of FB ZuLu): 3/D received 1 Chicom grenade from an unknown size enemy force 15m to the north of their position. The platoon returned organic weapons fire and the enemy withdrew in an unknown direction. A search of the area was conducted at 0700 with negative results. Results: 2 US WIA (E).

## March 2, 1971

**0856H** Co. D CO informed by 2-501 XC that he has to come in for the hearing on Bennet's court martial.

**1016H** (YD557106): 3/D found fresh grave containing 1 NVA KIA, killed an estimated two days prior, may have been a KIA from action in 4/D's area the night of Feb. 27-28. The body was missing left arm and appeared to have been hit by grenades or a claymore mine. Results: 1 NVA KIA.

## March 3, 1971

**1000H** (YD554096): 2/D spotted 5 NVA in the open about 400m south of their location, moving toward the west. The enemy wore green uniforms, helmets, and 2 had rucksacks. Arty was employed as a blocking force and a Pink Team was called in to assist. At 1300H 1/A and 3/A passed OPCON to Co. D as they moved into blocking positions for Co. D in an effort to intercept the 5 NVA spotted earlier. At 1950H (YD558098) 2/D observed flashlights 500m east of their position, Arty was employed on the suspected location. At 2038H Co. D reported flashlights still moving towards their location approximately 300m from the east moving west. At 2145H the Company reported the lights had gone out.

## March 4, 1971

**1200H** In checking the area where lights had been spotted the previous night, 2/D found 1 hole (10' in diameter & 4' deep), 6 bunkers approximately 2 weeks old, and a 3 foot wide trail running north-south used approximately 1 week prior. The area had been previously used by the 1st BDE of the 1st Cav. Div.

**1236H** CPT Roger L. Ebert (Co. D CO) requested a bird for 1 man to go on R&R and 1 man for medical reasons; he also requested Kaopectate for some of his people who have diarrhea.

**1948H** 1/D observed 2 flashlights 200m northwest of their location.

## March 5, 1971

**1700H** (YD561095): 2/D found 2 VC claymore mines placed in the ground with blasting caps ready to blow. The mines consisted of 15 lbs. of TNT each, one had a wire and blasting cap with no firing device, and the other was buried about 1' underground with a pressure type firing device. The mines, which were destroyed in place, were believed to have been at the location for approximately 1 month.

**1710H** 2/D and 3/D each received scout dog teams, and 1 scout dog team was extracted from 3/D.

## March 6, 1971

**1730H** (Y0568095): 4/D found a 3 foot wide trail, 24 hours old, oriented northwest to southeast. Footprints revealed 1 pack with possible rucksack had traveled the trail about 24 hours prior. The trail was not hardpacked and was not visible from the air because of thick vegetation.

## March 7, 1971

**0730H** (YD567099): 1/D found an AK-47 sticking in mud and rocks by a small stream. It appeared to have been there for a long time but was still operational. There were no signs of recent enemy activity. The weapon was evacuated.

## March 13, 1971

**1224H** 2/D and 3/D moved by air from YD587097 to FB Bastogne, closing at 1238H.

**1239H** 1/D and 4/D moved by air from YD585085 to FB Bastogne, closing at 1252H.

## March 18, 1971
**1213H** Co. D (- 3/D & 4/D) CA'd from FB Bastogne to YD564132, closing at 1233H.

**1236H** 3/D and 4/D CA'd from FB Bastogne to YD564132, closing at 1258H.

## March 29, 1971
**1055H** (YD541105): 1/D discovered a 4-month old cache covered with plastic containing 10 60mm or 61mm mortar rounds, 25 AK-47 rounds, some of the caps were off the rounds. There were no signs of recent enemy activity.

## April 1, 1971
**1221H** 1/D moved by air from YD540117 to FB Bastogne (complete at 1236H). At 1233H Co. D CP and 2/D moved by air from YD565096 to FB Bastogne (complete at 1248H). At 1515H 3/D and 4/D moved by air from YD554099 to FB Bastogne (complete at 1530H).

## April 2-6, 1971
Co. D responsible for security of FB Bastogne, taking over from Co. E, 2-501.

## April 6, 1971
**1419H** Co. D CP and 2/D CA'd from FB Bastogne to YD577077 (complete at 1428H). At 1407H 1/D CA'd from FB Bastogne to YD569108 (complete at 142DH). At 1432H 3/D and 4/D CA'd from FB Bastogne to YD578093 (complete at 1444H).

## April 11, 1971
**1200H** The 2-501 became OPCON to 2nd BDE.

## April 14, 1971
**1600H** (YD582025 - 4.5 KM E of FB Blaze): Co. D discovered a 3 foot wide trail oriented north-south. There were indications of enemy activity within the last 48 hours.

## April 15, 1971

**1305H** (YD582020 - Nam Hoa): 2/D and 3/D observed enemy movement at YD5SDD18, 250m from their position. Arty was employed on the enemy position. At 1325H an OH-6A received 1 RPG round from the same enemy element resulting in negative hits or casualties. Additional artillery fire and an airstrike were employed and a visual reconnaissance of the area had negative results.

**1848H** (YD583013 - 4 KM SE of FB Veghel): While enroute to a LZ where Co. A had contact on April 13, Co. D received RPG rounds and small arms fire from an unknown size enemy force in a tunnel complex 300m south of their position. The element returned organic weapons fire and then received heavy small arms fire, RPG rounds, and 60mm mortar rounds from an estimated reinforced NVA company surrounding their position. Artillery, ARA, a Nighthawk, flareships, a Shadow, FAC and a Basketball were employed to assist Delta Company.

Ground contact was broken at 2025H, with 4 US KIA, 2 US MIA, and 10 serious US WIA reported at that time. Urgent medevacs were requested with the first medevac completed to 85th Evac at 2042H and the second medevac completed at 2050H. The medevac aircraft received RPG rounds and small arms fire, and there still remained 8 wounded men in urgent need of extraction. The POL point at FB Birmingham was urgently opened up so that all aircraft involved in the support of Co. D could be refueled. At 2130H additional flareships were requested and additional gunships placed on standby, as the Division TOC was complaining that the emergency resupply for artillery illumination was not passed through their artillery channels.

At 2153H another medevac was completed, making a total of 3 US WIA evacuated to 85th Evac. The medevac aircraft received an unknown number of hits and small arms fire and mortar fire, with the fire appearing to come from all directions. At 2223H the fourth medevac aircraft (Dust-off 93) received an unknown number of small arms fire hits while making an extraction. 1 crew member received a minor wound in the leg and the medevac was forced to abort the extraction and return to home station. At 2243H the fifth attempted medevac (Dust-off 94) reported taking 10-12 hits by enemy fire. With its fuel gauge reading zero and internal radio problems the aircraft aborted its mission and returned to home base. At 2312H LTC Michael Boos (2-501 CO) reported that there would be no more medevacs attempted until daylight the next morning. At this time the Battalion TOC reported there remained 5 US WIA in need of a medevac and 10 US WIA that were "not serious".

## April 16, 1971

The medevac aircraft for Co. D were reported on station at 0614H and 0632H. At 0655H the first medevac attempt to Delta Company (Dustoff 92) received numerous hits of 12.7mm machine gun fire and the aircraft was forced to abort mission and return to FB Bastogne to check the damage. The ARA with the medevac engaged the enemy element and also received heavy machine gun fire. At 0710H Co. D moved east with patients on litters. At 0750H the Company received small arms fire from 360 degrees with negative casualties. The Company returned organic weapons fire. At this time the Company reports there remain 8 WIAs to be evacuated from previous contact. The Delta Company CO also reported it has enemy to their front and rear and in between them and 3rd Platoon. The BN CO advised the Company to "reduce enemy and move to the east. The Company continued to receive ARA and TAC AIR support.

At 0830H Dustoff 92 went back in and completed a medevac with 2 WIAs to 85th Evac, another dustoff to 85th Evac with 2 WIAs was completed at 0933H, and a third dustoff (Dustoff 90) was completed to 85th Evac with 3 WIAs at 0945H. Upon departure of the last medevac the Company again received heavy small arms and RPG fire, and an unknown number of mortar rounds at 1002H, resulting in an additional 3 US WIA (1 critical). An urgent medevac was requested. At 1016H a dustoff (Dustoff 92) was completed to FB Bastogne with 2 WIAs (1 US DOA at Bastogne), later taken to 85th Evac. Another dustoff (Dustoff 90) was completed at 1026H with 3 WIAs to 85th Evac, completing the extraction of all serious Co. D wounded.

At 0847H battalion requested an aircraft with a hoist for extraction of 5 Co. D KIAs, but the request was turned down because all available aircraft were working for the 2-501 extracting WIAs. Total casualties for Co. D for the April 15-16 contact: 14 US WIA (E), 6 US KIA (Ronald Eugene Bales, Rex Martin Daniels, Robert Charles Hein, Terry Willard Greene, Charles Dennis McGinnes, and William James Ward,. 2 US MIA (later changed to KIA: Paul McKenzie and Jerry Sheldon Stearns). The bodies of Paul McKenzie and Jerry Stearns were not recovered from the field until May 12 (along with 1 body from Co. A).

At 1544H an Engineer Team (0/326) repelled to YD581021 to cut a LZ for the extraction of Co. D. At 1645H the Company was moved by air from that location to FB Birmingham (complete at 1728H), and then moved again by air from FB Birmingham to Phu Bai.

The April 15-16 contact involving Delta Company was one of the last significant engagements involving U.S. ground troops in Vietnam.

## April 18, 1971
**1951H** (YD607061 - 3.5 KM SW of FB Bastogne): 3/D observed 1 light 1000m northwest of their position. Mortars were employed and the light went out. A search of the area was made the next morning with negative results.

## April 20, 1971
**0015H** (YD614057 - 3 KM SW of OP Checkmate): 3/D observed their mechanical ambush detonate 50m northwest of their position. A search of the area without illumination and a further search at first light revealed negative results.

## April 23, 1971
**1101H** Co. D moved by air from YD623050 to FB Bastogne (complete at 1629H) and assumed security of the firebase.

## April 28, 1971
**1010H** Co. D moved by vehicle from FB Bastogne to YD570053 to conduct screening operations and night ambushes in the AD (complete at 1032H).

## April 29, 1971
**1913H** (YD566044 - 2 KM E of FB Veghel): 1/2/D observed 3-5 enemy 1200m west of their position moving towards a light 200m west of the enemy position. The enemy wore khaki uniforms. Arty was employed and check of the area was made at first light with negative results.

**1943H** (YD566044 - 2 KM E of FB Veghel ): 1/2/D observed 8 lights 2200m southeast of their position. Arty was employed and the lights went out. At 1952H the element observed 4 lights 3100m south of their position. Arty was employed and the lights went out. At 1956H the element observed 5 trucks 2000m southwest of their position on Route 547, with 100m between vehicles and with lights going off and on, making it difficult to adjust arty. The trucks appeared to moving toward Veghel. Arty was fired into the area and at 2021H 2/D observed a large secondary explosion.

**2300H** (YD576D43 - 2.5 KM NE of FB Veghel): 3/D observed a light 1000m northwest of their position. Arty was employed and the light went out. A search of the area was made at first light with negative results.

## April 30, 1971
**0110H** (YD576043 - 2.5 KM NE of FB Veghel): 3/D observed a light 500m north of their position. Arty was employed and the light went out. A search of the area at first light was negative.

**0900H** (YDSS9D3S): A 2/D patrol reported movement 250m to the northwest and south of their position. The patrol pulled back to the 2/D NDP site (YD567044) so Arty could be employed on the area. A pink team was also requested.

**1945H** (YD562041 ): Co. D CP and 2/D observed 8-10 constant lights 1100m southwest of their position in the vicinity of YDSSSO2S. Arty was employed on the area and lights went out at 2106H.

## May 1, 1971
**2030H** (YD582037): 3/D observed 8-10 red lights 2-3 klicks northeast of their position moving northeast towards Bastogne. 1 of the lights was bright and flashing on and off. 1/D at YD567058 and 2/D at YD569D41 also observed 4 lights 2-3 klicks from their positions moving northeast towards Bastogne. 3/D reported the lights appear to be in long line spread apart in small groups of lights, west or southwest of Bastogne. Arty was employed on suspected location.

## May 5, 1971
**1730H** (YD577942 - Nam Hoa): 1/2/D moving toward a former log site received 4-5 rounds of small arms fire from 1 enemy 35m southeast of their location. The element employed organic weapons fire and arty and the enemy fled to the southeast. A search of the area was made with negative results.

## May 7, 1971
**0930H** Co. D moved by air from YD568053 to FB Birmingham, complete at 1042H. At 1029H Co. D moved by air from FB Birmingham to Phu Bai, complete at 1259H.

The 2-501 (relieved by the 1-327) moved from the Bastogne AO to Phu Bai for standdown and refresher training.

## May 8, 1971
**1416H** Co. D moved by CH-47 from Phu Bai (Liftmaster Pad) to Eagle Beach for standdown (complete. at 1430H).

**May 10, 1971**
1255H Co. D moved by CH-47 from Eagle Beach to Phu Bai (complete at 1400H).

**May 11-14, 1971**
The 2-501 (including Co. D) conducted refresher training at Phu Bai.

**May 12, 1971**
LTC Kenneth C. Leuer succeeded LTC Michael A. Boos as commander of the 2-501.
The BDE reported locating 3 US bodies and requested the 2-501 to confirm if they were members of their battalion. The 2-501 confirmed that 2 of the men, Jerry S. Stearns and Paul McKenzie, were men of Co. D killed on April 15, and 1 man, John Wentworth, was with Co. A, killed on April 13.

**May 14, 1971**
2-501 CP at FB Tomahawk (relieving the 1-501).

**May 15, 1971**
Co. D moved by air to FB Tomahawk, assuming security of the firebase. Squad size elements conducted night ambushes near Nuoc Ngot with 155 RF personnel.

**May 16, 1971**
2000H (FB Tomahawk): Co. D observed 3-4 lights moving north 3000m from the firebase in the vicinity of ZC090990. At 2005H the Company believed the lights were from the Village.

**May 17, 1971**
0050H (ZD118014 - FB Tomahawk): Co. D bunkerline personnel heard cans rattling tin the wire at 30m from their position on the southwest portion of the perimeter. Illumination was employed, the noise ceased and a first light check of the area was made with negative results.
0750H (20083986 - Phu Loc): 2/D discovered a 2'-3' wide north-south oriented trail with 2 sets of southerly oriented footprints. There was evidence of enemy activity within the past 6-12 hours.

## May 21, 1971

2031H (FB Tomahawk): The Co. D FO observed 2 lights 500m northeast of the firebase in the area of ZC115018, moving west toward Phu Loc. Phu Loc gave negative clearance to fire, and at 2100H the lights went out.

## May 22, 1971

Co. D provided security for FB Tomahawk and continued night ambushes with 191 RF Co.

## May 23, 1971

Co. D (- 2/D) CA'd from FB Tomahawk to YC953988 to conduct search and attack operations in AO with 1/1-54 ARVN. 2/D passed OPCON to BN HQ to conduct night ambush with 191 RF Co.

## May 24, 1971

1158H (YD939001): Co. D CP and 3/D found a fish net 3' in diameter along the side of a stream oriented east-west. The net was estimated to be 1-2 months old and there were no signs of recent activity in the area. Results: net destroyed.

## May 26, 1971

0600H Co. D (- 2/D) passed to the OPCON of 1-502.

2/D moved by air from FB Tomahawk to YC953997.

## May 28, 1971

0510H (YD942001 ): 2/D observed 3 lights moving southwest at 600m south-southwest of their position. Communications between 155mm Btry and 155mm BN FDC was inoperative at this time and firing data could not be checked, therefore arty could not be employed.

1010H (YD943001): 2/D discovered blood on a 1'-2' wide north-south oriented trail. The last activity estimated to have been 2-3 days.

1103H Co. D requested a medevac for a Kit Carson Scout who slipped and hit a rock, cut his lip and was bleeding profusely; medevac completed at 1145H.

## May 30, 1971
Co. D continued OPCON to 1-502 and continued search and attack operations in the AC with 3/1-54 ARVN.

## June 1, 1971
**1117H** (YD941012): 3/D had a man detonate a boobytrapped RPG round with a trip wire devise, located on a LZ. Results: 1 US KIA (Robert Dale McKinney) and 1 US WIA (E).

**1120H** (YD942013): 1/D discovered a boobytrap composed of one concussion type grenade with a trip wire device. The boobytrap was employed on a 2' wide trail oriented north-south. The devise failed to detonate when accidentally stepped on by a member of the element. There were no signs of recent enemy activity. Results: boobytrap destroyed.

## June 13, 1971
Co. D provided security for FB Tomahawk and conducted night ambushes in the vicinity.

## June 10, 1971
**2355H** (ZD11SO1S - FB Tomahawk): Co. D personnel occupying a bunker on the west side of FB Tomahawk detected movement to their front and employed illumination with negative results.

## June 11, 1971
**0040H** (ZD118015 - FB Tomahawk): Co. D security element observed through a Starlight scope 1 enemy carrying a package approximately 25m to their front. DTs were fired, hand grenades were employed and a check of the area revealed negative results.

**0515H** (ZD11SD1S - FB Tomahawk): A sensor was activated on the west side of the firebase perimeter and the area was engaged with M-79 fire by Co. D personnel. A first light check of the area was made with negative results.

## June 13, 1971
Co. D (- 3/D) CA'd from FB Tomahawk to AT797976 to conduct search and attack operations. 3/D moved by vehicle from FB Tomahawk to ZD015025 to provide security for arty (C/1-321).

## June 16, 1971
3/D CA'd from ZD015025 to ZC203983.

## June 21, 1971

Co. D (-2/D): continued search and attack operation with 153 RF Platoon in the area of AU7900. 2/D at Phu Bai for refitting.

## June 22, 1971

Co. D (- 2/D): continued search and attack operation with 153 RF Platoon at ATSD1991. 1/D moved by air from AT813988 to Phu Bai for refitting and 2/D moved by air from Phu Bai to rejoin the Company.

## June 23, 1971

**1735H** (AT805986): 3/D discovered 21 fighting positions (3'x3'x2') with no overhead cover. The area was estimated to be 3-4 months old and there were negative signs of recent activity. Results: positions destroyed.

## June 25, 1971

Co. D (- 3/D) located at AT801991. 3/D at Phu, Bai for refitting.

**0958H** (AT810984): A member of 2/D detonated a boobytrap composed of an unknown amount of C-4 and rocks contained by a plastic bag and trip wire devise. The boobytrap was employed on a 1.5' wide trail oriented north-south. The trail was estimated to be 1-3 months old and there were no signs of recent activity. Results: 1 US WIA (E), 1 US WIA (M), and 1 Luc Loung 66 WIA.

**1211H** (AT810984): 2/D and 153 RF discovered a boobytrap composed of an unknown type grenade and trip wire device. The boobytrap was estimated to be 6 months old and there were no signs of recent activity. Results: boobytrap destroyed.

**1475H** (AT810984): 2/D discovered a boobytrap marker composed of 9 rocks forming a V with its base oriented to the north. There were also 2 7" sticks forming an X and placed near the rocks. The marker was 15m south of the boobytrap discovered at 1211H. The last activity in the area could not be determined.

At 1525H a second boobytrap marker was discovered 2Dm west of the area where a boobytrap detonated at D958H. The marker was composed of a Y shaped stick leaning against a large rock. The branch of the Y was oriented upward and there was a V shaped stick on top of the rock with a straight stick lying diagonally across it.

**1800H** (AT815986): While firing prep fires tin the above grid, the Arty FO for Co. D observed 12 unknown type of secondary explosions.

## June 26, 1971
3/D moved by air from Phu Bai to AT8D1991 to rejoin the company.

## June 27, 1971
Co. D CA'd from AT801991 to 20065941.

**0935H** (20065974): 1/D discovered a boobytrap composed of an unknown amount of black powder contained in a plastic bag, with a pressure type firing device. The boobytrap was employed near an old LZ, age and last activity could not be determined. Results: destroyed.

**1330H** (ZC054961): 3/D discovered 3 trail markers spaced 50m apart on a 1.5' wide trail oriented east-west. The markers were made of 10". long Y shaped sticks and there were 15" long sticks placed in the branch of the Y oriented to the west. The markers were estimated to be one week old, and the last activity within one week.

**1415H** (20053962): 3/D discovered a trail marker on a 1.5' wide trail oriented east-west. The marker was made 5" long sticks arranged to form an H. The marker was estimated to be 1 week old and the last activity within one week. The element also discovered a trail marker made of 3 5" long sticks arranged to form an L. The bottom stick in the L was oriented to the west.

**1445H** (ZC051962): 3/D discovered 2 trail markers spaced 50m apart on a 1.5' wide trail oriented east-west. The markers were made of 10' long Y shaped sticks with a 15" long stick placed in the branch of the Y and oriented to the west. The markers were estimated to be 1 week old.

**1520H** (20050964): 3/D discovered 2 fighting positions (2'x2'x3'), both of which had overhead cover. The positions were estimated to be 1 month old and there were no signs of recent activity. Results: positions destroyed.

## June 28, 1971

**1055H** (2C052963): 3/D discovered a trail marker made of 2 8" sticks arranged to form a Y. The marker was in the center of the trail and the base of the V was oriented to the northwest. The last area activity was estimated to be about 48 hours.

**1335H** (20049965): 2/D discovered a 1' wide northeast-southwest oriented trail which was 50m in length and estimated to be approximately 12 hours old. There were indications that the trail had been recently used by 2 individuals moving northeast. At the northeast end of the trail was a trail marker made of 3 unknown type of small arms rounds which had been arranged to form a triangle with 1 point oriented to the southwest.

**1710H** (ZC064974): 1/D discovered a boobytrap composed of a US-type grenade and a pressure type firing device. The boobytrap was located on a 2' wide trail oriented northeast-southwest. The boobytrap was estimated to be about 6 months old and there were no signs of recent activity. Results: boobytrap extracted by EQO team which was on location at the time of discovery.

## June 30, 1971

**0930H** (ZC045943): 2/D discovered 3 trail markers spaced 30m apart on a 2' wide trail oriented east-west. 1 marker was made of an 18' vine which had a knot and a loop midway. A second marker was made of 2 18" sticks arranged to form an L and 1 12" stick standing upright at the bottom of the L. The bottom of the L was oriented to the west. The third marker was made of 2 18" sticks arranged to form an X and a 9" stick which had been placed on the west side of the X and oriented east-west. All markers had been placed in the center of the trail. The last activity in the area estimated to have been about 72 hours.

## July 1, 1971

**0920H** (20044975): 3/D discovered an old 2 foot wide trail, running north-south along a ridgeline. The trail was not hardpacked and was not visible from the air due to thick vegetation. No signs of recent enemy activity. The element found a trail marker on the trail consisting of 2 parallel 18" long sticks pointing north-south. 20m north of the marker the platoon found a detour trail also going north around some fallen logs and back onto original trail. Trail was 3 foot wide, cut in last 1-2 hours with negative footprints.

**1510H** (20044977): 3/D discovered a 3 foot wide trail running north-south along a ridgeline. The trail, estimated to be about 1 month old, is not hardpacked and is not visible from the air due to thick vegetation. The trail turned to the east at ZC044957. The trail had footprints of undetermined number of personnel moving south. The depth of the footprints, estimated to be about 3 days old, indicated the personnel were carrying heavy loads.

At 1528H the platoon discovered a trail marker on the trail. The marker, estimated to be about 1 week old, consisted of 2 18' sticks forming a V and 2 additional 18' sticks standing upright at the top of the V. The top of the V was pointing northwest 10m north of the marker was a vine with one knot in it. The vine was 10' long and lying in the middle of and parallel to the trail.

At 1553H (20040978) 3/D also found 1 fighting position (3'x3'x2'). The position was alongside the trail discovered earlier and did not have overhead cover. There were 4 sandbags in front of the open position. The age of the position could not be determined. At 1620H the platoon located another trail marker, consisting of 3 sticks 18" long forming an N. The marker was on the same north-south trail cited earlier.

At 2045H (2C038976) 3/D observed 3-5 lights flashing on and off, and at 2100H 2/D and 3/D reported a stationery light in the same general vicinity. Arty was employed and the lights went out.

**July 2, 1971**
1055H (ZC046978): 2/D and 3/D heard suspected enemy movement at ZC036877, 500m west of their position. Movement sounded like chopping and cutting of wood. Arty was employed and movement stopped at 1130H.

**July 4, 1971**
2015H (20041978): 2/D observed numerous stationary lights and fires 1000-1500m northwest of their position. Arty was employed on location.

**July 5, 1971**
0735H (2C044976): CP/D, 2/D, and 3/D discovered a boobytrap consisting of C-4 with pressure type firing device. Boobytrap was employed on westerly oriented 2-3 foot wide trail, 10-15m east of a landing zone. The most recent activity in the area was approximately 6 months prior. The boobytrap was destroyed.

**July 11, 1971**
1255H (2C0492): During a CA the CO of Co. D observed 1 75' long by 5-7' wide wooden bridge. The bridge appeared to be in good condition. Recent activity in the area and age of the bridge could not be determined. He suggested that a Pink Team check out the area.

## July 13, 1971
**1600H** (ZC048962): 2/D discovered and destroyed 1 two-month old bunker (3'x3'x1' with no overhead cover) along a stream. The last activity in the area was estimated to be about 2 months prior.

## July 15, 1971
**0820H** (ZC047964): 3/D discovered a 2-3' wide north-south trail which bypasses a waterfall. The trail was not hardpacked or visible from the air. Recent activity and age of the trail could not be determined.

## July 16, 1971
**0930H** (ZC043958): 2/D discovered 1 footprint on the east bank of a north-south intermittent stream. The footprint was 2-3 hours old and the direction could not be determined.

**1220H** (ZC043967): 1/D discovered an old 2-3' wide southeast-northwest trail on a ridgeline. The trail was not visible from the air due to thick vegetation. There were no footprints on the trail but recent activity was estimated to be 1 week. The platoon also discovered a trail marker consisting of a limb on a tree bent down pointing to the southeast. The limb was tied down with a vine. The marker was located on the east side of the trail and was estimated to be about 1 week old.

## July 17, 1971
**1927H** (ZC046959): CP/D and 3/D observed suspected enemy movement 700m west of their position moving to the north. Arty was employed on the location and the movement stopped at 1940H.

## July 18, 1971
**1430H** (ZC041957): 2/D found a piece of broken pottery near the edge of a north-south stream. There were no signs of recent enemy activity in the area.

## July 19, 1971
**1400H** (ZC033962): 2/D discovered and destroyed a Chicom grenade laying in an east- west stream. The grenade was very old and there were no signs of recent enemy activity.

## July 23, 1971
**1657H** Co. D requested an urgent medevac for 1 man, medevac was completed at 1745H.

## Aug. 7, 1971

**0745H** Co. D requested an urgent medevac for 1 man (Compton T. Dodson) who received fragmentation wounds in the face, medevac was completed to 95th Evac at 0826H.

## Aug. 22, 1971

Co. D moved to FB Tomahawk and assumed security for the firebase.

## Aug. 25, 1971

**1250H** 1/D point man stepped on a mine 10m east of an LZ, with negative casualties. At 1750H (2C098987) 1/D found a boobytrap marker on a 2' wide trail running north-south. The marker, attached to a 5' long stick stuck in the ground, was found south of an old NDP site. The sign, written on the back of a PRC 25 battery carton, stated in Vietnamese that there were boobytraps on trails and LZ.

## Aug. 31, 1971

The 2-501 CP moved from FB Tomahawk to FB Rifle (relieving the 1-501).

**1125H** (YD855020): 1/D found and destroyed 4 bunkers (9'x12'). One bunker had a cement top and the other three had logs for overhead cover. The bunkers had been badly burned and the age could not be determined. Rice was found in hollow trees near the bunkers and 1 pair sandals were found in one of the bunkers. Recent enemy activity estimated to be about 3 months. The platoon also found in the area 2 AK-47s, a set of human bones, pieces of a burned individual and five individual graves; all apparently killed by a flame drop since there were numerous barrels of the type used in flame drops found in the area. The AK-47s had been burned with rounds in the chamber. 200m south of this location the platoon found a northeast-southwest 18" wide trail. The hardpacked trail ran along the side of a hill and was estimated to be 3-4

months old with negative recent activity. The trail was 150m south of LZ. 2 fighting positions (4'x4'x5') were also located on the west side of the trail.

**1539H** (YD807021): 1/D found and destroyed 2 bunkers (6'x9'x5' with overhead cover) estimated to be 2 months old. The last enemy activity was estimated to be about 2 days prior. The bunkers were located on level terrain that had generally been burned off. Also found in the area was a "Y" shaped marker on a tree consisting of 2 strips of recently cut bamboo. The tree was on an east-west trail that was not visible from the air. The trail was 18" wide running along the side of a ridge.

## Sept. 2, 1971

**1045H** (YD854023): Co. D found and destroyed 4 bunkers. The Company found numerous trails in the area and there were indications that the enemy had been in the area during the previous 24 hours.

**1850H** (Y0854023): A man from 1/D detonated a "toe popper" boobytrap, receiving only minor powder burns.

## Sept. 5, 1971

**0915H** (YD851019): Co. D requested a disposal team for a located 500 lb. bomb.

**1116H** (YD852019): Co. D requested an urgent medevac for 1 man who hit a boobytrap amputating one foot, medevac completed to 85th Evac at 1142H. The boobytrap consisted of unknown quantity of C-4 with a pressure type firing device. The boobytrap, estimated to be about 6 months old, was buried in the ground on a 1.5' wide north- south trail running along a ridgeline. The man was 9th in file when he stepped on the boobytrap. Results: 1 US WIA (E: John W. Ash, 2/D).

**1341H** (YD852019): Co. D requested a medevac for a heat casualty (1Lt Terry Wayne Harter, 1st Platoon Leader), medevac completed to 85th Evac at 1410H. At 1430H 3/D requested a medevac for another heat casualty (Rudolf Beregsasi), medevac completed at 1447H.

## Sept. 6, 1971

**0550H** (YD849019): 3/D discovered a 3, wide trail running along the side of a hill, running southeast-northwest. Recent enemy activity was estimated to be about 3-4 weeks. The trail was not visible from the air due to heavy vegetation.

**0600H** (YD852019): 3/D found one shallow grave uncovered by arty, body estimated to be 2-3 months old. At YD849018 3/D also discovered a boobytrap, buried in the ground, consisting of approximately 2 lbs. of 0-

4 with a pressure type firing device. About 2' from the boobytrap was a stick (6-7' long) pointing toward the boobytrap. At the end of the stick was an uneven cut, estimated to be about 3-4 weeks old. A mine dog working with the platoon discovered the boobytrap.

**2000H** (YC878976): 3/D found a 2 trail intersection, with 18" wide trails running north- south and east-west through a swampy area. The trails were estimated to be about 6 months old with negative signs of recent enemy activity. The trails were not visible from the air due to thick vegetation. 1 old Ho Chi Minh type sandal found in the area.

### Sept. 8, 1971

**1120H** (YC884975): 1/D observed and engaged with organic weapons fire 1 enemy 150m south of their location. The enemy was stationary and was not wearing a shirt and the type of trousers could not be determined. The enemy was armed, but did not return fire and fled to the northwest. Arty and a pink team were also employed in the area. 1315H (YC879971 ): 3/D found an 18" wide trail running south along the side of a hill. The hardpacked trail could not be seen from the air due to thick vegetation. The trail was estimated to be about 5-6 months old with no signs of recent enemy activity.

### Sept. 26, 1971

**1020H** (YC878968): In what was described in the battalion journal as a minor incident, Bruce E. Warrick of 2/D was accidentally shot with an M-16 by William L. Carnahan, also of 2/D. Warrick received a M-16 wound to this lower right leg between the knee and ankle. Disciplinary action was to be taken on Carnahan.

### Sept. 28, 1971

**0201H** A 1/D ambush reported movement coming up the road toward their position (south-north).

**1120H** Co. D reports the combat loss of a M-203 (over and under) weapon.

**1605H** Co. D requested an extraction by log bird for 1 man from 2/D (Manuel E. Vaneych) who cut his hand on a piece of bamboo, extraction made at 1630H.

### Oct. 4, 1971

Co. D, along with part of HHC and other components of the 2-501, moved by air from Phu Bai to Cam Ranh Bay.

## Oct. 5, 1971
**0700H** 3/D moved by vehicle from Cam Ranh Bay to FB Kerry Lou.
**1415H** Co. D completed a medevac to 483rd Hospital for 1 man (James B. McKinney) with viral exanthema.

## Oct. 7, 1971
**1308H** Co. D requested an urgent medevac for 1 man from 3/2/D (Larry Pohlman) who fell and busted his knee open; man was extracted by log bird.

## Oct. 8, 1971
**1655H** Co. requested a medevac for 1 man from 1/1/D with infected lower extremities and 1 man from 2/1/D with a cut hand; the 2 men were extracted by log bird.

## Oct. 9, 1971
**2130H** Co. D CP and 1/D observed movement and received arty and illumination from FB Kerry Lou on BP008087.

## Oct. 10, 1971
**1931H** 1/1/D observed an estimated 2-3 enemy moving west approximately 150m south of their location. The squad observed a light, moving, going off and on. Illumination and 81mm mortars were fired on the suspected enemy location.

## Oct. 11, 1971
**0600H** 1/1/D heard 2 people in a small sampan moving south up a small inlet (BP989072) and at 0630H return and move into "large blue." Illumination was requested but clearance was not received in time.

## Oct. 12, 1971
**2100H** Co. D reported that 1 man (Beregsasi) had been struck by a Dodge pickup on the road while returning to the Company. He was taken to 6CC for examination and released in good condition.

## Oct. 14, 1971
**1237H** (BP980217): A Huey while bringing in troops from Co. D crashed and injured one of the doorgunners. The pilot said he lost control of the directional pedal and the Delta Co. CO (CPT Flavin) said that the chopper "approached too fast, the pilot tried to correct and crashed when the wind caught him."

## Oct. 15, 1971

**1330H** (BP979222): 3/3/D found 10 natural caves of various sizes. Recent enemy activity estimated to be about 2-3 weeks prior, based on 6 cans of NVA C-rations found near the entrance of the cave complex. The squad also found in the deepest cave 1 105 round without a fuse and 4 cans of US C-rations.

**1600H** (BP986220): 2/3/D found a 1 foot wide trail on a ridge running east-west, along with 6 stacks of wood 4.5' high. The trail could not been seen from the air due to thick vegetation. There were no footprints on the trail or signs of recent activity in the area. The squad could also hear 2 dogs barking 300-500m west of their position.

## Oct. 17, 1971

**1500H** (BP965242): 2/3/D found 6 foxholes (2'x2'x2') with no camouflage or overhead cover. The holes were estimated to be 6-8 months old, with no signs of recent enemy activity in the area. Also located near the foxholes was a 1 wide hardpacked trail running east-west. The trail could not be seen from the air due to heavy vegetation.

## Oct. 18, 1971

**1400H** (BP963226): 3/3/D found 12 fighting positions (4'x4') consisting of rocks piled 12- 18" high with level floors. The positions, estimated to be 2 weeks old, were located on top of a hill with natural camouflage. The squad also found in the area 1 radio antenna, 1 A type radio frame, 6 slashed rice bags, 6 C- rations, fruit and meats, and red tinfoil bands with Vietnamese writing on them.

## Oct. 19, 1971

**0920H** Co. D requested a medevac for 1 man from 3/3/D (Gilbert Goldberg) with a swollen arm (possibly cellulitis). The Company is socked in and will need a penetrator since the nearby LZ is not useable.

**1025H** 3/D sighted 4 Vietnamese moving south at BP982205. They appeared to be rummaging through an old NDP site. They did not have weapons and were wearing straw hats.

**1659H** Co. D informed by BN that they will not be able to extract the man with a swollen arm until the next morning due to bad weather.

## Oct. 20. 1971

**0703H** Co. D requested a medevac for 1 man from 3/3/D (John Begay) with a broken wrist, in addition to the man with cellulitis waiting extraction. A medevac for the 2 men was completed to 483rd AF Hospital at 0935H.

## Oct. 28, 1971
**1000H** Co. D reported that 3/3/D had been without communication with Co. D CP since the previous night. A patrol was sent to the squad and a radio was requested and received, reestablishing radio communication.

## Oct. 29, 1971
**1500H** (BP998079): 2/3/D found a 2' wide north-south oriented trail. The trail was old and hardpacked and had been used within the last 24 hours by 2 people moving south. Due to vegetation the trail could not be seen from the air. The squad also found in the area 1 bag of rice and 3 empty rice bags. The footprints were bare and deeply embedded as if they were carrying something heavy. The footprints went from the trail about 200m to the beach and back to the trail again. The battalion advised Co. D to thoroughly check the area.

## Oct. 31, 1971
**1330H** (CP034064): 3/1/D found a trail next to the ocean made out of rocks oriented east- west. The squad also found 1 105mm round with shipping plug still in it. At 1515H 3/1/D reported seeing a sampan coming into shore at CPD27062.

## Nov. 2. 1971
**0810H** Co. D reported that they will not need an EOD team to blow a 105 round found by 3/1/D, the squad would back haul the plugged round.

## Nov. 4, 1971
**1520H** Co. D requested their 3rd Platoon leader be brought to Co. D CP's location to take over the Company since the Co. CO has a high temperature and needs to be extracted.

## Nov. 8, 1971
**1220H** (BP943176): 1/2/D found 1 bunker (2.5'x4'x4' with overhead cover and camouflage). The age of the bunker could not be determined. There were no signs of recent enemy activity in the area.
**2005H** A mechanical ambush went off at Co. D's location, but a check of the area under illumination was negative.

## Nov. 9, 1971
**1000H** (BP939167): 2/2/D found a 1' wide trail oriented north-south, estimated to be about 1 day old, that was used by an unknown number of people moving south-north. The trail, located in thick vegetation, was

not hardpacked. At 1041H the squad at BP941169 spotted 1 an unarmed individual 50m north of their position.

## Nov. 10, 1971

**074QH** (CP124205): 3/3/D sighted a fishing boat 1000m to the southeast of their position. The boat wasn't fishing but sailing around the island: the 26th CG checked it out.

**1200H** (CP019D94): A man from 2/1/D cut himself with a machete and was extracted by log bird.

**1250H** (CP041422): 1/1/D requested an urgent medevac for 1 man (Monroe Conerly) with a possible fractured leg, medevac completed to 483rd Hospital at 1335H.

**1830H** (CP112223): 1/3/D found a boobytrap consisting of a pepsi can filled with C-4 and an unknown type of firing device. The boobytrap was found above ground.

## Nov. 11, 1971

**1400H** (CP1282120) 3/3/D found a dud 81mm illumination round.

**2150H** Co. D had a mechanical ambush detonate, possibly by high wind. The area was checked under illumination with negative results.

## Nov. 12, 1971

**0730H** (BP937171 ): 1/2/D found what appeared to be a RPG round.

**1150H** 1/D reported that it was not safe to move troops due to the heavy rain and elephant grass. The platoon indicated that it would stay in location until further notice.

## Nov. 16, 1971

**0615H** (CP107144): 1/D heard what it believed to be 20 rounds of M-16 fire, 500m northeast of their NDP.

## Nov. 20, 1971

**1830H** Co. D requested a medevac for 1 man (Kenneth Pogue) with 2nd and 3rd degree burns caused by a trip flare, the medevac arrived at 1945H but the man was not extracted because the LZ didn't have sufficient lights. The medevac was completed the following morning.

**1850H** (BP966204): 2/3/D found 1 155mm round laying on the end of a LZ; EOD team disposed of the round.

The 101st ABN DIV was placed on standdown and directed to conduct a phased redeployment (over 3-5 months) of division units from Vietnam to Ft. Campbell, Kentucky, and concurrently reorganize the remainder of the division for continued operations in RVN under OPCON of the CG XXIV Corps.

## Nov. 21, 1971

**1055H** (BP980210): Co. D inquired whether there were any RFs in the area, since they had heard the shooting of M-16s throughout the night and morning. The reply from Battalion was negative. 3/3/D checked out the area and found a Vietnamese with a M-16 dressed in a green uniform, hat, and jungle boots. He appeared to be guarding 2 POL tanks, 2000m southeast of 3/3/D's location. He was walking up and down the road firing his weapon.

## Nov. 22, 1971

**0900H** (BP964205): 2/3/D found 3 foxholes 6-12 months old, with no overhead cover or natural camouflage. 1 was 2'x2'x5' and the other 2 were 3'x2'x3'. There were signs of recent enemy activity in the area. Nearby the squad also found a 1-2' wide trail running north-south. The trail, estimated to be about 1 year old, was not hardpacked or visible from the air.

**1240H** (BP965206): 2/3/D saw 1 individual 50m north of their location. The Squad followed but lost him as they searched the area.

**1710H** Co. D requested a priority medevac for 1 man (Harry Vandiver of 3/1/D) with possible malaria and a temperature of 104 degrees. The man was picked up by log bird the following morning (11/23).

**1750H** 3/3/D observed ROK troops working on a tank and firing M16s in their AO. Co. D requested that the firing stop.

## Nov. 24, 1971

**1635H** (BP993209): 3/3/D requested an urgent medevac for 1 man (Tommy D. Zinn) who cut his right wrist on bamboo, medevac completed to 483rd Evac at 1754H.

## Nov. 26, 1971

**1050H** 2/1/D found natural caves that were not used by the Vietnamese. The 1st Platoon Leader made sketches to show S-2.

**1400H** 2/1/D found and destroyed a boobytrap consisting of a 4" piece of C-4 in a tree, with an unknown type of firing device. The boobytrap was estimated to be about 1 year old.

## Nov. 27, 1971
**1030H** (BP986207): 2/1/D found a 2 wide hardpacked trail running north-south. The trail, about 1 year old with signs of activity 2 weeks prior, was in double canopy and could not be seen from the air.

## Nov. 30, 1971
**1800H** 3/1/D was sent to pull security for two stuck trucks until wreckers could be sent to get them unstuck. At 1940H 1/2/C reviewed 3/1/D of security duty for the stuck trucks.

Harry Vandiver of 3/1/D died of malaria. A memorial service was conducted at Cam Ranh Bay on December 16.

## Dec. 6, 1971
**0950H** Co. D reported that a sampan landed on the beach at BP987071, where 4 men in black clothing got out and moved southwest along the beach.

**1145H** (BP989072): 2/2/D found a 2' wide east-west trail. Evidence of 3-4 personnel moving west to east on the trail within the previous two days. The squad also located a trail marker consisting of 2 forked sticks stuck in the ground with a stick about 1 long laying the vortex of each stick.

**1600H** (BP983069): 2/2/D observed 3 men in black clothing, 1 woman and 1 child approximately 600m from their location. The Vietnamese were walking north along the beach. When the squad started down the hill, the Vietnamese fled west to the vicinity of villages at BP962073. The Co. D CO believed the people are probably fisherman from the village, but possibly could be unfriendly since they run whenever they see a G.I.

## Dec. 7, 1971
**0945H** 1/3/D pursued 2 Vietnamese sighted at CP025053, approximately 600m south of their position. The Vietnamese were carrying a large unidentified flag (4'x4') and boarded a helicopter at CP029057.

**1210H** (BP999072): 2/2/D apprehended 4 Vietnamese (1 old man, 2 young girls, and 1 young boy). They apparently were fishing as they had a net in the water and one on the ground. They were instructed by CTOC to release them since they were woodcutters.

## Dec. 8, 1971
**1730H** (BP991074): 3/2/D found a 1-3' wide trail running east to west on a ridgeline going up a hill. The trail, estimated to be 4-6 months old, was located in single to double canopy. The trail led to a natural cave (15'x6'x4'). Located outside the cave was a black box (9"x6"x2.5") in

excellent condition. The box had 2 battery poles and "52V" written on it. A pottery bowl was also located inside the cave. The box and bowl were extracted.

### Dec. 9, 1971
**0830H** (BP979067): 3/2/D saw 4 people (2 on the beach and 2 in the water) and 2/2/D was sent to pursue them. When the people saw the squad they fled to the southwest toward a village. Co. D thinks they were just woodcutters.

### Dec. 19, 1971
**0845H** (BP941161): 3/3/D reported finding a 1 foot wide trail in lowlands, estimated to be one year old. The hardpacked trail, running north to south, had a trail marker consisting of 5 rocks pointing southwest.
**1925H** (CP115237): 1/1/D spotted 2 fishing boats with one light on each boat about 200m from their position.

### Dec. 20, 1971
**1725H** (CP113243): 1/1/D sighted 6 sampans 50m off shore.

### Dec. 21, 1971
**1330H** (CP109230): 1/1/D found a hand grenade with trip wire firing device along a ridge. The boobytrap, estimated to be 2-3 years old, was hanging low to the ground. An EOD team destroyed the grenade at 1115 the following morning.
**1628H** (CP124205): 3/1/D spotted a boat with 2 people about 400m offshore.

### Dec. 22, 1971
**1015H** (CP018047): 2/3/D found a 2' wide trail estimated to be one day old. An estimated 4 people, based on footprints, had used the trail moving to the east.
**2050H** (BP921164): Co. D saw red lights signal for 3 minutes followed by a green light up a hill that signaled for 30 seconds; followed by the red light again for another 20 seconds. Co. D estimated the location of the red light to be about 2000m-6000m from their location.

### Jan. 9, 1972
**2030H** Co. D reports that Pvt 1 Frederick Johnson had wandered away from his bunker without permission, leaving his weapon and gear.

## Jan. 10, 1972

**1200H** The Co. D CO reported that 3 tripflare wires had been cut just outside the wire in the vicinity of bunkers 34 and 35.

**2135H** Co. D reported that a CS 40mm canister was fired in a bunker. Apparently the men got excited and fired one red star cluster.

## Jan. 12, 1972

**1000H** (YD782173): Co. D located a 40mm HE round and 2 20mm rounds linked together with the powder removed. The Company also found a claymore without C-4, 1 spare M-60 barrel, and 5 hand grenades (without caps); all along a trail. Also found was a trail marker consisting of 6 stones in a circle, with the 7th stone oriented east approximately 90 degrees.

## Jan. 15, 1972

**0400H** Co. D at Bunker 42 spotted movement 100-150mm from their location. They engaged the area with 40mm HE and illumination.

## Jan. 16, 1972

**1245H** 3/D reported finding 1 40" long and .5" wide bamboo stick pointing to 3 openings in the wire in front of Bunker 44. The stick was located 50-60m in front of the bunker and 1' outside the outer strand of wire. The stick was estimated to be in place about 1 day.

## Jan. 18, 1972

**2025H** 2/D heard small arms fire 1000m to the north of their position, sounding like a small fire fight.

## Jan. 19, 1972

**1530H** Co. D sent 1 man (Bennie Thompson) to the 616th medical hospital with an eye injury. The injury was due to an accident while he was on a work detail; he was hit by another man swinging a pick mallet.

## Jan. 20, 1972

**0850H** (YD852091 ): 2/D received 40mm rounds landing 300m from their NDP.

## Jan. 22, 1972

**1135H** 2/D saw one Vietnamese moving northwest along a ridgeline at YD854124. A White Team checked out the area with negative results.

## Jan. 31, 1972

**2215H** Co. D sighted 1 enemy in outer wire approximately 100m from Bunker 13. 40mm NE was fired in the vicinity and 1 round hit within 10m of the enemy, possibly wounding him. Then 30 AK-47 rounds were received from the same general area.

## Feb. 1 1972

**0910H** 1/D found the concertina wire trampled down around bunkers 8 and 10. Barefoot prints (about 48 hours old) were also found in the area.

**1135H** A 3/D RIF patrol found an AK-47 magazine and a 7.62 round.

## Feb. 12, 1972

**0708H** Co. D was released from "E" sector security at Camp Eagle and replaced by ARVN elements. Later in the day the Company, along with other elements of the 2-501 (the last US combat battalion to leave I Corps), was moved by air from Phu Bai back to Cam Ranh Bay.

The 2-501 departed Vietnam (Cam Ranh Bay) on March 1 and 2, 1972.

# 17.
# Vietnam: A Father's Story

## Erin Elizabeth Policz

*Dedicated to all the POW's and MIA's,
to my Dad, Richard C. Policz,
and all the people who fought in Vietnam.*

### Foreword

My dad was drafted into the United States Army in March of 1969 at the age of nineteen. He served in Vietnam from December of 1969 to November of 1970. This is his story.

### Contents
Foreword
1. We Want You
2. Training
3. Next Stop: Vietnam
4. In the Field
5. Baptism by Fire
6. Hill 805
7. Friends
8. Coming Home
9. Looking Back
Glossary

Ch. 17 / A Father's Story

# Chapter 1
# We Want You

In March of 1969, I was drafted into the United States Army. I had come home from work and was looking at my mail. When I opened the last envelope I read, "Greetings, we want you for military service." I had been expecting this because my draft status was I-A. Then the reality hit me. I was scared. Then I got really scared. There was a war going on in a small country called Vietnam in Southeast Asia. I knew that I would probably go there. "I'm only nineteen years old! I'm not old enough to go to war!" I thought. A lot of people don't even think we should be fighting in Vietnam. Greg went to Canada to avoid the draft. No! That's the easy way out. I wasn't brought up that way." I could never live with myself if I didn't do my duty to my country. So it was settled. I was going. Sure, I didn't want to get killed but I wouldn't be a coward either. If anyone said they weren't scared to go to Vietnam, then they were lying, maybe even to themselves. It was a confusing time for me and for the country too.

# Chapter 2
# Training

After saying goodbye to my family and friends for the second time, I was finally on my way to Fort Campbell, Kentucky, for basic training. I was glad because I just wanted to get it over with. The first time I went to the recruiting office they had sent me back home.

Basic training was like nothing I'd ever experienced before. It was still cold, so we wore heavy coats and we ran. We ran for shots. We ran for haircuts. We got up at 5:00 a.m. and ran a couple of miles before breakfast. We ran to breakfast, lunch and dinner. We did push-ups and pull-ups before every meal. There was night training, gas-mask training, learning how to fire a rifle, and throwing hand grenades. Eight weeks of this was just to get us in shape for advanced infantry training.

Advanced infantry training was twelve weeks in Fort Polk, Louisiana. Most of the things we did there was to help us to know what to expect when we got to Vietnam. In the escape and evade class they sent me out into the swamps one night. I had to get to an objective by morning. There were other soldiers there trying to capture me and put me in a POW camp where I would be tortured until I talked. I was lucky. I got to my objective without getting caught but I was wet, hot, and worried about poisonous snakes. In the rest of the jungle training, we learned about booby traps, night fighting, getting on and off helicopters, and assaulting enemy positions.

For ten weeks at Fort Benning, Georgia, I trained with the Army Rangers. Most of those guys had been to Vietnam, so they tried to teach us what they knew to keep us alive there. For me, this was the hardest part of my training because I'm afraid of heights. I learned how to repel down ropes from a high tower. I had to climb two telephone poles, one on top of the other, handwalk a wire out to the middle of a river, and drop in. I did all of this with full gear. In late September 1969 I got a thirty-day leave. After my leave, the next stop would be Vietnam. I was ready.

## Chapter 3
## Next Stop: Vietnam

My thirty-day leave had gone too fast. It was hard saying goodbye to my loved ones not knowing if I'd ever see them again. When I arrived in Fort Lewis, Washington, I was put on hold. After twenty days, on December 20, 1969, I shipped out for Vietnam. It is a lonely feeling sitting on a plane heading for a war. There were other people with me, but somehow I felt isolated. We stopped in Alaska to refuel. It was twenty degrees below zero there and we were in lightweight clothing. There were some Christmas carolers there and they gave us some hot chocolate. I thought about the people back home and wondered what they were doing. After a brief stop in Yokota, Japan, we headed for Cam Ranh Bay, Vietnam. Now I was getting scared and wondered what it would be like there. Would there be shooting or bombs exploding or what? We landed with no problem. I arrived at night and I really couldn't see much of the country so my first impression of Vietnam was the stifling heat and the smell of jet fuels. From the airfield, I rode in a bus to the replacement center where we got more shots. The bus had wire mesh on the windows to keep people from throwing hand grenades or other things in on us.

It was hard to believe there was a war going on. I had expected bombs and bullets going off all the time. What I saw was a beautiful country with white sand beaches, blue ocean, green mountains, and miles of rice paddies.

Most of the people of Vietnam are fishermen or farmers. The older people bowed to us while the small kids mobbed us for food or candy. Mostly they seemed to be quiet and very polite.

I would soon find out where the war was. After a week of training to get me used to the climate, I was flown north in a Chinook helicopter to meet my company. My company was the 101st Airborne Division in Northern I Corps. We met at Eagle Beach on the China Sea.

## Chapter 4
## In the Field

When I was first out in the field, I was just an infantry man or a "grunt" as they called us. Then I became a radio operator. I carried a radio for two different men over an eight-month period. It was my job to call and order supplies and things we needed in the field. I would have to talk the helicopter pilots into our locations so they could drop food and supplies through the trees to us. Sometimes I would have to bring in jets or helicopters for air strikes. Helicopters were our lifeline in Vietnam. They fired up an area before we went in, they dropped us into an area, they resupplied us every five to seven days, they gave us fire support during battles, they medevaced us out when we were wounded, and they flew us back to the rear. Even now, I get excited when I hear a helicopter.

I only weighed one hundred fifty pounds then, and I carried at least ninety pounds of supplies and equipment. I carried an M-16 rifle with fifteen magazines of ammunition, a colt 45 automatic pistol, four hand grenades, two smoke grenades, a poncho, a poncho liner, a seven-day supply of C-rations, and personal items like a razor, soap, and writing paper. Because I was a radio operator I also had a twenty-three pound radio, two antennas and at least two extra batteries. We carried two M-60 machine guns per squad. We had M-79 grenade launchers which looked like big shotguns and some of the pointmen carried 12 gauge shotguns. The enemy used AK 47 assault rifles, SKS Russian rifles, and Chi Com (Chinese) grenades.

Our area of operation was in Northern South Vietnam about twenty or thirty miles south of the DMZ. We worked the mountains overlooking the A Shau Valley and the Ho Chi Minh Trail. The country was green and lush and at times we had to use machetes to cut through the jungle. The mountains had plenty of rivers and streams with fresh water to drink and bathe in. Some of the hills were so steep we had to climb them on our hands and knees. We slept wherever we decided to stop for the night. I tried to find a level flat place to sleep but a few times I actually had to tie myself to a tree to keep from rolling back down the hill. I usually slept on the ground except during the monsoons, when I had an air mattress to sleep on. One morning

I woke up and saw a three to four foot earthworm under my air mattress. I thought it was a snake and it scared me half to death. All the guys laughed at me. It seemed like everything in Vietnam was big except the people.

The monsoons always started with a typhoon. There was a heavy fog and it rained in torrents. We tried to stay dry but never could and our feet always looked like prunes. One of the worst things about the monsoons was the leeches. They got all over me! Sometimes I wouldn't even know they were there until they burst from sucking so much blood.

Sometimes, during the monsoons season, the helicopters had trouble flying our supplies in to us. One time we had to go without food for a few days. A few days might not seem like a long time, but when you're walking up and down mountains carrying ninety pounds you can get mighty hungry. The monkeys were starting to look good to eat.

Another incident with monkeys occurred one night when we had set up our defensive perimeter in an old ARVN base camp. There were a lot of foxholes there for protection. After dark we always had one or two men awake pulling security. We started seeing movement to our front. We thought we were being probed or set up for an attack. We started throwing hand grenades out. We did this all night long. In the morning we searched the area and found out we had been fighting monkeys. The monkeys had been trying to get in to the old foxholes to get food from the C-ration cans which had been left behind. It wasn't funny that night but we had a good laugh the next day.

Usually our missions lasted two to three weeks. One time we were out for almost two months. Then we would come to the rear and get to eat some real food and drink real white milk.

## Chapter 5
## Baptism by Fire

January 29, 1970, on Firebase Bastogne, we got a call saying that one of our sister companies in the bush (jungle) was in trouble. We prepared to go help them. My chopper was the first one in and the landing zone was "hot." We ran off the LZ as fast as we could, found cover, and returned fire. As soon as we were all safely on the ground, the enemy had disappeared. Hit and Run — that was their way of doing things. We headed into the jungle. About fifteen minutes down the trail, we walked right into an enemy ambush. Machine guns opened up on us from right beside the trail not ten feet away from me. I carried the radio for my platoon leader, LT Rufty, and we were third and fourth in line. LT Rufty was hit and dropped to the ground. We opened up with everything we had. I called in the Cobra Gunships and they worked the area over with rockets and mini guns. The medevac chopper came in, we put LT Rufty on, and they flew him out. He died on the way to the rear. Afterwards, while searching the area, we found out that we had walked into an enemy base camp. We had killed one enemy, captured two machine guns, some AK-47 rifles, some rice, and ammunition. After it was over, I felt really sad and scared. I had become very close to LT Rufty in the short time I had known him. The NVA usually try to shoot the platoon leader and the radio man first. I had been standing right next to LT Rufty. I don't know how they missed me! That was my baptism by fire which earned me my Combat Infantry Badge.

## Chapter 6
## Hill 805

The worst week of my life started on July 12, 1970, my twenty-first birthday. The NVA had been using Hill 805 to mortar Fire Support Base Ripcord. We were to go in and take the hill from them. We combat assaulted a hill not far from 805 with no problem. Hill 805 had been bombed by B-52s the night before so there wasn't much left but a few big boulders and a few scraggly trees. Our job was to hold the hilltop. It was tough going because the hill was very steep, the temperature was one hundred five degrees, and we had on full packs with extra ammunition. We made it to the top of the hill with no enemy resistance. All we found there was a couple of bunkers with some dead bodies in them. We figured we had it made and would just kick back and enjoy ourselves, so we didn't dig our foxholes very deep. At 10:20 p.m. rocket-propelled grenades and rifle fire came in on us. The only birthday present I got was a piece of shrapnel in the arm. It was a small piece so I didn't leave the field. There were sixteen of us wounded that night and thirteen were evacuated to the rear for treatment. The next day we dug our foxholes a lot deeper.

The second night was quiet until 2.30 A.M. when the enemy hit us with everything they had. The firefight lasted about an hour. The noise was deafening with F-4 Phantom jets, artillery firing from Firebase Ripcord, aerial rocket artillery from Cobra gunships, mortars, and quad fifty caliber machine guns. All this was lit up by flares dropped from a C-130. The first platoon needed replacement because they had gotten hit the hardest on their side of the hill. Their lieutenant, Terry Palm, had gotten killed. SGT Jim Hembree, the man I carried the radio for, who was also one of my best friends, went over with some replacements. I didn't know that night that when SGT Hembree got to the other side of the hill he had gotten shot by a sniper. The next morning I walked to the center of the hill and saw some bodies covered up. I saw the black boots sticking out of the cover. All of us wore green jungle boots, but SGT Hembree liked the old army black boots. I was in total shock, I sat down on the hill and cried. I had reached an all-time low. That was the last time I cried over there. I was angry, but like most of the guys over there, I began to numb my emotions. We had a saying over there. We'd say, "It don't mean nothin'." There were many wounded and six killed that night.

The third night, we were hit again and had everything firing support for us. My buddy, SGT Schneider, was killed that night. The enemy was so close they threw a satchel charge into his foxhole. He died from the concussion. There wasn't a scratch on him.

The fourth day we had a resupply helicopter shot down on the LZ. A sky crane helicopter came to haul it back to the rear. As they started lifting, the sling broke and the small chopper crashed back to the LZ. The pilots got out on another chopper but the door gunners had to stay the night with us. At 2:45 a.m. that night we were hit again. The fight lasted about forty-five minutes with no casualties.

Day five at about 11:00 p.m. we were notified that an NVA message had been intercepted. The message said that NVA were massing for an attack on Hill 805. We were going to get hit again! At about 2:30 a.m., the enemy started probing our perimeter. We called in artillery and Cobra gunships to fire up the area. Again we had no casualties. We found out much later that there had been three regiments or five thousand NVA soldiers massing near Hill 805.

Out of one hundred twelve men, forty-five of us walked off that hill on July 17. As we were leaving the hill, one of the Vietnamese scouts killed himself with a grenade. We were going down into the jungle and he was afraid he would be captured by the VC and tortured. Two men were killed and seven were wounded as a result of this. We moved along a trail until dark. No one slept that night. No one had slept for five nights. We thought for sure we would get hit again but we didn't.

The next morning we made it to a landing zone. As the choppers came in to the LZ they were taking enemy fire but they picked us up anyway. When we landed in the rear the door gunners got out and counted the bullet holes in the choppers. I was just glad to be in a rear area. We had given all we had to give.

## Chapter 7
## Friends

I was close, very close to many of the men in my platoon. After spending almost a year in the jungle, fighting side by side with them, we were as they say, "Bonded together by the brotherhood of war." We did everything together. We laughed together, cried together, ate together, and much more. We shared everything. We depended on each other for our very lives. We didn't know prejudice. We were all one and we tried to lift each other up. I'm still in touch with some of them today. John Shipley, who lives in Knoxville, Tennessee, is probably my best friend. I can always talk to him and feel he understands because he went through the war with me. We spent our youth and innocence together. I saw two of my very closest friends, LT Rufty and SGT Jim Hembree, killed in Vietnam. In Vietnam there is little time to mourn for your friends or even react to their death. In the years that have followed, I have mourned. I remember my friends. I always will!

## Chapter 8
## Coming Home

In September, 1970, I was taken out of the field. My job now was to fly resupply to my company. I was SHORT! Being SHORT means you have a short time left to serve. When we got SHORT in Vietnam, we got really nervous. Two really scary things happened to me during this time in the rear. The first incident occurred when we were flying some dynamite into my company so they could clear an LZ. We got lost in a monsoon fog. Still carrying a full load of dynamite, we had to be guided in and land by radar. I was really glad to see ground again. The second incident was in a rear area. The siren sounded that there were incoming rockets so we went to our bunkers. Some of the rockets were landing close to our bunker. We heard one come in, but no explosion. When the all clear sounded, we stepped outside. There, not ten feet from our door, was a rocket stuck in the ground! Needless to say, we got out of there quickly! A special demo team was called in to defuse it.

Finally, my time was up. I was going back to the "world" as we called it. I was going home! I had mixed feelings. I was never so happy to get out of a place in all my life, but I was sad because some of my friends didn't make it out. Three hundred forty-five days and my tour of duty was over, but part of me stayed in Vietnam.

# Chapter 9
# Looking Back

I believe going to Vietnam was the right thing to do. The Americans who fought there never lost a battle but we lost the war. We didn't lose it, our government gave it away. We were too limited. I say if you're going to fight a war, then you'd better fight to win or don't get involved. The guys in Vietnam hated the protesters. We felt like they turned this country against the war and against the men who fought the war. We were bitter. We were actually glad when the Kent State shootings happened. I'm sorry it happened now. They were just kids, like us, who happened to be in the wrong place at the wrong time. I had a few close calls myself and looking back I wonder if it was divine protection. I wasn't a Christian then. I didn't even know how to pray except for "HELP!" and "HELP ME!" All I knew about the Bible was the twenty-third Psalm, but if that's all you know that's what you say when you get scared.

## About the Author

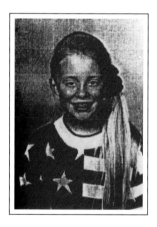

The author of VIETNAM: A FATHER'S STORY is Erin Elizabeth Policz of Sheffield Lake, Ohio. She is a fifth grade student at Open Door Christian School in Elyria, Ohio. Her favorite subjects are Reading, Math, and Science. Her hobbies include ballet, reading, playing the piano, and listening to classical music.

# Faces

Vietnam Veterans 6th Reunion, Melbourne, Florida 1993
I went to on this fine day.
Drove some 110 miles or so
Just to hear what they had to say.

Went there not knowing
What all would take place.
Ran into some "Screaming Eagles"
I was looking for one face.

An old friend and Brother
That I haven't seen in 25 years.
For three long days I searched
Till my face turned to tears.

What I found wasn't my old friend and Brother
Who in Vietnam had fought by my side,
But faces of other Brothers, Sisters and Families
To honor those who fought and died.

                                        Written by Roy J. Moore
                                      April 26, 1993
                                      101st Airborne, All the Way
                                      D Co. 2/501st
                                      Class of 68-69

# Roster of Delta Raiders

| * | PLT | YEAR | RANK | LAST NAME | FIRST NAME |
|---|---|---|---|---|---|
| Unl. | Unk. | 1968 | | Abernathy | (first name?) |
| Dec. | HQ | 1969 | SGT | Abram | William M. |
| Loc. | 2nd | 1967/68 | SGT | Acra | Larry R. |
| Unl. | Unk. | 1968/69 | SSG | Adams | James A. |
| Unl. | 1st | 1970 | PFC | Adams Jr., | Joseph A. |
| Loc. | 3rd | 1970/71 | PFC | Aguirre | Rodofo |
| Unl. | Unk. | 1971/72 | SP4 | Akers | Albert F. |
| Unl. | 1st | 1969/70 | SP4 | Alicia-Torres | Jose A. |
| Loc. | 3rd | 1970/71 | PFC-RTO | Allen | Alan D. |
| Loc. | 3rd | 1970/71 | SP4 | Allen | Michael B. |
| Loc. | 3rd | | | Allen | Willie Lee |
| Unl. | 3rd | 1970 | SP4 | Allison | James W. |
| Unl. | 1st | 1969 | SP4 | Alston | Eugene C. |
| Unl. | Unk | 1970/71 | SP4 | Alvarado | Alberto |
| Unl. | 1st | 1970 | SSG | Anderson | Bobby |
| Unl. | 1st | 1970/71 | | Anderson | Richard L. |
| Loc. | 4th | 1967/68 | | Anderson | William E. |
| Loc. | 2nd | 1969/70 | SP4 | Andre | Jerome F. |
| Unl. | HQ | 1967/68 | SGT | Andrews | Thomas A. |
| Unl. | Unk. | 1970 | | Andriunas | Joseph |
| Dec. | 2nd | 1967/68 | SP4 | Anslow | Walter Harold |
| Loc. | 2nd | 1970/71 | SGT | Anthony | Robert |
| Unl. | Unk. | 1972 | SP4 | Argraves | Edward F. |
| Unl. | 1st | 1969/70 | PFC | Arimont-Rosa | Angel A. |
| Loc. | 2nd | 1970 | 1LT | Arndt | Victor E. |
| Unl. | Unk. | 1967/68 | PFC | Arnold | Richard |
| Loc. | HQ | 1968 | 1LT-XO | Aronow | William Fred |
| Loc. | 3rd | 1969/70 | SP4-Medic | Aschilman | Ralph E. |
| Unl. | 2nd | 1971 | | Ash | John W. |
| Loc. | 3rd | 1970 | | Ash | Tom |
| Loc. | 1st | 1967/68 | SSG | Ashton | Michael D. |
| Unl. | Unk. | 1971 | SP4 | Atkinson | Thurman |
| Unl. | 3rd | 1969/70 | | Atteberry | Charles M. |
| Unl. | 1st | 1971 | SP4 | Audet | Raymond |
| Loc. | 3rd | 1969 | SFC | Avelino | Jose J. |

| *    | PLT  | YEAR    | RANK    | LAST NAME      | FIRST NAME      |
|------|------|---------|---------|----------------|-----------------|
| Unl. | Unk. | 1971/72 | SP4     | Ayala          | Estrada Angel   |
| Loc. | 1st  | 1967/68 | SP4     | Ayala          | Samuel R.       |
| Unl. | Unk. | 1971    | SP4     | Ayala/Richards | Jose I.         |
| Loc. | 2nd  | 1970/71 | SP4     | Ayers          | Jerry L.        |
| Unl. | Unk. | 1972    | 1LT     | Bailey         | Cecil E.        |
| Loc. | 3rd  | 1970/71 |         | Bailey         | William H.      |
| Dec. | 3rd  | 1970/71 | 1LT     | Baker          | John C.         |
| Unl. | Unk. | 1967    | SSG     | Bakoe          | James           |
| Unl. | Unk. | 1969    |         | Baldwin        | Bobby           |
| Dec. | Unl. | 1971    | SSG     | Bales          | Ronald Eugene   |
| Unl. | 2nd  | 1968    | PFC     | Ball           | Laverne T.      |
| Unl. | Unk. | 1969    |         | Banks          | Larry           |
| Loc. | 1st  | 1967/68 | SGT     | Barber II      | Roy L.          |
| Loc. | 3rd  | 1971/72 | SP4     | Barcus         | Harold R.       |
| Unl. | Unk. | 1971/72 | SP4     | Barnard        | David A.        |
| Loc. | 2nd  | 1970    |         | Barnes         | Barry L.        |
| Loc. | 3rd  | 1967/68 | SGT     | Barnett        | Billy R.        |
| Loc. | 2nd  | 1968/69 | SP4     | Barr           | Bobby E.        |
| Unl. | Unk. | 1971/72 | PFC     | Barry          | Robert V.       |
| Loc. | 3rd  | 1970    | 1LT     | Bass           | Franklin K.     |
| Loc. | 1st  | 1969/70 | PFC     | Bates          | Earl G.         |
| Loc. | 2nd  | 1970/71 | SGT     | Baugh          | Terry L.        |
| Unl. | Unk. | 1971/72 | SP4     | Baur           | Thomas M.       |
| Unl. | Unk. | 1970    |         | Bealer         | Carl            |
| Unl. | 3rd  | 1971    | SP4     | Begay Jr.      | John            |
| Dec. | 1st  | 1967/68 | SP4     | Begody         | Harold L.       |
| Unl. | Unk. | 1970/71 | PFC     | Bell           | Thomas          |
| Loc. | 1st  | 1969/70 | SP4     | Belt           | Dennis W.       |
| Unl. | 2nd  | 1969/70 | SP4     | Beneduce       | Angelo N.       |
| Unl. | Unk. | 1969    | SP4     | Bennett        | William J.      |
| Loc. | 4th  | 1967/68 | PSG     | Benoit         | Robert J.       |
| Loc. | 1st  | 1969/70 | PFC     | Benward        | George T.       |
| Dec. | 3rd  | 1970/71 | SP4     | Beregsasi      | Rudolf          |
| Unl. | 2nd  | 1971    | PFC     | Berg           | Danial          |
| Unl. | Unk. | 1969    | SFC     | Bermodez       | Justino         |
| Unl. | Unk. | 1971/72 | PFC     | Berrones       | Juan J.         |
| Loc. | 2nd  | 1967/68 | SP4     | Besosa Jr.     | Charles W.      |
| Loc. | 3rd  | 1968/69 | PFC-RTO | Bevins         | Jimmy B.        |
| Unl. | 1st  | 1968/69 | 1LT     | Bevis Jr.      | Stanford J.D.   |
| Dec. | 1st  | 1969/70 | SP4     | Beyl           | David R.        |

| * | PLT | YEAR | RANK | LAST NAME | FIRST NAME |
|---|---|---|---|---|---|
| Dec. | 2nd | 1969/70 | SP4 | Biasin | Silvio |
| Loc. | 1st | 1967/68 | PFC | Bickel | David W. |
| Loc. | 3rd | 1967/68 | 2LT | Bischoff | David G. |
| Loc. | 3rd | 1970/71 | SGT | Blackman | Raymond H. |
| Loc. | 3rd | 1970/71 | SP4 | Blaskiewicz | Harry |
| Unl. | Unk. | 1969 | Medic | Bledsoe | Richard |
| Dec. | 1st | 1969 | SP4 | Blend | William L. |
| Unl. | Unk. | 1969 | PSG | Block | William D. |
| Unl. | Unk. | 1970 | | Blunt | Ken |
| Loc. | 1st | 1970/71 | SP4 | Boeve | Oliver |
| Loc. | 3rd | 1969/70 | PFC | Bolden | Albert |
| Dec. | 1st | 1968 | SGT | Bolden | Bobby J. |
| Loc. | HQ | 1969/70 | SP4 | Bolton | Gary L. |
| Loc. | 2nd | 1967/68 | SP4 | Bongiorno | Salvator |
| Unl. | Unk. | 1970/71 | PFC | Bonner | Garland |
| Loc. | 1st | 1970/71 | SP4 | Boostrom | Larry |
| Unl. | Unk. | 1971/72 | PFC | Bourbanis | Gerald |
| Unl. | Unk. | 1969 | SP4 | Bourquin | Ronald C. |
| Loc. | 2nd | 1967/68 | PFC | Bowling | Hirshel |
| Loc. | 3rd | 1969/70 | SGT | Bowling | Kindred |
| Loc. | 2nd | 1967/68 | SP4 | Bowman | James B. |
| Dec. | 2nd | 1968/69 | SSG | Bowman | Ronald H. |
| Unl. | Unk. | 1970/71 | SP4 | Bradford | Tommy W. |
| Unl. | 1st | 1967/68 | SP4 | Bradshaw | Ernest |
| Loc. | Unk. | 1971/72 | PFC | Brailsford | Robert L. |
| Loc. | 2nd | 1969/70 | SP4 | Brannen | Bobby R. |
| Unl. | Unk. | 1971/72 | SSG | Bratt | Gary L. |
| Loc. | HQ | 1971 | SP4-RTO | Breckenridge | Berlyn |
| Loc. | 1st | 1967/68 | PFC | Brewer | Lawrence |
| Loc. | 3rd | 1970/71 | SP4 | Briggs | David C. |
| Unl. | 1st | 1968/69 | | Bright | Willard |
| Unl. | Unk. | 1969 | SP4 | Bright, Jr. | Lee A. |
| Unl. | 2nd | 1969/70 | PFC | Brinkley | William R. |
| Unl. | 3rd | 1971 | 1LT | Britt | Kermit J. |
| Unl. | 4th | 1967/68 | SP4 | Britt | Phillip D. |
| Dec. | 2nd | 1967/68 | PFC | Brockman | Robert David |
| Loc. | Unk. | 1972 | SP4 | Brooks | Louis D. |
| Unl. | Unk. | 1968 | PFC | Brown | David J. |
| Loc. | Unk. | 1968 | PFC | Brown | Francisco A. |
| Unl. | 3rd | 1970/71 | SGT | Brown | James M. |

Roster of Delta Raiders

| *    | PLT  | YEAR    | RANK | LAST NAME | FIRST NAME |
|------|------|---------|------|-----------|------------|
| Loc. | 2nd  | 1970/71 | SP4  | Broxton   | Coy A.     |
| Dec. | 3rd  | 1967/68 | 2LT  | Brulte    | Robert Franci |
| Unl. | 2nd  | 1969    | SP4  | Brumbelow | Jackie M.  |
| Loc. | 3rd  | 1970/71 | SP4  | Brumitt   | Philip E.  |
| Unl. | Unk. | 1967    | PVT  | Brund     | Larry M.   |
| Unl. | Unk. | 1968    | PFC  | Bryan     | Michael A. |
| Unl. | 3rd  | 1971    | SP4  | Bryant    | Collie     |
| Unl. | 3rd  | 1968/69 | SSG  | Buchman   | Robert J.  |
| Loc. | 3rd  | 1969/70 | SP4  | Bull      | Jerry K.   |
| Loc. | 3rd  | 1970/71 | SGT  | Bullard   | Henderson  |
| Unl. | 1st  | 1967/68 | SP4  | Burke     | Land T.    |
| Unl. | Unk. | 1967    | PVT  | Burnam    | Anthony C. |
| Unl. | 1st  | 1969    | SSG  | Burnham   | William J. |
| Loc. | 1st  | 1970/71 | SP4  | Burns     | Robert J.  |
| Loc. | 3rd  | 1969/70 | PFC  | Burrell   | Rodney C.  |
| Dec. | 3rd  | 1967/68 | SP4  | Burroughs | Emanuel Fero |
| Loc. | 2nd  | 1968/69 | SP4  | Bussell   | Richard A. |
| Loc. | Unk. | 1968    | PFC  | Bussey    | Henry      |
| Unl. | Unk. | 1971    | SP4  | Butteris  | William    |
| Loc. | 1st  | 1967/68 | SP4  | Buzzini   | Richard L. |
| Loc. | 2nd  | 1970/71 | SSG  | Cain      | Charles W. |
| Unl. | Unk. | 1969    | SP4  | Caldwell  | Clayton R. |
| Unl. | Unk. | 1971    | SSG  | Caldwell  | Jerry      |
| Loc. | 3rd  | 1968/69 | SP4  | Calhoun   | Donald E.  |
| Unl. | 3rd  | 1967/68 | SGT  | Calhoun   | James E.   |
| Unl. | 2nd  | 1967/68 | PFC  | Calvert   | Michael R. |
| Unl. | 2nd  | 1968/69 | SP4  | Camacho   | Raul F.    |
| Unl. | 1st  | 1970/71 | SGT  | Camden    | Harold L.  |
| Unl. | 3rd  | 1968/69 |      | Camera    | James C.   |
| Loc. | Unk. | 1970/71 | SP4  | Canty     | Leroy      |
| Loc. | 1st  | 1969/70 | SP4  | Capps     | Earl D.    |
| Unl. | Unk. | 1971/72 | SP4  | Cardial   | Larry D.   |
| Unl. | Unk. | 1970    |      | Care      | James B.   |
| Unl. | 1st  |         |      | Carlson   | Gene H.    |
| Unl. | 2nd  | 1971/72 | SP4  | Carnahan  | William L. |
| Loc. | 3rd  | 1970/71 | SP4  | Carr      | Mickey A.  |
| Loc. | 1st  | 1970/71 | 1LT  | Carroll   | Ronald L.  |
| Unl. | Unk. | 1971/72 | PFC  | Carter Jr.| Ralph D.   |
| Loc. | 3rd  | l969/70 | SP4  | Caruso    | James V.   |
| Unl. | Unk. | 1967    | PFC  | Case      | Raymond    |

| *    | PLT  | YEAR    | RANK    | LAST NAME  | FIRST NAME    |
|------|------|---------|---------|------------|---------------|
| Dec. | 3rd  | 1967/68 | SGT     | Cash       | David Manfred |
| Unl. | Unk. | 1970/71 | SP4     | Castro     | Ernest F.     |
| Unl. | Unk. | 1968/69 | SP4     | Cervantes  | Antonio       |
| Unl. | Unk. | 1969/70 | SGT     | Chandik    | Gerald P.     |
| Unl. | 1st  | 1970    | SP4-RTO | Chandler   | Bruce A.      |
| Unl. | Unk. | 1971    | PFC     | Chandler   | John L.       |
| Unl. | Unk. | 1968/69 | SP4     | Chartier   | Daniel J.     |
| Loc. | 4th  | 1970/71 | Medic   | Chiaro     | George        |
| Loc. | 1st  | 1970    | SP4     | Chilton    | Gary L.       |
| Loc. | Unk. | 1971/72 | SP4     | Chin       | Eugene        |
| Unl. | Unk. | 1970/71 | PFC     | Chiparo    | Charles       |
| Unl. | Unk. | 1971/72 | PSG     | Chisolm    | Nathaniel     |
| Unl. | Unk. | 1971/72 | SP4     | Church     | John C.       |
| Dec. | 3rd  | 1971    | 1LT     | Church     | Ralph Lee     |
| Loc. | 1st  | 1970    | PFC-RTO | Cirrincoine| Martin        |
| Unl. | 3rd  | 1971    | PFC     | Clark      | Eugene        |
| Unl. | Unk. | 1967    | PVT     | Clark      | Kenneth D.    |
| Unl. | Unk. | 1971    | SGT     | Clark      | Michael S.    |
| Unl. | Unk. | 1969    | PFC     | Clauder    | Rick          |

## Roster of Delta Raiders

| *    | PLT  | YEAR    | RANK      | LAST NAME    | FIRST NAME    |
|------|------|---------|-----------|--------------|---------------|
| Loc. | 2nd  | 1970/71 | SP4       | Clemens      | Thomas H.     |
| Unl. | Unk. | 1971/72 | SGT       | Clements     | Ralph D.      |
| Dec. | Unk. | 1968    | SGT-Medic | Cleveland    | James Arthur  |
| Loc. | 2nd  | 1970    | SGT       | Cluff        | Keith A.      |
| Unl. | 1st  | 1967/68 | SGT       | Cobb         | O'Dell E.     |
| Unl. | Unk. | 1969    | SP4       | Cochran, Jr. | Arthur        |
| Unl. | Unk. | 1971    | SP4       | Cole         | William S.    |
| Unl. | Unk. | 1971/72 | PFC       | Collins      | Leon          |
| Unl. | 1st  | 1970    | SP4       | Collins      | Rodney B.     |
| Unl. | Unk. | 1967    | SP4       | Comer        | Earnest       |
| Loc. | 2nd  | 1971    | PFC       | Condran      | Patrick J.    |
| Unl. | 1st  | 1971    | PFC       | Conerly      | Monroe        |
| Unl. | Unk. | 1970/71 |           | Connell      | Victor F.     |
| Unl. | HQ   |         | PSG       | Cook         | Jerry         |
| Dec. | 1st  | 1969/70 | SSG       | Cooksley     | Michael       |
| Unl. | Unk. |         | SP4       | Coons        | Ronald        |
| Unl. | 2nd  | 1969/70 | SP4       | Cooper       | Joseph        |
| Unl. | 1st  | 1970    |           | Cooper       | Terry         |
| Unl. | Unk. | 1970    |           | Copeland     | Alan          |
| Unl. | 3rd  | 1969    | PFC       | Coppens      | Gregory R.    |
| Unl. | Unk. | 1968    | PFC       | Cornette     | Jerry D.      |
| Loc. | 1st  | 1970/71 | SSG       | Corts        | George A.     |
| Unl. | 2nd  | 1969    | SP4       | Cossette     | Thomas B.     |
| Dec. | 2nd  | 1969    | PFC       | Courtney     | Jimmy Darrell |
| Loc. | 3rd  | 1969/70 | SP4       | Cowen        | Andrew R.     |
| Unl. | 3rd  | 1970/71 |           | Crawford     | Harry C.      |
| Loc. | 3rd  | 1969/70 | PFC       | Crills       | Jay S.        |
| Loc. | 2nd  | 1970/71 | PFC       | Croyle       | Philip J.     |
| Unl. | Unk. | 1968    | SP4       | Cudd II      | John W.       |
| Unl. | Unk. | 1968/69 | SP4       | Culp         | Arthur E.     |
| Unl. | 2nd  | 1968/69 | SP4       | Cure         | Frank B.      |
| Unl. | HQ   | 1969    | CPT       | Curtis       | Thomas M.     |
| Unl. | 3rd  | 1969    | 1LT       | Cushing      | Patrick       |
| Loc. | 3rd  |         |           | Dailey       | Douglas H.    |
| Unl. | Unk. | 1970/71 | SP4       | Daisey       | Richard L.    |
| Unl. | Unk. | 1969    | PFC       | Dalton       | James A.      |
| Unl. | Unk. | 1969/70 | PFC       | Danders      | Robert L.     |
| Unl. | HQ   | 1969    | 1SG       | Danials      | (first name?) |
| Dec. | 2nd  | 1971    | SP4       | Daniels      | Rex Martin    |
| Unl. | Unk. | 1971/72 | SP4       | Dankert      | Wayne S.      |

| *    | PLT  | YEAR    | RANK    | LAST NAME    | FIRST NAME   |
|------|------|---------|---------|--------------|--------------|
| Unl. | Unk. | 1968    | PFC     | Darensburg   | Gerald G.    |
| Unl. | 2nd  | 1969/70 | SP4     | Darmiento    | John A.      |
| Loc. | HQ   | 1967/68 | SGT-Arty| Davidson     | Larry P.     |
| Unl. | Unk. | 1968    | PFC     | Davis        | Alvin P.     |
| Unl. | 1st  | 1967/68 | SGT     | Davis        | Hubert L.    |
| Unl. | 1st  | 1967/68 | SSG     | Davis        | John H.      |
| Unl. | 2nd  | 1970/71 | SP4     | Davis        | Lynn O.      |
| Loc. | 2nd  | 1970    | SP4     | Davis        | Randy C.     |
| Loc. | 2nd  | 1970/71 | SP4     | Day          | Mark E.      |
| Unl. | Unk. | 1971/72 | PFC     | Dean         | Ronnie E.    |
| Loc. | 1st  | 1969    | SP4     | Deegan       | Joseph R.    |
| Loc. | 3rd  | 1970/71 | Medic   | Dehorney     | Thurman C.   |
| Unl. | 3rd  | 1967/68 | PSG     | Deland       | James        |
| Unl. | 1st  | 1967/68 | PFC     | Delaney      | Henrie L.    |
| Unl. | Unk. | 1967    | SP4     | Delgado      | Rafael I.    |
| Unl. | Unk. | 1970    |         | Dellwo       | Bruce        |
| Unl. | Unk. | 1968    |         | Demarco      | Ralph        |
| Unl. | Unk. | 1968    | SP4     | Depoint      | Lewis F.     |
| Loc. | 2nd  | 1968/69 | PFC     | Des Jarden   | William      |
| Loc. | 2nd  | 1970/71 |         | Dotty        | Ronnie D.    |
| Unl. | Unk. | 1971/72 | SP4     | Dicicco      | Robert L.    |
| Loc. | 3rd  | 1968    | PFC     | Dickens II   | Eugene J.    |
| Loc. | 2rd  | 1970    | SP4     | Dickerson    | Samuel D.    |
| Unl. | 1st  | 1970    | PFC     | Diepenbrock  | Richard A.   |
| Unl. | 3rd  | 1969    | PFC     | Dillard      | James C.     |
| Unl. | HQ   |         | 1LT-FO  | Dion         | Paul G.      |
| Unl. | Unk. | 1969    | SP4     | Dirschberger | David R.     |
| Dec. | 3rd  | 1971    |         | Diters       | Grady G.     |
| Unl. | Unl. | 1969    | PFC     | Dixon        | Lloyd        |
| Unl. | Unk. | 1971/72 | PFC     | Dodge        | Robert B.    |
| Unl. | Unk. | 1971    | SP4     | Dodson       | Compton T.   |
| Unl. | Unk. | 1968    | PFC     | Dolan        | Charles D.   |
| Loc. | 2nd  | 1969    | PFC     | Domain       | Robert       |
| Unl. | 3rd  | 1970/71 | SGT     | Dominque     | James A.     |
| Unl. | Unk. | 1968    | PFC     | Donatone     | Dominick S.  |
| Loc. | 3rd  | 1971    | SGT     | Dornbush     | Gerald       |
| Unl. | Unk. | 1969    | PFC     | Doster       | Robert       |
| Loc. | 3rd  | 1969/70 | SSG     | Dotson       | Raymond T.   |
| Unl. | Unk. | 1972    | PFC     | Dozier       | Ronald T.    |
| Unl. | 4th  | 1967/68 | SGT     | Driffill     | Martin E.    |

| * | PLT | YEAR | RANK | LAST NAME | FIRST NAME |
|---|---|---|---|---|---|
| Loc. | 2nd | 1971 | PFC | Duarte | William S. |
| Loc. | 3rd | 1967/68 | SSG | Dunlap | Joe W. |
| Unl. | 2nd | 1968/69 | SP4 | Dunlap | John C. |
| Dec. | Unk. | 1969 | SGT | Dunn | Robert Terrence |
| Unl. | Unk. | 1968/69 | SP4 | Duquette | Robert W. |
| Unl. | 2nd | 1968/69 | SP4 | Dykes | Richard R. |
| Loc. | HQ | 1967/68 | SGT | Eastburn III | David R. |
| Unl. | Unk. | 1969 | SP4 | Easterly | Led |
| Loc. | HQ | 1971 | CPT | Ebert | Roger L. |
| Loc. | Unk. | 1968 | SP4 | Eccleston | Sheldon L. |
| Unl. | Unk. | 1969 | | Echols | William R. |
| Unl. | Unk. | 1968 | PFC | Eckrote | David C. |
| Unl. | Unk. | 1968/69 | SP4 | Eggles | Thomas J. |
| Dec. | 2nd | 1968 | PFC-RTO | Eller | Lawrence William |
| Unl. | Unk. | 1971/72 | SP4 | Ellison | Ezekiel R. |
| Loc. | HQ | 1968/69 | 1SG | Embrey | Edward E. |
| Unl. | HQ | 1968 | 1SG | Emory | Robert |
| Unl. | Unk. | 1969 | SGT | Encarmacion | Colon A. |
| Unl. | Unk. | 1969 | SGT | Endfinger | Darryl |
| Unl. | HQ | 1971/72 | SP4 | Engle | Richard D. |
| Loc. | 2nd | 1969 | PFC | Englerth III | William J. |
| Unl. | Unk. | 1969/70 | SP4 | Engram | David J. |
| Unl. | Unk. | 1971 | SP4 | Epling | Donald R. |
| Loc. | 2nd | 1970 | SP4 | Ertel | Larry |
| Loc. | Unk. | 1968 | SP4 | Escobedo | Perfecto A. |
| Loc. | 1st | 1969/70 | SP4 | Espada | Porfirio F. |
| Unl. | 1st | 1969 | | Estevez | Jose R. |
| Unl. | 1st | 1969 | PFC | Estevez-Cabrera | Jose R. |
| Unl. | Unk. | 1967/68 | SP4 | Eubanks | James |
| Loc. | 2nd | 1970/71 | SP4 | Evans | Eugene |
| Loc. | HQ | 1969 | 1LT | Evans | Robert |
| Unl. | Unk. | 1972 | SP4 | Evans | Stephen D. |
| Loc. | 3rd | 1970/71 | PFC | Evers | Wayne M. |
| Loc. | 1st | 1969/70 | PFC | Ewing | Eldon N. |
| Unl. | Unk. | 1971 | PFC | Eyck | Manuel Van |
| Loc. | 1st | 1971 | SP4 | Fail | Cedric E. |
| Unl. | Unk. | 1968 | PFC | Fantasia | Richard |
| Unl. | Unk. | 1968/69 | SP4 | Faulk | Charles |
| Unl. | 2nd | 1970/71 | PFC | Faulkner | William E. |
| Unl. | Unk. | 1969 | PFC | Ferm | Timothy J. |

| * | PLT | YEAR | RANK | LAST NAME | FIRST NAME |
|---|---|---|---|---|---|
| Loc. | 2nd | 1968/69 | SGI | Ferrell | Eugene |
| Unl. | 1st | 1971 | SP4 | Fertitta | Anthony |
| Loc. | HQ | 1968 | CPT | Feurer | Michael H. |
| Unl. | Unk | 1969 | SP4 | File | Howard |
| Unl. | Unk. | 1972 | PFC | Fincers | George |
| Unl. | Unk. | 1968/69 | SGT | Findley | John M. |
| Loc. | 2nd | 1970 |  | Finn | Michael W. |
| Unl. | Unk. | 1971 | PFC | Finones | George A. |
| Loc. | 3rd | 1970/71 | SSG | Fisher | Douglas E. |
| Dec. | Unk. | 1967/68 | SGT | Fitzgerald | James J. |
| Loc. | 3rd | 1968/69 | SGT | Fitzgerald | James M. |
| Unl. | HQ | 1971 | CPT | Flavin | William J. |
| Loc. | Unk. | 1968/69 |  | Fletcher | Bobby G. |
| Loc. | 2nd | 1968/69 | SP4 | Flett | Richard W. |
| Unl. | Unk. | 1968 | SP4 | Flores | James F. |
| Unl. | 2nd | 1970/71 | SGT | Flores | Jerry S. |
| Dec. | 3rd | 1967/68 | SGT | Flores | Joseph |
| Loc. | 3rd | 1970/71 | SP4 | Flynn | Jerry |
| Unl. | Unk. | 1971/72 | 1LT | Forbes | John M. |
| Unl. | Unk. |  | SP4 | Ford | Thurlow J. |
| Unl. | Unk. | 1968/69 | PFC | Foreman | John M. |
| Unl. | HQ | 1970 | Medic | Fowler | (Everett G. ?) |
| Unl. | Unk. | 1971/72 | SGT | Fowlkes | Ronald L. |
| Unl. | Unk. | 1969 | PFC | Fox | Russell E. |
| Loc. | Unk. | 1970/71 | SP4 | Fox | Stephen R. |
| Loc. | 3rd | 1968/69 | SGT | Foytich | Richard B. |
| Unl. | 2nd | 1967/68 | SP4 | Franklin | Glenn M. |
| Loc. | HQ | 1968 | SP5-Medic | Frawley | James J. |
| Unl. | Unk. | 1968 |  | Freeling | Joe |
| Loc. | 1st | 1968 | 1LT | Frick | John E. |
| Unl. | Unk. | 1968/69 | SSG | Frisby | Charles |
| Loc. | 1st | 1970/71 | SP4 | Frost | Irvin M. |
| Unl. | 3rd | 1970/71 | PFC | Fueston | Robert A. |
| Loc. | 2nd | 1969/70 | SP4 | Fusia | Richard J. |
| Loc. | 4th | 1967/68 | SGT | Fyffe | James M. |
| Unl. | Unk. | 1968 | PFC | Gafford | Arthur L. |
| Loc. | 3rd | 1967/68 | PFC | Gagne | Bradford J. |
| Unl. | 3rd | 1969 |  | Gagnon Jr. | Raymond J. |
| Loc. | 1st | 1967/68 | PFC | Gaines | Frank D. |
| Unl. | Unk. | 1970 |  | Galindo | Armando |

| *    | PLT  | YEAR    | RANK      | LAST NAME | FIRST NAME   |
|------|------|---------|-----------|-----------|--------------|
| Loc. | 3rd  | 1968/69 | SP4       | Gamboa    | Robert R.    |
| Loc. | 4th  | 1968/69 | SSG       | Garcia    | Gilbert      |
| Unl. | Unk. | 1967/68 | PVT       | Garcia    | Ralph        |
| Loc. | 2nd  | 1967/68 | PFC       | Garland   | Hugh S.      |
| Unl. | Unk. | 1970    |           | Garner    | Lawrence     |
| Unl. | 2nd  | 1969    |           | Garrett   | James L.     |
| Unl. | 4th  | 1967/68 | 2LT       | Gash      | Reed A.      |
| Loc. | 1st  | 1969/70 | SGT       | Gaster    | Kerry D.     |
| Unl. | HQ   | 1969    |           | Gates     | Robert E.    |
| Unl. | 3rd  | 1967/68 | SP4       | Gay       | Dean F.      |
| Loc. | 3rd  | 1970/71 | PFC       | Gay       | Teddy        |
| Unl. | Unk. | 1969/70 |           | Gebinger  | Charles J.   |
| Loc. | 3rd  | 1969/70 | PFC       | Gerew     | Terrence P.  |
| Loc. | 3rd  | 1970/71 | SP4       | Gervasi   | Robert       |
| Loc. | 1st  | 1971    | 1LT       | Gervin Jr.| Jack E.      |
| Loc. | 1st  | 1969/70 |           | Gibson    | Billy        |
| Unl. | Unk. | 1967    | PFC       | Gilbert   | Arthur A.    |
| Loc. | Unk. | 1968    | SGT       | Gillard   | Michael      |
| Unl. | 2nd  | 1970    | Medic     | Gilliland | Gary D.      |
| Unl. | 3rd  | 1969    | SP4-Medic | Gilmar    | Jerry W.     |
| Loc. | 3rd  | 1967/68 | SSG       | Gingery   | John Bernard |
| Loc. | Unk  | 1968/69 | SSG       | Ginn      | Joe A.       |
| Unl. | HQ   | 1968/69 | SP4-RTO   | Gipson    | Danny W.     |
| Loc. | 1st  | 1968/69 | SP4       | Gischel   | Richard L.   |
| Unl. | Unk. | 1971    | PFC       | Givens    | Willie C.    |
| Unl. | 1st  | 1969    | SP4       | Gobert    | James R.     |
| Unl. | Unk. | 1970/71 | SGT       | Godby     | Charles      |
| Loc. | 1st  | 1970    |           | Godwin    | Jack L.      |
| Loc. | 2nd  | 1969/70 | SGT       | Goeckel   | William G.   |
| Unl. | 3rd  | 1969    | SP4       | Goldbeger | Joseph P.    |
| Unl. | 3rd  | 1971/72 | PFC       | Goldberg  | Gilbert G.   |
| Loc. | Unl. | 1968/69 | PFC       | Gomez     | Anselmo      |
| Unl. | 1st  | 1967/68 | SGT       | Gonzales  | Benjamin     |
| Dec. | 1st  | 1968/69 | PFC       | Gonzales  | Raymond L.   |
| Unl. | 1st  | 1969/70 | PFC       | Goodman   | Robert J.    |
| Loc. | Unk. | 1971/72 | SP4       | Goodnight | Robert F     |
| Unl. | Unk. | 1971    | SP4       | Goodwin   | Roy W.       |
| Unl. | 3rd  | 1967/68 | PVT       | Gould     | Robert       |
| Loc. | Unk. | 1971/72 | SGT       | Graham    | John E.      |
| Unl. | 2nd  | 1969    | SP4       | Grant     | Sylvester    |

| *    | PLT  | YEAR    | RANK  | LAST NAME    | FIRST NAME    |
|------|------|---------|-------|--------------|---------------|
| Unl. | 1st  | 1967/68 | SSG   | Grant Jr.    | Franklin      |
| Loc. | 3rd  | 1967/68 | SGT   | Gravett      | Jody          |
| Loc. | 2nd  | 1970/71 | PFC   | Gray         | David I.      |
| Loc. | 1st  | 1967/68 | SP4   | Gray         | Tex W.        |
| Unl. | 1st  | 1969/70 |       | Grayson      | William R.    |
| Unl. | Unk. | 1971/72 | SP4   | Greathead Jr.| Thomas C.     |
| Unl. | 3rd  | 1969    | SGT   | Grebinger    | Charles J.    |
| Unl. | 3rd  | 1971    | SSG   | Green        | Alvin         |
| Unl. | 1st  | 1969/70 | SGT   | Green        | George L.     |
| Loc. | 1st  | 1970/71 | SGT   | Green        | Glen A.       |
| Loc. | 2nd  | 1971    | SGT   | Green        | Jody A.       |
| Dec. | Unk. | 1971    | PFC   | Greene       | Terry Willard |
| Loc. | 2nd  | 1967/68 | SSG   | Gregory      | Eulas Fay     |
| Loc. | 1st  | 1969/70 | SGT   | Grelle       | Paul J.       |
| Loc. | 3rd  | 1968/69 | PFC   | Grieco Jr.   | Frank A.      |
| Loc. | 3rd  | 1970/71 | SGT   | Griffin      | Alto          |
| Unl. | Unk. | 1971    | PFC   | Griffin      | Thomas W.     |
| Unl. | Unk. | 1968/69 | SGT   | Grimmett     | Joel T.       |
| Dec. | 1st  | 1967/68 | 2LT   | Grimsley     | Lee Eldrige   |
| Loc. | 1st  | 1970    | Medic | Grubidt      | Ronald W.     |
| Unl. | Unk. | 1970    |       | Gubis        | Donald        |
| Unl. | 1st  | 1969/70 | PFC   | Guerena      | Robert G.     |
| Unl. | 3rd  | 1970    | 1LT   | Guerra       | Joseph L.     |
| Unl. | 3rd  | 1969    | SGT   | Guild        | William R.    |
| Loc. | 1st  | 1969/70 | SP4   | Guimond      | Paul Gerald   |
| Unl. | Unk. | 1971    | PFC   | Gulas        |               |
| Unl. | Unk. | 1971/72 | PFC   | Gurcharran   | Padarath      |
| Unl. | Unk. | 1971/72 | PFC   | Gutierrez    | Michael V.    |
| Dec. | 3rd  | 1967/68 | SGT   | Hacker       | Bernard B.    |
| Unl. | 3rd  | 1970    | PFC   | Hager        | Mark G.       |
| Unl. | 1st  | 1969    |       | Hall         | Paul D.       |
| Unl. | Unk. | 1971    | 1LT   | Hall         | Timothy J.    |
| Loc. | Unk. | 1968/69 | SGT   | Hamlin       | Jerry C.      |
| Unl. | Unk. | 1969    | SGT   | Hankins      | Ronald D.     |
| Unl. | Unk. | 1968    | PFC   | Hanna        | Lony J.       |
| Loc. | 2nd  | 1970    | SGT   | Hanrahan     | Warren R.     |
| Unl. | Unk. | 1969    | SP4   | Harding      | Bernard J.    |
| Unl. | Unk. | 1972    | SP4   | Hargraves    | Edward F.     |
| Loc. | 2nd  | 1969/70 | PFC   | Harper       | Ryan E.       |
| Loc. | 2nd  | 1968    | SSG   | Harris       | Billy R.      |

## Roster of Delta Raiders

| *    | PLT  | YEAR    | RANK   | LAST NAME | FIRST NAME     |
|------|------|---------|--------|-----------|----------------|
| Unl. | Unk. | 1971/72 | SGT    | Harris    | Phillip B.     |
| Unl. | 1st  | 1969    | SGT    | Harrison  | Charles E.     |
| Unl. | Unk. | 1971/72 | SP4    | Harrison  | John J.        |
| Unl. | 2nd  | 1969    | SP4    | Hart      | Leroy H.       |
| Unl. | Unk. | 1969    | PFC    | Harvey    | Elwin M.       |
| Unl. | 3rd  | 1967    | PFC    | Harvey    | William D.     |
| Unl. | 2nd  | 1970    | SGT    | Harvin    | Willie E.      |
| Unl. | Unk. | 1971    | SP4    | Hass      | Paul J.        |
| Loc. | HQ   | 1969    | 1LT-FA | Hayes     | Carl E.        |
| Unl. | 2nd  | 1967/68 | SP4    | Hayes Jr. | Clarence       |
| Unl. | Unk. | 1970/71 | PFC    | Hayworth  | William E.     |
| Unl. | 3rd  | 1969    | PFC    | Head      | Gerald D.      |
| Unl. | Unk. | 1968/69 | PFC    | Head      | John R.        |
| Dec. | 2nd  | 1970/71 | SP4    | Hein      | Robert Charles |
| Loc. | 2nd  | 1967/68 | PFC    | Heiserman | Lester H.      |
| Loc. | Unk. | 1967    | PFC    | Helson    | Paul D.        |

## Roster of Delta Raiders

| *    | PLT  | YEAR    | RANK    | LAST NAME   | FIRST NAME      |
|------|------|---------|---------|-------------|-----------------|
| Dec. | 2nd  | 1969/70 | SSG     | Hembree Jr. | James Thomas    |
| Unl. | Unk. | 1971/72 | PFC     | Hemphill    | James A.        |
| Loc. | 2nd  | 1967/68 | PFC     | Henderson   | James T.        |
| Unl. | 2nd  | 1969    | SP4     | Henderson   | Thomas W.       |
| Loc. | 3rd  | 1967/68 | PFC-RTO | Hendricks   | Ronald E.       |
| Unl. | Unk. | 1969/70 | PFC     | Hendrix     | Dale E.         |
| Unl. | Unk. | 1969/70 | PFC     | Henze       | Kenneth H.      |
| Unl. | 1st  | 1969    | SP4     | Herman      | Frank J.        |
| Unl. | Unk. | 1972    | SP4     | Hernandez   | George J.       |
| Unl. | Unk. | 1968/69 | SSG     | Hernandez   | Rivera L.       |
| Unl. | 1st  | 1968/69 | SP4     | Hess        | Clarence E.     |
| Loc. | 1st  | 1969    | SGT     | Hess        | Harold D.       |
| Loc. | 2nd  | 1968/69 | SP4     | Hilderbrand | Tommy           |
| Loc. | 2nd  | 1969/70 | SP4     | Hill        | Bobby G.        |
| Unl. | 3rd  | 1969    | SP4     | Hill        | Montez R.       |
| Unl. | Unk. | 1969/70 | PFC     | Hilton      | Stephen K.      |
| Loc. | 2nd  | 1967/68 | PSG     | Hines       | Bernard Z.      |
| Unl. | Unk. | 1969/70 | PFC     | Hinkley     | Ralph E.        |
| Loc. | 3rd  | 1967/68 | SGT     | Hinz        | William J.      |
| Unl. | Unk. | 1969    | SP4     | Hiott       | Dennis J.       |
| Loc. | 2nd  | 1969/70 | SP4     | Hirt II     | Mathew P.       |
| Unl. | Unk. | 1969    | Medic   | Hochlin     | Gary H.         |
| Unl. | Unk. | 1969    |         | Hoffman     | Gordon H.       |
| Loc. | HQ   | 1967/68 | CPT     | Hogan Jr.   | Cleo C.         |
| Unl. | 2nd  | 1968/69 | 1LT     | Hogenauer   | Edward L.       |
| Loc. | HQ   | 1968/69 | 1LT-FO  | Holden      | Dwight A.       |
| Loc. | 2nd  | 1970/71 | SGT     | Holgersen   | Kenneth A.      |
| Unl. | 1st  | 1970/71 | SP4     | Hollamon    | Edgar (Eugene?) |
| Unl. | 2nd  | 1970/71 | PFC     | Holloway    | Clarence        |
| Dec. | 2nd  | 1967/68 | PFC     | Holmes      | Ernest Paul     |
| Unl. | 2nd  | 1967/68 | SSG     | Holmes      | John Henry      |
| Unl. | Unk. | 1967/68 | PFC     | Holmes      | Victor A.       |
| Unl. | Unk. | 1971    | SGT     | Holt        | John N.         |
| Unl. | Unk. | 1971    | SGT     | Holtz       | John H.         |
| Unl. | Unk. | 1969    |         | Hoof        | Earnest         |
| Dec. | 1st  | 1967/68 | SSG     | Hooper      | Joe R.          |
| Unl. | 1st  | 1969/70 | SP4     | Hoosier     | Hernan D.       |
| Unl. | 1st  | 1967/68 | PFC     | Hopkins     | Thomas A.       |
| Unl. | HQ   | 1969    | PFC     | Hopper III  | William G.      |
| Unl. | Unk. | 1971    | SGT     | Horn        | Terrence O.     |

## Roster of Delta Raiders

| *    | PLT  | YEAR    | RANK    | LAST NAME  | FIRST NAME  |
|------|------|---------|---------|------------|-------------|
| Loc. | 3rd  | 1967/68 | SGT     | Horne      | Wayne A.    |
| Unl. | Unk. | 1967/68 | PFC     | Horton     | John C.     |
| Unl. | Unk. | 1972    | SP4     | Hoskins    | John W.     |
| Unl. | 3rd  | 1967/68 | SP4     | House      | Haskelle P. |
| Unl. | Unk. | 1969    | PFC     | Howard     | Charles B.  |
| Unl. | Unk. | 1970/71 | SP4     | Howard     | Kent S.     |
| Unl. | Unk. | 1969    | SP4     | Howell     | Scott A.    |
| Unl. | 1st  | 1969    | SP4     | Hubbert    | Kenny D.    |
| Unl. | 2nd  |         |         | Hudson     | Albert J.   |
| Unl. | 2nd  | 1969/70 | SP4     | Hudson     | Gary        |
| Loc. | 1st  | 1970/71 | SP4     | Hudson     | Gregory A.  |
| Loc. | 1st  | 1969/70 | SP4     | Huels      | Alvin P.    |
| Loc. | 3rd  | 1969/70 | SP4     | Hughes     | Danny W.    |
| Loc. | 3rd  | 1971    | 1LT     | Humphrey   | George J.   |
| Unl. | Unk. | 1969    | SP4     | Hunley     | Timothy J.  |
| Unl. | Unk. | l971/72 | PFC     | Hunsucker  | Dudley M.   |
| Dec. | 1st  | 1970/71 | SP4     | Hurst      | Richard T.  |
| Loc. | Unk. | 1969/70 | Medic   | Hyatt      | Kerry       |
| Loc. | 3rd  | 1968/69 | SP4     | Hyche      | Alton       |
| Loc. | 3rd  | 1969/70 | SP4     | Inderrieden| George D.   |
| Loc. | 3rd  | 1968/69 | PFC     | Inness     | Dwain C.    |
| Unl. | Unk. | 1969    | PFC     | Jackson    | Steven D.   |
| Unl. | 2nd  | 1970/71 | SP4     | Jackson    | Theobold A. |
| Unl. | Unk. | 1972    | PFC     | Jackson    | Thomas G.   |
| Loc. | 1st  | 1967/68 | PFC-RTO | James      | Ava A.      |
| Unl. | Unk. | 1971/72 | PFC     | Jaramillo  | Marin R.J.  |
| Unl. | 3rd  | 1969    | SP4     | Jarnegan   | Arthur R.   |
| Unl. | 2nd  | 1970    |         | Jasinski   | George      |
| Loc. | 2nd  | 1970    |         | Jasso      | Maximo G.   |
| Loc. | 1st  | 1969/70 | SP4     | Jenkins    | Albert      |
| Loc. | 2nd  | 1967/68 | PFC     | Jenkins    | James E.    |
| Loc. | 1st  | 1969    | PFC     | Jennings   | Steven R.   |
| Unl. | lst  | 1970    | SP4     | Jennings   | Terry J.    |
| Unl. | Unk  | 1972    |         | Johnson    | Fredrick    |
| Unl. | 3rd  |         |         | Johnson    | Glen L.     |
| Unl. | Unk. | 1971    | PFC     | Johnson    | Jackie      |
| Loc. | Unk. | 1970/71 | PFC     | Johnson    | Jimmie      |
| Unl. | Unk. | 1968/69 | SP4     | Johnson    | Larry S.    |
| Loc. | 3rd  | 1967/68 | PFC     | Johnson    | Lorin W.    |
| Unl. | Unk. | 1971/72 | PFC     | Johnson    | Robert J.   |

## Roster of Delta Raiders

| *    | PLT  | YEAR    | RANK | LAST NAME    | FIRST NAME    |
|------|------|---------|------|--------------|---------------|
| Unl. | 1st  | 1969    | SP4  | Johnson      | Wayne L.      |
| Unl. | Unk. | 1969    | PVT  | Johnson Jr.  | Robin         |
| Unl. | HQ   |         | 1SG  | Jones        | Frank N.      |
| Unl. | Unk. | 1970    |      | Jones        | Walter        |
| Dec. | 1st  | 1970    | SSG  | Jones        | Willam Edward |
| Unl. | Unk. | 1969    | SGT  | Joplin       | William F.    |
| Loc. | 2nd  | 1969/70 | SP4  | Jurva        | Leland K.     |
| Loc. | 3rd  | 1970/71 | SP4  | Kallio       | John S.       |
| Unl. | Unk. | 1971/72 | SP4  | Kanaby       | Paul E.       |
| Loc. | 3rd  | 1967/68 | SP4  | Kearns       | James R.      |
| Dec. | 1st  | 1969/70 | PFC  | Keister      | John Lay      |
| Unl. | 3rd  | 1969/70 | PFC  | Keller       | Robert J.     |
| Loc. | 2nd  | 1970/71 | SP4  | Kelley       | Ronald K.     |
| Loc. | 1st  | 1969/70 | PFC  | Kelley       | Sanford L.    |
| Unl. | Unk. | 1970/71 | PFC  | Kelly        | Edward        |
| Loc. | 2nd  | 1970/71 | PFC  | Kelly        | William C.    |
| Dec. | HQ   | 1969    | CPT  | Kelly Jr.    | John Edward   |
| Unl. | 2nd  | 1969    |      | Keogh        | Terence J.    |
| Unl. | Unk. | 1972    | SSG  | Kilgore      | Clifford D.   |
| Unl. | Unk. | 1972    | PFC  | Killner      |               |
| Unl. | Unk. | 1971/72 | SGT  | Kimble       | Donald L.     |
| Loc. | 3rd  | 1969/70 | PFC  | Kimsey       | Clarance K.   |
| Unl. | Unk. | 1969    | PFC  | King         | George L.     |
| Loc. | 1st  | 1970/7l | SGT  | King Jr.     | Harry E.      |
| Dec. | 3rd  | 1969/70 | PFC  | Kinsey       | William D.    |
| Unl. | Unk  | 1972    | PFC  | Kirby        | Mark R.       |
| Loc. | 3rd  | 1970/7l | SP4  | Kirk         | Stephen J.    |
| Loc. | 2nd  | 1970/71 | SSG  | Kirklin      | Stephen M.    |
| Loc. | 1st  | 1969/70 | 1LT  | Kirmse       | James T.      |
| Unl. | Unk. | 1972    | PFC  | Kirtley      | Roger D.      |
| Unl. | HQ   | 1971    | 1SG  | Klaer        |               |
| Unl. | Unk. | 1968/69 | SP4  | Kleckley     | Emanuel       |
| Loc. | Unk. | 1969    | PFC  | Klingaman    | Ronald L.     |
| Unl. | Unk. | 1971/72 | SP4  | Klinkman     | William R.    |
| Unl. | Unk. | 1972    | SP4  | Knapp        | John K.       |
| Dec. | 1st  | 1970    | PFC  | Knickerbocker| Robert J.     |
| Unl. | Unk. | 1972    | PFC  | Knight       | Jesse E.      |
| Unl. | 4th  | 1967/68 | SP4  | Koage1       | Bernard C.    |
| Unl. | Unk. | 1968    | SP4  | Kolesar      | Albert J.     |
| Loc. | 1st  | 1969    | PFC  | Kolodzey     | Leslie J.     |

## Roster of Delta Raiders

| *    | PLT  | YEAR    | RANK      | LAST NAME     | FIRST NAME   |
|------|------|---------|-----------|---------------|--------------|
| Loc. | 3rd  | 1971    | Medic     | Konkal        | Roger        |
| Loc. | 3rd  | 1967/68 | SGT       | Kopay         | Michael V.   |
| Loc. | 2nd  | 1969/70 |           | Kosa#W59871 J7 | Charles G.  |
| Loc. | 1st  | 1970/71 | SSG       | Kron          | Charles      |
| Loc. | Unk. | 1971-72 | SP4       | Kucera        | Laddie       |
| Loc. | 3rd  | 1971    | PFC       | Kusiak        | Randall J.   |
| Unl. | Unk. | 1969    | PFC       | Lasanta-Rolon | Jos.         |
| Unl. | 1st  | 1971    | PEC       | Labelle       | Joseph       |
| Unl. | Unk. | 1968    | SP4       | Ladue         | Joseph B.    |
| Unl. | 3rd  | 1967/68 | SP4       | Laing Jr.     | William H.   |
| Unl. | Unk. | 1969    | SP4       | Lamb          | Jack E.      |
| Unl. | Unk. | 1972    | PFC       | Lambert       | Jerry L.     |
| Unl. | 2nd  | 1969    |           | Larson        | Michael J.   |
| Unl. | 3rd  | 1971    | PFC       | Lauver        | James W.     |
| Loc. | 3rd  | 1968/69 | SP4       | Lawley        | Tommy R.     |
| Unl. | 3rd  | 1967/68 | SP4       | Leaf          | David R.     |
| Unl. | Unk  | 1971/72 | SP4       | Lee           | Oscar R.     |
| Unl. | Unk. | 1968/69 | SGT       | Leon          | Wallace J.   |
| Unl. | Unk. | 1967/68 | PFC       | Leonzi        | Thomas E.    |
| Loc. | Unk. | 1968/69 | 1LT       | Leshikar      | Todon C.     |
| Unl. | Unk. | 1972    | PFC       | Levario       | Adolpho P.   |
| Unl. | Unk  | 1972    | PFC       | Lewis         | James        |
| Unl. | 2nd  |         |           | Lewis         | Willie J.    |
| Unl. | 3rd  | 1971    | PFC       | Lewis Jr.     | Tommy        |
| Unl. | HQ   | 1968/69 | SP4       | Leysath       | Thurmond K.  |
| Loc. | 1st  | 1971    |           | Lieby         | Charles J.   |
| Unl. | Unk. | 1968/69 | PFC       | Livingston    | David C.     |
| Unl. | Unk. | 1968/69 | PFC       | Livingston    | William      |
| Unl. | Unk. | 1972    | PFC       | Loftin        | Alan M.      |
| Loc. | 2nd  | 1967-68 | 2LT       | Loftin        | William D.   |
| Loc. | 1st  | 1969/70 | SP4       | Logan         | James E.     |
| Unl. | 1st  | 1967/68 | SP4       | Longbottom    | Harry P.     |
| Unl. | 2nd  | 1967-68 | SP4       | Lopez         | Luis F.      |
| Loc. | 2nd  | 1967/68 | PFC       | Losinger      | Chester L.   |
| Loc. | 1st  | 1968/69 | SP5-Medic | Loucks        | Terry L.     |
| Loc. | 1st  | 1969    | SGT       | Lovell        | Larry D.     |
| Unl. | 2nd  | 1967/68 | PFC       | Lucas         | Rufas E.     |
| Unl. | Unk. | 1971    | SGT       | Luke          | James L.     |
| Unl. | 2nd  | 1969/70 | SSC       | Lusk          | Roger D.     |
| Unl. | HQ   | 1969    | SP4       | Lynch         | Carlos J.    |

| *    | PLT  | YEAR    | RANK      | LAST NAME  | FIRST NAME     |
|------|------|---------|-----------|------------|----------------|
| Unl. | Unk. | 1969    | SP4       | Lyons      | David E.       |
| Unl. | 3rd  | 1970/71 | PFC       | Lyons      | Russell I.     |
| Unl. | 1st  | 1969/70 | PFC       | Mack       | Jimmy R.       |
| Unl. | Unk. | 1970    | PFC       | Maguire    | Ronald         |
| Unl. | Unk. | 1969    | PFC       | Mahoney    | David B.       |
| Unl. | Unk. | 1972    | PFC       | Malcom     | George N.      |
| Unl. | Unk. | 1971/72 | SP4       | Maldonado  | Luis           |
| Loc. | 2nd  | 1969/70 | SGT       | Mallard    | Vaughn T.      |
| Loc. | 2nd  | 1969/70 | SP4       | Mangum     | Lee A.         |
| Unl. | Unk. | 1972    | PFC       | Mara       | John R.        |
| Unl. | 1st  | 1969    | SGT       | Marquez    | Clemente       |
| Dec. | 2nd  | 1968    | PFC       | Marron     | Bruce A.       |
| Unl. | Unk. | 1968    | SP4       | Marrow     | Charles E.     |
| Loc. | 3rd  | 197071  | SP4       | Marsh      | Donald L.      |
| Loc. | 2nd  | 1967/68 | SP4       | Martin     | David W.       |
| Unl. | 1st  | 1967/68 | SSG       | Martin     | James L.       |
| Loc. | 1st  | 1971/72 | 1LT       | Martin     | Perry W.       |
| Loc. | 2nd  | 1968/69 | SP4       | Martin     | Robert R.      |
| Unl. | Unk. | 1969    | SP4       | Martin     | Tony L.        |
| Dec. | Unk. | 1969    | PVT       | Martinez   | Alex Esequiel  |
| Unl. | 1st  | 1967/68 | SP4       | Martinez   | Glenn          |
| Unl. | 2nd  | 1970/71 | PFC       | Martinez   | Nick           |
| Loc. | HQ   | 1967/68 | SGT-RTO   | Marunchuck | Lawrence       |
| Unl. | Unk  | 1971    | SP4       | Massey     | Vernal         |
| Unl. | 3rd  | 1969/70 | SP4       | Mastro     | Mark S.        |
| Unl. | 1st  | 1969/70 | PFC       | Masunaga   | Clifford M.    |
| Unl. | Unk. | 1971    | PFC       | Matheu     | Francisco M.   |
| Unl. | Unk. | 1972    | SP4       | Mathews    | Charles D.     |
| Unl. | Unk. | 1972    | SP4       | Mauer      | Jack A.        |
| Dec. | Unk. | 1970    | PFC       | Maynard    | Richard Lee    |
| Unl. | Unk  | 1970/71 | PFC-Medic | McCants    | Henry L.       |
| Unl. | Ist  | 1969/70 | SGT       | McCarthy   | Joseph M.      |
| Unl. | Unk. | 1971    | SP4       | McClellan  | Harry H.       |
| Unl. | 3rd  | 1969/70 | SSG       | McCloskey  | Donald W.      |
| Loc. | 3rd  | 1969/70 | SP4       | McCreight  | Kenneth W.     |
| Unl. | 3rd  | 1970/71 | SP4       | McDonald   | Orie S.        |
| Unl. | Unk. | 1969    | 1LT       | McEachern  | Robert         |
| Unl. | Unk. | 1968    | SP4       | McGee      | Eddie          |
| Loc. | 2nd  | 1970/71 | SGT       | McGee      | George T.      |
| Unl. | Unk. | 1969    | SP4       | McGill     | Jimmy D.       |

| *    | PLT  | YEAR    | RANK      | LAST NAME    | FIRST NAME     |
|------|------|---------|-----------|--------------|----------------|
| Dec. | 2nd  | 1971    |           | McGinnes     | Charles Dennis |
| Unl. | 3rd  | 1969/70 | SP4       | McGowans     | Norman D.      |
| Unl. | 3rd  | 1968/69 | SP4       | McGowen      | Jimmy D.       |
| Unl. | 3rd  | 1969    | PFC       | McIntyre     | Harry J.       |
| Dec. | 2nd  | 1971    | 1LT       | McKenzie     | Paul           |
| Unl. | Unk. | 1967/68 | SP4-Medic | McKieghan    | David H.       |
| Loc. | 2nd  | 1971    | PFC       | McKinney     | James B.       |
| Loc. | 2nd  |         |           | McKinney     | Joel           |
| Unl. | Unk. | 1971/72 | 1LT       | McKinney     | Joseph W.      |
| Dec. | 3rd  | 1971    | PFC       | McKinney     | Robert Dale    |
| Unl. | Unk. | 1972    | SP4       | McKinney     | Stanley A.     |
| Unl. | Unk. | 1969    | PFC       | McLaughlin   | Thuron B.      |
| Unl. | Unk. | 1968    | SP4-Cook  | McManee      | Dennis M.      |
| Dec. | 1st  | 1967/68 | SGT       | McManus      | Ernest         |
| Loc. | HQ   | 1967/68 | CPT       | McMenamy     | Charles Wayne  |
| Loc. | 2nd  | 1967/68 | SP4       | McMichael    | Howard R.      |
| Loc. | 2nd  | 1971    | PFC       | McMillen     | Jimmie D.      |
| Loc. | 3rd  | 1970/71 | PFC       | McNeil       | Luther         |
| Unl. | Unk. | 1970    |           | McVey        | James          |
| Loc. | 1st  | 1971/72 | SP4       | Meador       | Garrett C.     |
| Loc. | 2nd  | 1970/71 | PFC-RTO   | Medina       | Martin L.      |
| Unl. | 2nd  | 1967/68 | SGT       | Medina-Diaz  | Julio          |
| Loc. | 2nd  | 1968/69 | PFC       | Meeks        | Thomas J.      |
| Unl. | Unk. | 1968    | PFC       | Mejia        | John R.        |
| Unl. | 2nd  | 1969    | SGT       | Menhorn      | Ronald L.      |
| Unl. | 2nd  | 1969    | PFC       | Mercado      | Jose E.        |
| Loc. | 1st  | 1969/70 | SGT       | Mergentharer | Randy          |
| Unl. | HQ   | 1967/68 | SSG       | Merrett      | Carlton G.     |
| Unl. | 1st  | 1970    |           | Messman      | Thomas         |
| Loc. | HQ   | 1967/68 | SP4-RTO   | Meyer        | Virgil S.      |
| Unl. | Unk. | 1971/72 | SGT       | Michael      | Daniel         |
| Loc. | 2nd  | 1970/71 | SGT       | Michael      | James          |
| Loc. | 1st  | 1969/70 | SP4-Medic | Michener     | Dan            |
| Unl. | Unk. | 1971/72 | SP4       | Mickles      | Eddie D.       |
| Unl. | 3rd  | 1967/68 | PFC       | Miles        | Thomas L.      |
| Unl. | 3rd  |         |           | Miles        | Vincent W.     |
| Unl. | Unk. | 1971/72 | SP4       | Milford      | Edward M.      |
| Unl. | Unk. | 1968    | SP4       | Milla        | Gutierrez R.   |
| Unl. | 3rd  | 1969    | SP4       | Miller       | Bernard F.     |
| Unl. | HQ   | 1970    | 1LT       | Miller       | Dallas         |

Roster of Delta Raiders

| * | PLT | YEAR | RANK | LAST NAME | FIRST NAME |
|---|---|---|---|---|---|
| Unl. | Unk | 1971 | SGT | Miller | Franklin D. |
| Loc. | 3rd | 1970/71 | SGT | Miller | Gary P. |
| Unl. | Unk. | 1967/68 | SP4-Medic | Miller | Harold |
| Unl. | Unk. | 1971/72 |  | Miller | Paul |
| Unl. | Unk. | 1970 | PFC | Milligan | Emery |
| Unl. | Unk. | 1971/72 | SGT | Milliken | Robert F. |
| Unl. | Unk. | 1970/71 | PFC | Mills | Gregory H. |
| Unl. | Urk. | 1971/72 | PFC | Milner | Neal A. |
| Unl. | Unk. | 1970/71 | SP4 | Mineff | Steve C. |
| Loc. | 3rd | 1970/71 | SGT | Mitchell | C. David |
| Unl. | Unk. | 1969 | SP4 | Mitchell | David D. |
| Unl. | 2nd |  |  | Mitchell | James R. |
| Unl. | 1st | 1968/69 | SP4 | Mitchell | Jerry E. |
| Unl. | 3rd | 1969/70 | PFC | Mitchell | Larry R. |
| Unl. | Unk. | 1971 | SGT | Mitchell | Leslie C. |
| Unl. | 2nd | 1969 | PFC | Mitchell Jr. | James |
| Loc. | HQ | 1968/69 | SP4 | Mitotes | Harry |
| Unl. | HQ | 1972 | CPT | Montano | James J. |
| Loc. | 1st | 1968/69 | SP4 | Moore | Roy J. |
| Loc. | 2nd | 1970/71 | SGT | Moore | Terry B. |
| Unl. | 2nd | 1968/69 | 1LT | Moore II | Van H. (John ?) |
| Dec. | 1st | 1969/70 | SP4 | Morace | Leon J. |
| Unl. | Unk. | 1968 | SP4-Medic | Morauske | Paul D. |
| Loc. | 2nd | 1969 | PFC | Moreno | Michael E. |
| Loc. | 3rd | 1969/70 |  | Morgan | Robert L. |
| Unl. | 1st | 1967/68 | PFC | Morris | James L. |
| Unl. | 1st | 1967/68 | SSG | Morris Jr. | William |
| Unl. | Unk. | 1968 | SP4 | Morrow | Charles E. |
| Unl. | 1st | 1970 | 1LT | Morton | Bruce B. |
| Loc. | 1st | 1969/70 |  | Morton | Paul M. |
| Unl. | 2nd | 1969 | SP4 | Moses | Lawrence R. |
| Unl. | Unk. | 1971 | PFC | Mosley | Albert D. |
| Unl. | 2nd | 1969 | SP4-Medic | Motter | Jacob |
| Loc. | 1st | 1967/68 | SGT | Mount | Alfred M. |
| Unl. | Unk | 1971 | PFC | Mullins | Willard R. |
| Dec. | 1st | 1970 | PFC | Muncey | Jay Allen |
| Unl. | Unk. | 1969 | SP4 | Murray | Danny R. |
| Loc. | 2nd | 1969 | SP4-Medic | Musewicz | John J. |
| Loc. | 1st | 1969/70 | SP4 | Myles | Roger |
| Loc. | HQ | 1967/68 | SP4 | Nale Jr. | Lonnie |

| * | PLT | YEAR | RANK | LAST NAME | FIRST NAME |
|---|---|---|---|---|---|
| Unl. | Unk. | 1971/72 | PFC | Nava | John R. |
| Loc. | 1st | 1969/70 | SGT | Neal | Jeffrey A. |
| Unl. | Unk. | 1971/72 | PFC | Necaise | Phillip M. |
| Loc. | HQ | 1967/68 | SGT-RTO | Nelson | Clark E. |
| Loc. | 3rd | 1970/71 | | Neubert | David A. |
| Unl. | Unk. | 1970/71 | PFC | Neuendorff | Marvin T. |
| Loc. | 2nd | 1970/71 | SP4 | Neumiller | Daryl R. |
| Unl. | Unk. | 1968 | SP4 | Newsome | Ermil R. |
| Unl. | 2nd | 1968/69 | SGT | Nichol | Edward E. |
| Unl. | Unk. | 1972 | PFC | Nickel | Charles R. |
| Unl. | Unk. | 1971/72 | PFC | Nieves-Morales | Luis |
| Unl. | Unk. | 1972 | SP4 | Niggles | Eddie D. |
| Unl. | 2nd | 1969 | PFC | Nissen | Gerald L. |
| Loc. | 3rd | 1971 | PFC | Nix | Rex |
| Loc. | 2nd | 1969 | SGT | Noble | James P. |
| Unl. | HQ | 1967-68 | SGT-RTO | Noe | James H. |
| Dec. | Unk. | 1968/69 | SP4 | Nordell Jr. | John E. |
| Loc. | 1st | 1968/69 | SGT | Northrup | Clarence V. |
| Unl. | Unk. | 1971 | SP4 | Nowell | Bradley S. |
| Unl. | Unk | 1972 | PFC | Nowlin III | William C. |
| Unl. | Unk. | 1971/72 | SGT | Noyes | Don 0. |
| Loc. | 4th | 1967/68 | SP4 | Nunez-Perez | Isreal |
| Unl. | 2nd | 1969 | Medic | OHarra | James |
| Loc. | 1st | 1967/68 | Medic | Oak | Brian |
| Unl. | Unk. | 1969 | SP4 | Oakley | Richard P. |
| Unl. | Unk. | 1971 | SGT | Obryan III | John L. |
| Unl. | 2nd | 1968/69 | SP4 | Oerman Jr. | Richard E. |
| Unl. | Unk. | 1972 | SP4 | Oldmixon | Alan E. |
| Unl. | Unk. | 1971/72 | SP4 | Oliveria | John E. |
| Unl. | 1st | 1969/70 | SSG | Ormsby | Keith |
| Unl. | Unk. | 1969 | SGT | Orr | William G. |
| Unl. | 1st | 1968/69 | SP4 | Osborne | William L. |
| Loc. | 3rd | 1970/71 | SGT | Padilla | Richard L. |
| Loc. | 1st | 1970/71 | SP4 | Pagan | Monzon S. |
| Unl. | 1st | 1969 | SP4 | Page | Eugene |
| Loc. | 3rd | 1970/71 | PFC | Page | Frank L. |
| Unl. | Unk. | 1972 | PFC | Paines | Dwight L. |
| Unl. | Unk. | 1968/69 | SGT | Painter | Kerry A. |
| Dec. | 1st | 1970 | 1LT | Palm | Terry Alan |

| * | PLT | YEAR | RANK | LAST NAME | FIRST NAME |
|---|---|---|---|---|---|
| Unl. | 2nd | | | Paprocky | Eugene N. |
| Unl. | Unk. | 1967 | PFC | Parish | Donald N. |
| Unl. | Unk. | 1969 | PSG | Parker | George W. |
| Unl. | Unk. | 1971/72 | SP4 | Parker | Kimball B. |
| Loc. | 1st | 1967/68 | PSG | Parker Jr. | George R. |
| Unl. | Unk. | 1971/72 | PFC | Parks | Lawrence H. |
| Loc. | 2nd | 1968/69 | SP4-RTO | Parlier | Kenneth A. |
| Unl. | Unk. | 1971/72 | PFC | Parmes | Dwight L. |
| Loc. | 2nd | 1967/68 | SGT | Parnell | Gary O. |
| Unl. | Unk. | 1969 | SP4 | Parnell | Paul S. |
| Loc. | 3rd | 1970 | | Pascale | James E. |
| Unl. | Unk. | 1971 | SGT | Patterson | Carl F. |
| Unl. | Unk. | 1969/70 | SP4 | Patterson | Regg K. |
| Unl. | 3rd | 1971 | | Pavelich | David |
| Loc. | 1st | 1967/68 | SGT | Payne | Gary L. |
| Unl. | Unk. | 1971 | SP4 | Payne | John C. |
| Unl. | Unk. | 1971/7 | SP4 | Pearson | Ronald |

## Roster of Delta Raiders

| *    | PLT  | YEAR    | RANK     | LAST NAME    | FIRST NAME   |
|------|------|---------|----------|--------------|--------------|
| Loc. | 3rd  | 1967/68 | SP4      | Pechacek     | Glenn S.     |
| Unl. | 2nd  | 1968/69 | PFC      | Peck         | James F.     |
| Unl. | Unk. | 1969/70 | 1LT      | Peele        | Robert A.    |
| Unl. | Unk. | 1968    | PFC      | Penick       | Tommy R.     |
| Unl. | Unk. | 1971    | PFC      | Perdue       | Doug         |
| Unl. | Unk. | 1971/72 | PFC      | Perez        | Dometrio M.  |
| Unl. | 1st  | 1967/68 | SGT      | Perez        | Ernest       |
| Unl. | Unk. | 1968    | PFC-Cook | Perez        | Ricardo      |
| Unl. | 3rd  | 1970    | PFC      | Perez Jr.    | Albert       |
| Unl. | Unk. | 1968    | PFC      | Perez-Torres | Ricar        |
| Unl. | 1st  |         |          | Perry        | Martin       |
| Unl. | Unk. | 1967    | SP4      | Petcker      | Robert L.    |
| Loc. | 1st  | 1967/68 | SGT      | Peterson     | Dwight E.    |
| Unl. | 1st  | 1967/68 | SSG      | Petitt       | Edward E.    |
| Unl. | Unk. | 1968    | PFC      | Phillips     | George D.    |
| Loc. | 2nd  | 1968/69 | 1LT      | Phillips     | Ronald E.    |
| Loc. | 1st  | 1968/69 | SP4      | Pickett      | Donald R.    |
| Loc. | 2nd  | 1969/70 | PFC      | Pierce       | William H.   |
| Unl. | Unk. | 1969    | SGT      | Pimentel     | Richard K.   |
| Unl. | Unk. | 1967/68 | SP4      | Piotrowski   | Longin       |
| Loc. | 2nd  | 1970    |          | Plenderleith | James        |
| Unl. | Unk. | 1971    | SGT      | Pogne        | Kennet W.    |
| Unl. | Unk. | 1967/68 | PFC      | Pogue        | Ken W.       |
| Unl. | Unk. | 1971/72 | SP4      | Pohlman      | Larry H.     |
| Unl. | Unk. | 1970/71 | 2LT      | Polach       | John J.      |
| Loc. | 2nd  | 1970    | SP4      | Policz       | Richard C.   |
| Unl. | 1st  | 1969    | SP4      | Pondi        | Bruce A.     |
| Loc. | HQ   | 1971    | CPT      | Post         | Francis W.   |
| Unl. | Unk. | 1970    |          | Postreil     | William      |
| Loc. | HQ   | 1970    | 319th FA | Potter       | James M.     |
| Unl. | 2nd  | 1970    | SGT      | Poullard     | James L.     |
| Unl. | 2nd  | 1969/70 | SP4      | Powell       | Jimmy L.     |
| Unl. | 2nd  | 1968/69 | SP4      | Powers       | Henry L.     |
| Loc. | 1st  | 1970    |          | Pressley     | Marty G.     |
| Loc. | Unk. | 1968/69 | Medic    | Preston      | HMCS David R.|
| Unl. | Unk. | 1971    | PFC      | Pribble      | Ronald E.    |
| Unl. | Unk. | 1971/72 | PFC      | Primrose     | Niles L.     |
| Unl. | Unk. | 1972    | PFC      | Pritt        | Dometrio M.  |
| Dec. | 1st  | 1967/68 | SSG      | Probert Jr.  | Donald K.    |
| Unl. | Unk. | 1970    |          | Putnay       | Larry        |

## Roster of Delta Raiders

| *    | PLT  | YEAR    | RANK      | LAST NAME    | FIRST NAME  |
|------|------|---------|-----------|--------------|-------------|
| Unl. | 1st  | 1967/68 | SGT       | Rachell      | James C.    |
| Unl. | HQ   | 1969    | SP5-Medic | Raemaker     | John L.     |
| Unl. | 3rd  | 1967/68 | PFC       | Rainey       | Barry       |
| Unl. | 2nd  | 1967/68 | SP4       | Rainwater    | Robert L.   |
| Loc. | 1st  | 1967/68 | SP4       | Rakestraw    | Bobby L.    |
| Unl. | Unk. | 1971    | SGT       | Ralph Jr.    | Patrick F.  |
| Unl. | 3rd  | 1970/71 | SP4       | Ramey        | Clinton A.  |
| Unl. | Unk. | 1969/70 | PFC       | Ramos-Roman  | Ismeal      |
| Loc. | 3rd  | 1969/70 | SP4       | Rasmussen    | Max D.      |
| Loc. | 3rd  | 1968/69 | PFC       | Raterman     | Ronald J.   |
| Unl. | 2nd  | 1969/70 | SP4       | Rathman      | Howard V.   |
| Loc. | 3rd  | l971    | SP4       | Raynor       | Jerry L.    |
| Unl. | 2nd  | 1968/69 | SP4       | Rector       | Roger G.    |
| Loc. | 3rd  | 1969    | 1LT       | Rector Jr.   | John M.     |
| Unl. | Unk. | 1967/68 | PVT       | Reed         | Arthur R.   |
| Unl. | 1st  | 1967/68 | SP4       | Reese Jr.    | Simon B.    |
| Unl. | Unk. | 1971    | SGT       | Reid         | Barry M.    |
| Loc. | 1st  | 1969/70 | SP4       | Reitz        | Douglas N.  |
| Loc. | 2nd  | 1971    | SP4       | Remmick      | Raymond F.  |
| Loc. | 3rd  | 1967/68 | PFC       | Remund       | Donald N.   |
| Unl. | Unk. | 1971    | SGT       | Repik        | Robert T.   |
| Unl. | 2nd  | 1969    | 2LT       | Reyes        | Rudy P.     |
| Unl. | Unk. | 1971/72 | SP4       | Reynoldson   | Donald J.   |
| Unl. | Unk. | 1971/72 | SGT       | Rhodes       | Thomas A.   |
| Unl. | Unk. | 1968/69 | SP4       | Rhoton       | Curtis D.   |
| Unl. | Unk. | 1970/71 | PFC       | Rice         | Gary M.     |
| Unl. | Unk. | 1968    | SP4-Cook  | Rice         | John E.     |
| Unl. | Unk. | 1971    | SGT       | Richards     | Donald M.   |
| Loc. | 2nd  | 1969/70 | SP4       | Richardson   | Larry R.    |
| Loc. | HQ   | 1968/69 | PFC       | Rife         | Wilbur M.   |
| Loc. | 1st  | 1967/68 | PFC       | Riley        | Stanley W.  |
| Unl. | Unk. | 1971/72 | SP4       | Rivera       | Albert      |
| Unl. | Unk. | 1971/72 | SP4       | Rivera       | William     |
| Unl. | Unk. | 1971/72 | SP4       | Robbins      | David L.    |
| Unl. | Unk. | 1970/71 | PFC       | Robbins      | Leonard E.  |
| Loc. | 2nd  | 1968/69 | SP4       | Roberts      | John K.     |
| Loc. | 2nd  |         |           | Roberts      | Reginald W. |
| Loc. | Unk. | 1971/72 | PFC       | Roberts      | Ronald      |
| Loc. | 2nd  | 1967/68 | SGT       | Robertson    | Eugene E.   |
| Unl. | 1st  | 1969    |           | Robetzke     | Richard     |

| *    | PLT  | YEAR    | RANK      | LAST NAME  | FIRST NAME    |
|------|------|---------|-----------|------------|---------------|
| Loc. | 2nd  | 1970    | PFC       | Robinson   | Carl E.       |
| Loc. | 3rd  | 1970/71 | SSG       | Robinson   | George M.     |
| Unl. | 3rd  | 1969/70 | SSG       | Robinson   | James E.      |
| Unl. | 2nd  | 1969/70 | PFC       | Robinson   | Johnny G.     |
| Dec. | 3rd  | 1971    | SSG       | Rochester  | Philip        |
| Loc. | 2nd  | 1967/68 | PFC       | Rockel     | Noah R.       |
| Unl. | 1st  | 1970    | SP4       | Rodriguez  | Luis A.       |
| Dec. | 3rd  | 1970/71 | PFC       | Rolland    | Terry L.      |
| Dec. | 1st  | 1969/70 | SP4       | Rollason   | William David |
| Loc. | 1st  | 1968/69 | SPS-Medic | Rolls      | Tomas E.      |
| Unl. | HQ   | 1969/70 |           | Rosas      | Carlos        |
| Loc. | Unk. | 1968    | SGT       | Royer      | Samuel P.     |
| Loc. | 2nd  | 1967/68 | PFC       | Rubbelke   | Donald P.     |
| Dec. | 2nd  | 1969/70 | 1LT       | Rufty      | Joe Hearne    |
| Unl. | Unk. | 1971    | SP4       | Ruiz       | Ronald S.     |
| Loc. | 3rd  | 1969/70 | SP4       | Rundquist  | Carl W.       |
| Loc. | 3rd  | 1967/68 | PFC       | Ryan       | Richard       |
| Unl. | Unk. | 1969    | SP4       | Ryan       | Thomas J.     |
| Loc. | HQ   |         | FO        | Saitta     | Tom           |
| Unl. | Unk. | 1968    | PFC       | Salisbury  | Francis C.    |
| Loc. | 2nd  | 1969/70 | SP4       | Salzman Jr.| Arthur J.     |
| Unl. | Unk. | 1971/72 | SP4       | Sanders    | Marshall O.   |
| Unl. | 1st  | 1969    | PFC       | Sanderson  | Jimmy R.      |
| Loc. | 2nd  | 1969/70 |           | Sanford    | James T.      |
| Unl. | 3rd  | 1969/70 | SP4       | Sanford    | Lloyd L.      |
| Unl. | 2nd  | 1970    |           | Sardina    | James A.      |
| Unl. | Unk. | 1971    | SSG       | Sarraeino  |               |
| Dec. | 3rd  | 1968    | PFC       | Saunders   | Michael Joseph|
| Loc. | 3rd  | 1970/71 | SP4       | Sautter    | Gary D.       |
| Loc. | lst  | 1970    | SP4       | Savage     | Ira L.        |
| Unl. | HQ   | 1967/68 | SGT       | Savic      | George        |
| Unl. | 2nd  |         |           | Savoy      | Lionel J.     |
| Loc. | 2nd  | 1967/68 | PFC       | Saxiones   | Nicholas      |
| Loc. | 3rd  | 1970/71 | SP4       | Schaaf     | Francis G.    |
| Loc. | 3rd  | 1971/72 | SPS-Medic | Schaefer   | Terry L.      |
| Unl. | 3rd  | 1970    |           | Schaub     | Herbert P.    |
| Loc. | 2nd  | 1968/69 | SP4       | Scherger   | Arlen A.      |
| Unl. | Unk. | 1972    | PFC       | Schiberl   | Timothy L.    |
| Dec. | 2nd  | 1969/70 | SSG       | Schneider  | Gary Lee      |
| Loc. | HQ   | 1969/70 | 1SG       | Schuelke   | John T.       |

| * | PLT | YEAR | RANK | LAST NAME | FIRST NAME |
|---|---|---|---|---|---|
| Unl. | Unk. | 1971 | SGT | Schultz | Victor L. |
| Unl. | Unk. | 1972 | PFC | Schumpert | Dale R. |
| Unl. | Unk. | 1972 | SP4 | Schupp | Stephen A. |
| Loc. | Unk. | 1970/71 | SGT | Schweikert | Gary |
| Unl. | 3rd | 1969/70 | PFC | Scillia | Mario |
| Unl. | 4th | 1967/68 | SGT | Scott | Harold |
| Unl. | Unk. | 1971 | PFC | Scott | Joe D. |
| Loc. | 3rd | 1967/68 | SGT | Scott | Ronald D. |
| Loc. | HQ | 1967/68 | 1SG | Scott Jr. | Arthur |
| Unl. | 1st | 1970 | SGT | Scrova | |
| Loc. | 2nd | 1969/70 | SGT | Seaborn | Jeffery A. |
| Unl. | 1st | 1969 | SP4 | Searcy | Arnold |
| Unl. | Unk. | 1968 | PFC | Seib | Leroy R. |
| Loc. | 3rd | 1969/70 | 1LT | Selvaggi | Ralph L. |
| Unl. | Unk. | 1971/72 | PFC | Settles | Michael E. |
| Unl. | Unk. | 1970/71 | SP4 | Sexton | Gordon A. |
| Loc. | 1st | 1970 | SP4 | Shannon | Carlton C. |
| Unl. | 3rd | 1969/70 | PFC | Sharp | Herman E. |
| Loc. | 2nd | 1970/71 | PFC | Shaw | Willard A. |
| Dec. | Unk. | 1968 | SP4 | Sheldon | Leroy Eldan |
| Unl. | Unk. | 1968/69 | | Sheraco | |
| Unl. | Unk. | 1969 | SP4 | Sheridan | James J. |
| Unl. | Unk. | 1972 | PFC | Sherman | Russel N. |
| Unl. | Unk | 1968 | PFC | Sherrell | Jimmy |
| Loc. | 3rd | 1970/71 | SGT | Shilling | Giles W. |
| Loc. | 2nd | 1970 | 1LT | Shipley | John D. |
| Unl. | 1st | 1969/70 | PFC | Shirk | Bert E. |
| Unl. | Unk. | 1971/72 | SP4 | Shoffner | Roy R. |
| Loc. | 1st | 1969/70 | SP4 | Silvus | Francis D. |
| Unl. | 3rd | 1967/68 | PFC | Simmons | Dennis C. |
| Unl. | Unk. | 1969/70 | SP4 | Simpson | John J. |
| Unl. | HQ | 1970/71 | 1SG | Simpson | L.N. |
| Unl. | Unk. | 1971/72 | SP4 | Sims | Bobby J. |
| Dec. | 2nd | 1967/68 | SSG | Sims | Clifford Chester |
| Unl. | 2nd | 1970 | PFC | Sims | Robert J. |
| Unl. | Unk. | 1970/71 | PFC | Sinzi | John N. |
| Unl. | Unk. | 1971/72 | SSG | Skipwith Jr. | Leon |
| Loc. | 2nd | 1970/71 | PFC | Sklanka | Bernard M. |
| Loc. | 3rd | 1968/69 | SGT | Sloan | Thomas L. |
| Loc. | 3rd | 1970/71 | SP4 | Small | Craig E. |

# Roster of Delta Raiders

| *    | PLT  | YEAR    | RANK | LAST NAME | FIRST NAME   |
|------|------|---------|------|-----------|--------------|
| Unl. | Unk. | 1970/71 | SP4  | Small     | Judson       |
| Unl. | 3rd  | 1971    | PFC  | Smith     | Barry R.     |
| Unl. | Unk. | 1971/72 | SGT  | Smith     | Brent F.     |
| Loc. | HQ   | 1971    | SFC  | Smith     | Buford W.    |
| Unl. | Unk. | 1969    | PFC  | Smith     | Jacob J.     |
| Loc. | 1st  | 1970/71 | SGT  | Smith     | Jeffery A.   |
| Unl. | Unk. | 1968    | PFC  | Smith     | Larry J.     |
| Loc. | 2nd  | 1968/69 | PFC  | Smith     | Marvin       |
| Loc. | 3rd  | 1970/71 | PFC  | Smith     | Paul         |
| Loc. | 2nd  | 1970/71 |      | Smith     | Timothy J.   |
| Loc. | 2nd  | 1968/69 | SSG  | Smith     | Volney T.    |
| Unl. | Unk. | 1971/72 | SP4  | Smith Jr. | William E.   |
| Unl. | Unk. | 1968/69 | SP4  | Smothers  | Ronald L.    |
| Unl. | Unk. | 1972    | PFC  | Smouse    | Cliff D.     |
| Unl. | 1st  | 1967/68 | SP4  | Snead     | Michael P.   |
| Loc. | 1st  | 1968/69 | SGT  | Snyder    | Arthur M.    |
| Unl. | Unk. | 1970/71 | SSG  | Snyder    | Clyde R.     |
| Unl. | HQ   | 1969    |      | Snyder    | James M.     |
| Unl. | Unk. | 1970/71 | SP4  | Somerville| George A.    |
| Dec. | 2nd  | 1969    | PFC  | Sommer    | Douglas John |
| Unl. | 1st  |         |      | Sorenson  | (Jim?)       |
| Unl. | Unk. | 1968    | PFC  | Sorrell   | Jimmy C.     |
| Loc. | 1st  | 1969/70 |      | Soubers   | Richard R.   |

| * | PLT | YEAR | RANK | LAST NAME | FIRST NAME |
|---|---|---|---|---|---|
| Unl. | 3rd | 1969 | SP4 | Speakman | Terry D. |
| Unl. | Unk. | 1971/72 | PFC | Spear | Rodney W. |
| Unl. | 3rd | 1970 | | Spears | Lanny W. |
| Loc. | 3rd | 1967/68 | SP4 | Speer | Jack |
| Unl. | 2nd | 1969/70 | | Spiars | Donald E. |
| Loc. | 3rd | 1967/68 | SP4-Medic | Spivey | Alex D. |
| Unl. | 3rd | | | Spivey | Lawrence C. |
| Unl. | Unk. | 1971/72 | SSG | Spooner | Lawrence W. |
| Unl. | Unk. | 1971/72 | PFC | Sprouse | Glenn D. |
| Loc. | HQ | 1971/72 | 2LT | St. Peter | Albert J. |
| Unl. | Unk. | 1972 | SP4 | Stanley | Gary L. |
| Loc. | 2nd | 1970/71 | SP4-RTO | Stapleton | Ronald L. |
| Unl. | 4th | 1967/68 | SP4 | Starks | Victor I. |
| Dec. | 2nd | 1970/71 | SGT | Stearns | Jerry Sheldon |
| Unl. | HQ | 1969 | SGT | Stegman | Adolph J. |
| Unl. | 3rd | 1969/70 | SGT | Stehman | Edward L. |
| Loc. | Unk. | 1968 | PFC | Stengle | Dale Leroy |
| Unl. | Unk. | 1969/70 | PFC | Stephens | Carlton L. |
| Unl. | Unk. | 1972 | SP4 | Stephens | Stephen W. |
| Unl. | Unk. | 1972 | SP4 | Stevens | Rickey A. |
| Loc. | 1st | 1970 | SP4 | Stewart | Garrett E. |
| Unl. | HQ | 1968/69 | SP4 | Stewart | Robert E. |
| Unl. | Unk. | 1968 | PFC | Stickle | James H. |
| Unl. | Unk. | 1971/72 | SGT | Stirewalt | Terry G. |
| Unl. | Unk. | 1971 | SGT | Stokes | Doyle D. |
| Loc. | 2nd | 1969/70 | SP4 | Stone | Patrick W. |
| Unl. | Unk. | | | Strafer | Ken |
| Loc. | HQ | 1970 | CPT | Straub | Christopher C. |
| Unl. | 2nd | 1971 | SSG | Studdard | Robert E. |
| Unl. | Unk. | 1971 | SP4 | Studier | Ronald E. |
| Loc. | 2nd | 1967/68 | SGT | Sturgess | Craig S. |
| Unl. | 2nd | 1969/70 | SGT | Sullivan | Ronald J. |
| Unl. | HQ | | | Sutherland | Donald L. |
| Unl. | Unk. | 1972 | PFC | Swanson | John J. |
| Loc. | 2nd | 1968/69 | SP4 | Sykes | Francis T. |
| Dec. | 3rd | 1967/68 | SP4 | Tabet | Henry Marsial |
| Unl. | Unk. | 1969 | PVT | Taborn | Leo |
| Unl. | 2nd | 1969 | ILT | Tailor | Charles |
| Unl. | Unk. | 1968/69 | PFC | Tailor | James A. |
| Unl. | 2nd | 1970/71 | PFC | Tailor | Larry Carl |

| *    | PLT  | YEAR    | RANK | LAST NAME    | FIRST NAME      |
|------|------|---------|------|--------------|-----------------|
| Unl. | 2nd  |         |      | Tailor       | Larry E.        |
| Unl. | Unk. | 1968/69 | PFC  | Tamel        | Henry M.        |
| Unl. | Unk. | 1969    |      | Taterman     | Ronald J.       |
| Unl. | Unk. | 1969    | SP4  | Taunton      | Charles E.      |
| Unl. | Unk. | 1971/72 | SGT  | Taylor       | Benjamin        |
| Unl. | 3rd  | 1968/69 | SGT  | Taylor       | James F.        |
| Unk. | Unk. | 1971    | PFC  | Taylor       | Marvin          |
| Unl. | 3rd  | 1969/70 | SP4  | Taylor Jr.   | Harvey          |
| Unl. | 2nd  | 1968/69 | PFC  | Tealer Jr.   | Eddie           |
| Loc. | 2nd  | 1968/69 | SP4  | Teel         | Terry A.        |
| Loc. | HQ   | 1969    | CPT  | Terrel       | Douglas         |
| Dec. | Unk. | 1968    | PFC  | Terrell      | Robert Earl     |
| Unl. | Unk. |         |      | Thacher      | Harold          |
| Unl. | 2nd  | 1969/70 | PFC  | Thacher II   | Frank B.        |
| Dec. | 3rd  | 1967/68 | PFC  | Thackrey Jr. | Wade E.         |
| Loc. | 3rd  | 1971    | SGT  | Thill        | Paul D.         |
| Loc. | 1st  | 1968/69 | SP4  | Thomas       | David P.        |
| Unl. | 1st  | 1967/68 | SP4  | Thomas       | Donald A.       |
| Unl. | Ist  | 1967/68 | SSG  | Thomas       | Lonnie G.       |
| Loc. | 3rd  | 1970/71 | SP4  | Thomas       | Myle G.         |
| Unl. | Unk. | 1972    | PFC  | Thompson     | Bennie          |
| Unl. | Unk. | 1967/68 | PFC  | Thompson     | Charles         |
| Unl. | HQ   | 1969/70 | CPT  | Thompson     | John T.         |
| Unl. | Unk. | 1968    | SP4  | Thompson Jr. | Marvin M.       |
| Loc. | Ist  | 1967/68 | PFC  | Tobiness     | Joseph L.       |
| Loc. | 2nd  | 1967/68 | SGT  | Todd         | Donald A.       |
| Unl. | Unk. | 1968/69 | SP4  | Tomczuk      | Richard S.      |
| Unl. | Unk. | 1971/72 | PSG  | Tomlin Jr.   | Edster          |
| Loc. | 2nd  | 1970    | SSG  | Tompkins     | Willian Gregory |
| Dec. | 2nd  | 1969/70 | SP4  | Toth         | Frankie D.      |
| Loc. | 2nd  | 1967/68 | SGT  | Towns Jr.    | Grady L.        |
| Dec. | 3rd  | 1968    | 1LT  | Trabert      | Thomas W.       |
| Unl. | Unk. | 1971    | SP4  | Trapp        | William P.      |
| Unl. | Unk  | 1971/72 | SP4  | Trask        | Mark L.         |
| Unl. | 3rd  | 1970/71 | SP4  | Trembley     | Steve J.        |
| Unl. | Unk. | 1971    | PFC  | Trift        | Charles W.      |
| Loc. | 1st  | 1970/71 | SP4  | Triplett     | Richard F.      |
| Unl. | Unk. | 1967    | PFC  | Trotter      | Warren          |
| Loc. | 2nd  | 1967/68 | SGT  | Troutman     | David L.        |
| Unl. | 3rd  | 1970    |      | Trujillo     | Richard D.      |

| * | PLT | YEAR | RANK | LAST NAME | FIRST NAME |
|---|---|---|---|---|---|
| Loc. | 3rd | 1967/68 | SP4 | Tucker Jr. | Kyle L. |
| Unl. | Unk. | 1972 | PFC | Tumbling | James M. |
| Unl. | Unk | 1969 | SP4 | Turman | James T. |
| Unl. | HQ | 1967/68 | SP4 | Tye | Patrick |
| Unl. | Unk. | 1968 | SP4 | Underdown | David R. |
| Unl. | Unl. | 1971/72 | SP4 | Unthank | Robert P. |
| Unl. | Unk. | 1971 | SGT | Untreg | Gregg E. |
| Loc. | 3rd | 1967/68 | SGT | Urban | Dale A. |
| Unl. | Unk. | 1968 | PFC-Cook | Urquhart | Eugene |
| Dec. | 2nd | 1970 | PFC | Utter | Keith Edward |
| Unl. | Unk. | 1969 | SP4 | Valtinson | Larry A. |
| Unl. | 2nd | 1969 | LT | Van More | |
| Unl. | 2nd | 1971 | SP4 | VanEych | Manuel F. |
| Loc. | 3rd | 1969/70 | SP4 | Varderbloomin | Dale T. |
| Dec. | 1st | 1971 | SP4 | Vandiver | Harry Melborn |
| Unl. | Unk. | 1968 | PFC | Vaasques | John J. |
| Loc. | 3rd. | 1971/72 | SGT | Veitch | Andrew G. |
| Loc. | 1st | 1970/71 | PFC | Verken | Gary L. |
| Unl. | 2nd | 1968 | SGT | Veverka | Dannie D. |
| Unl. | 2nd | 1971 | SGT | Villapando | Gus |
| Unl. | Unk. | 1971 | SGT | Vindiver | Stanley |
| Loc. | 1st | 1969/70 | SP4 | Viola | Michael J. |
| Loc. | 1st | 1969/70 | SP4 | Viserta | Joseph R. |
| Unl. | 3rd | 1969/70 | PFC | Viveros | Danial J. |
| Unl. | Unk | 1968/69 | CPL | Vizina | Joseph Vinc |
| Unl. | Unk. | 1968 | PFC | Vogel | Thomas H. |
| Loc. | 3rd | 1971 | | Voytek | Donald M. |
| Unl. | Unk. | 1970 | | Waage | Jared |
| Dec. | 2nd | 1967/68 | PFC | Wagner | David Frederick |
| Loc. | 2nd | 1971 | SP4 | Wagner | Leslie |
| Unl. | Unk. | 1967/68 | PFC | Wagner | Ronald O. |
| Unl. | 1st | 1970/71 | SGT | Waites | Donnie D. |
| Unl. | 1st | 1969/70 | PFC | Walbeck | Forrest E. |
| Loc. | 2nd | 1967/68 | SP4 | Walker | Kurtland |
| Unl. | Unk. | 1968/69 | PFC | Walker | Robert L. |
| Unl. | HQ | 1969/70 | 1LT-FO | Wall | Christopher |
| Unl. | HQ | 1971 | 1SG | Wallace | Charles S. |
| Loc. | 3rd | 1968/69 | PFC | Wallace | Davis |
| Unl. | Unk. | 1971 | PFC | Walleck | Jimmy L. |
| Unl. | Unk. | 1971 | SP4 | Walsh | Richard M. |
| Unl. | Unk. | 1971/72 | SGT | Walter | Larry L. |

# Roster of Delta Raiders

| *    | PLT  | YEAR    | RANK      | LAST NAME  | FIRST NAME     |
|------|------|---------|-----------|------------|----------------|
| Unl. | 2nd  | 1969/70 | SGT       | Walters    | Steven R.      |
| Unl. | 3rd  | 1969    | SGT       | Ward       | Jerry E.       |
| Dec. | 2nd  | 1971    | PFC       | Ward       | William James  |
| Unl. | 2nd  | 1971    | PFC       | Warfield   | Christopher    |
| Dec. | 3rd  | 1969/70 | SP4       | Warner     | Wilfred Wesley |
| Unl. | Unk  | 1968    | PFC       | Warren Jr. | Fredrick J.    |
| Unl. | 2nd  | 1971    | PFC       | Warrick    | Bruce C.       |
| Loc. | HQ   | 1968/69 | 1LT       | Warywoda   | Steven M.      |
| Unl. | Unk. | 1971/72 | SP4       | Washington | Curtis F.      |
| Unl. | 2nd  | 1967/68 | SGT       | Washington | Robert B.      |
| Loc. | 1st  | 1968    | SP4-Medic | Wasley     | Robert P.      |
| Unl. | Unk. | 1969    | PFC       | Watkins    | Jimmie L.      |
| Loc. | HQ   | 1967/68 | 2LT-FO    | Watson     | Michael        |
| Loc. | 3rd  | 1969/70 | SGT       | Weaver     | David L.       |
| Unl. | Unk. | 1971/72 | PFC       | Webster    | William F.     |
| Unl. | 1st  | 1968    | PFC       | Weimer     | Henry J.       |
| Loc. | 2nd  | 1969/70 | SSG       | Weir       | Eric W.        |
| Unl. | 2nd  | 1971    |           | Weller     | William D.     |
| Unl. | 1st  | 1970/71 | SP4       | Wells      | Frank O.       |
| Loc. | 1st  | 1969/70 | SP4       | West       | Charles D.     |
| Unl. | 2nd  | 1970    |           | Weston     | Dave           |
| Unl. | Unk. | 1971/72 | SGT       | Whaley     | James W.       |
| Loc. | 3rd  | 1967/68 | PFC       | Wheat      | John W.        |
| Unl. | 3rd  |         |           | Whelan     | Charles        |
| Loc. | 2nd  | 1970    |           | Whipkey    | Ronald R.      |
| Loc. | HQ   | 1968/69 | SP4       | Whitaker   | James H.       |
| Unl. | Unk. | 1969    | PFC       | White      | Kenneth R.     |
| Loc. | 2nd  | 1968/69 | PFC       | White      | Thomas L.      |
| Loc. | 2nd  | 1968/69 | SP4       | White Jr.  | William        |
| Unl. | Unk. | 1968    | SP5-Cook  | Whitehead  | Clarence       |
| Loc. | 3rd  | 1970    | SP4       | Whitehead  | Dwight R.      |
| Unl. | Unk. | 1971    | SGT       | Willbanks  | James E.       |
| Unl. | Unk. | 1971    | SGT       | Williames  | George R.      |
| Unl. | Unk. | 1969/70 | SP4       | Williams   | Bradley T.     |
| Unl. | Unk. | 1971    | SP4       | Williams   | Clarence H.    |
| Dec. | Unk. | 1968    |           | Williams   | Clifford Leroy |
| Unl. | 2nd  | 1969    | SFC       | Williams   | Don R.         |
| Unl. | 2nd  | 1969/70 | Medic     | Williams   | Jimmy R.       |
| Unl. | Unk. | 1971    | SP4       | Williams   | John           |
| Unl. | Unk. | 1970/71 | SP4       | Williams   | Rayford        |

| * | PLT | YEAR | RANK | LAST NAME | FIRST NAME |
|---|---|---|---|---|---|
| Unl. | Unk. | 1971 | PFC | Williams | Robert |
| Unl. | 1st | 1969 | PFC-Medic | Williams | Ronald A. |
| Unl. | Unk. | 1969 | PFC | Williams | Sterling |
| Unl. | Unk. | 1967 | PVT | Williams | Virlin J. |
| Unl. | Unk. | 1968 | PFC | Williams Jr. | Robert |
| Dec. | Unk. | 1968 | PFC | Williams, Jr. | Arthur |
| Unl. | 3rd | 1967/68 | SP4 | Williamson | Glenn P. |
| Unl. | 2nd | 1970 | SP4 | Willis | Albert S. |
| Unl. | Unk. | 1971/72 | SGT | Wilson | David E. |
| Unl. | Unk. | 1971 | SSG | Wilson | Gary T. |
| Unl. | Unk. | 1968 | SP4 | Wilson | Scott |
| Loc. | 3rd | 1970 | PFC | Wilson | Tommy W. |
| Loc. | 2nd | 1967/68 | SGT | Wingo | Frank H. |
| Loc. | 2nd | 1969/70 | PFC | Winny | George U. |
| Unl. | Unk. | 1971/72 | PFC | Wintburger | Gary J. |
| Unl. | Unk. | 1971/72 | PFC | Winter | Mark R. |
| Loc. | Unk. | 1971/72 | PFC | Winterowd | Randy D. |
| Loc. | 2nd | 1970/71 | SGT | Wojciechowski | Henry P. |
| Dec. | 1st | 1969 | SFC | Woods | Freddie |
| Unl. | Unk. | 1971 | SP4 | Wooten | John D. |
| Unl. | Unk. | | | Wright | Bob B. |
| Loc. | 3rd | 1970/71 | SP4 | Wright | Jack C. |
| Loc. | HQ | 1968/69 | 1SG | Wright | Jerrel F. |
| Unl. | HQ | 1969 | SGT | Wright | Robert L. |
| Unl. | Unk. | 1971 | PFC | Wright | Timothy D. |
| Unl. | Unk. | 1968 | SSG Cook | Wyatt | Charles L. |
| Unl. | 1st | | Medic | Yeager | |
| Unl. | 1st | 1970/71 | PFC | Young | Gerald A. |
| Unl. | Unk. | 1972 | SP4 | Zaskington | Curtis F. |
| Loc. | 2nd | 1967/68 | PFC | Zielke | Mike |
| Unl. | 3rd | 1971/72 | SP4 | Zinn | Tommy D. |
| Unl. | 2nd | 1968/69 | SP4 | Zoller | Kenneth L. |
| Loc. | 3rd | 1970/71 | SP4 | Zwit | James R. |

**308** • *Delta Raiders*

# Glossary

**ABN**: Airborne abbreviation.

**Airmobile**: Helicopter-borne. Those who jump from helicopters without parachutes.

**Airborne**: Parachutist. Those who jump from airplanes with parachutes.

**AIT**: Advanced Individual Training.

**AK-47**: Also known as Kalashnikov AK-47. The most widely used assault rifle in the world. A Soviet produced semi-automatic or automatic 7.62mm assault rifle. Known as the TYPE 56 to Chinese forces. Characterized by an explosive popping sound.

**AO**: Area of Operation. In rear areas this may connote a sleeping area or bunk. "MY AO…"

**ARA**: Aerial Rocket Artillery. A Cobra AG-1H helicopter with four XM-

159C 19-rocket (2.75 inch rocket) pods.

**Arty**: Artillery.

**ARVN**: Army of the Republic of Vietnam. Also a South Vietnamese soldiers as in Marvin in the ARVN.

**AT**: Anti Tank.

**B-40**: A communist bloc rocket-propelled grenade launcher. Also the rounds fired—B-40 rockets.

**B-52**: Heavy American bomber.

**BDA**: Bomb Damage Assessment.

**BDE**: Brigade.

**bird**: A helicopter.

**Bivouac**: Camp Area.

**boonies**: The field, the bush, the jungle. Any place the infantry operates not a firebase, basecamp or ville. From boondock.

**BOQ**: Bachelors Officers Quarters.

**BN**: Battalion.

**C-4**: A powerful plastic explosive.

# Glossary

**C-130**: A medium cargo airplane.

**C-141**: A large cargo airplane.

**CA**: Combat Assault.

**CA'd**: Combat Assaulted.

**Cav.**: Cavalry.

**CG**: Commanding Officer.

**CH-47**: A Chinook.

**Charlie**: The Viet. Cong.

**Cherry**: A new troop.

**Chi-Com**: Also Chicom. Chinese communist. Used in conjunction with an object this denoted manufactured in Red China. Used alone Chi-com usually meant a Chinese manufactured

hand grenade.

**Chieu Hoi**: Vietnamese for Open Arms. An amnesty program to encourage enemy soldiers to rally to the GVN.

**Chinook**: A large twin-rotor cargo helicopter, CH-47. The rotor wash caused discomfort to anyone in the vicinity of its landing. Wind velocity at the tip of the rotors reportedly is 130 mph.

**CIB**: Combat Infantrymans Badge.

**Claymores**: Anti-personnel mines with one-pound charge of C-4 behind 600 small steel balls.

**CO**: Commanding Officer.

**Cobra gunships**: An assault helicopter.

**Commo**: Communication.

**CP**: Command Post.

**C-rats**: Combat rations. After two weeks they all taste the same.

**CS**: Tear Gas.

**Cs**: C-rats.

**dicks**: A derogatory expression meaning or referring to the enemy.

**DMZ**: Demilitarized zone.

**DOA**: Dead on Arrival.

**DROVA**: Delta Raiders of Vietnam Association.

**DTs**: Defensive Targets.

Dust-Off: Medical evacuation by helicopter.

**elements**: Part of a military unit.

**Eleven Bravo**: Also 11-B. The MOS of an infantryman.

**EM**: Enlisted Man.

**F-4s**: Phantom Jet fighter-bombers. Range—100 miles. Speed—1400 mph. Payload—16,000 lbs. The workhorse of the tactical air support fleet. Often called a fast mover.

**FAC**: Forward Air Controller; usually in a small, maneuverable single-engine prop airplane.

**FB**: Firebase.

**FDC**: Fire Direction Control. (Artillery).

# Glossary

**flareship**: C-47.
**FO**: Forward Observer.
**frag**: A fragmentation hand grenade.
**ghosting**: Goofing off.
**GI**: Slang for solider.
**gook**: An NVA soldier. Also, any Oriental human being.
**grunt**: An infantryman.
**gunship**: Early in the war this means any; extra heavily armed helicopter used primarily to support infantry troops. Later, it referred to a Cobra AH-1H equipped with a particular configuration of rockets, 40mm cannons and mini-guns.
**HE**: High Explosive. (Artillery).
**heat tabs**: An inflammable tabled used to heat C-RATS. Always in short supply.
**HHC**: Headquarters and Headquarters Company.
**hootch**: A billet, sometimes a bunker, sometimes an office building.
**HQ**: Headquarters.
**Hueys**: UH-1 helicopters of various series. This Utility helicopter was the primary troop insertion/extraction

aircraft for the 101st. Also used as Dust-Off birds and C&C birds. Called Slicks.
**Hump**: To patrol carrying a rucksack; to walk; to perform any arduous task.
**I Corps**: (The Roman numeral I here is pronounced "eye"). The northernmost military region of South Vietnam.
**KBA**: Killed By Artillery.
**KBAF**: Killed by Artillery fire.
**KIA**: Killed In Action.
**Kit Carson Scout**: Also KCS. A Vietnamese working with an American infantry unit as an interpreter and scout under the Luc Long 66 Program.
**klick**: A kilometer.
**LAW**: Light Anti-tank Weapon. A 66mm rocket in a collapsible, discardable firing tube. Effective against bunkers.
**lit-up**: Fired upon.

# Glossary

**LMG**: Light Machine Gun-the Soviet made RPD, a bi-pod mounted, belt fed weapon similar to the American M-60 machine gun. The RPD fires the same cartridge as the AK-47 and the SKS carbine.

**Loach**: Light Observation Helicopter or LOH.

**Log Bird**: Logistical (resupply) helicopter.

**log ship**: Logistical resupply helicopter.

**log sorties**: Logistical flights - more than one.

**LOH**: Light Observation Helicopter.

**LRRP**: Long Range Reconnaissance Patrol.

**LSA**: Lubricant, Small Arms.

**LZ**: Landing Zone.

**M-14**: A gas operated 308 cal rifle.

**M-16**: A gas-operated, air cooled automatic/semi-automatic assault weapon weighing 7.6 pounds with a 20-round magazine. Maximum range 2350m. Maximum effective range 460m. Automatic firing rate 650-700 rounds/minute, sustained automatic firing rate 100-200 rounds/minute.

**M-203**: (over and under weapon).

**M-60**: The standard American light machine gun. A gas-operated, air cooled, belt fed, automatic weapon. Often referred to by grunts as THE GUN.

**M-79**: An American single-shot 40mm grenade launcher.

**MEDCAP**: Medical Civilian Action Program.

**Medevac**: Medical evacuation by helicopter.

**MG**: Major General.

**MIA**: Missing In Action.

**MOS**: Military Occupational Speciality. Job title code.

**Nam**: Vietnam.

**NCO**: Non-Commissioned Officer.

**NCOCS**: Non Commissioned Officers Candidate School.

**NDP**: Night Defensive Position.

**NVA**: North Vietnamese Army. Also, a North Vietnamese soldier.

**NVA Regt.**: Also known as the Thu Ben Regiment.

**OD**: Olive drab.

**OP**: Observation Post.

**OPCON**: Operational Control.

**PF**: Popular Force - Vietnamese National Guard.

**PFC**: Private First Class Rank/E-3.

**Pink Team**: LOH and two COBRA

Gunships.

**point or pointman**: The first man of a patrol.

**POW**: Prisoner Of War.

**PRC**: Radio.

**PSYOPS**: Psychological Operations.

**PZ**: Pick-up Zone.

**Quad 50s**: A four-barrelled assembly of a .50 caliber machine guns.

**RA**: Regular Army.

**Raiders**: Delta Raiders.

**Regt.**: Regiment.

**REMF**: (rim-ph) Rear Echelon Mother Fucker.

**RIF**: Recon in force, a heavy reconnaissance patrol. Later, Reduction in force, an administrative mechanism for retiring career soldiers prior to the end of their 20 year term.

**ROK**: Republic of Korea.

**RPG**: Rocket Propelled Grenade.

**RRF**: Ready Reaction Force.

**R&R**: Rest and Relaxation.

**RTO**: Radio-Telephone Operator.

**ruck, rucksack**: Backpack issued to infantry in Vietnam.

**RVN**: Republic of Vietnam. (South)

**S-2**: Battalion Intelligence Office.

**sampan**: Small fishing boat.

**sappers**: Enemy demolition/assault teams.

**SERTS**: Screaming Eagle Replacement Training School.

**SKS**: A Simonov 7.62mm semi-automatic carbine. A Russian rifle.

**Slicks**: Hueys.

**SMG**: Sergeant Major.

**SOP**: Standard Operating Procedure.

**Springfield rifle**: 1903A3 - 30-06 Caliber.

**standdown**: An infantry unit's return from the boonies to base camp for refitting and training. Later, a unit being withdrawn from Vietnam and redeployed to the US.

**steel pot**: A GI helmet.

**TAC Air**: Tactical air (Air Force) support. Fighter-bombers.

**TOC**: Tactical Operations Center.

**UH-1H**: A Huey slick.

**VC**: Viet Cong.

**ville**: A village.

**WIA**: Wounded In Action.

**World**: The USA or any place other than NAM.

**XO**: Executive Officer.

# Index

## A

Adams, Joseph A. 158, 200
Aguirre, Rodofo 224
Allen, Michael (Allen) B. 6, 219
Alston, Eugene C. 150
An Lo Bridge 35, 46
Anslow, Walter 12, 67
ARA (Aerial Rocket Artillery) 174
Ash, John W. 251
Ayala, Samuel 49

## B

Bailey, Lori 7
Baker, LT 224
Bales, Ronald Eugene 12, 14, 239
Banks, Larry 138
Barber, Roy L. 107
Barnes, Barry L. 199
Barnett, Billy 34, 46
Barsanti, Olivito 68, 82
Bass, Lieutenant 172
Begay, John 254
Begody, Harold L. 12, 14, 32, 45
Belt, Denny 200
Benoit, SFC Robert 26
Beregsasi, Rudolf 251, 253
Bevis, 1LT Stanford 128
Beyl, David R. 12, 14, 158, 208
Bien Hoa 27, 39, 66
Bischoff, 2LT 51, 53, 55
Blackman, Raymond H. "Blackie" 6, 167
Bohn, Sgt. 53
Bolden, Albert 160
Boos, LTC Michael A. 214, 238, 242
Borman, Frank 146
Bowman, James B. 49, 56
Bradley, COL 160
Brashears, LT Bobby P. 160
Brashears, LTC Bobby P. 143
Brewer, Lawrence, Jr. 94
Brockman, Robert David 12, 70, 86
Broxton, Coy A. 179

Brulte, Robert Francis 12, 14, 32, 34, 46
Brumbelow, Jackie M. 199
Bull, Jerry 170
Burroughs, Emanuel Fero 12, 46
Bush, 1LT 55, 56
Buzzini, Richard 70
Byfield, Terry 7

## C

Calhoun, James 49, 56
Cam Ranh 39
Camera, James C. 127
Camp Eagle 203
Camp Evans 31, 44, 47, 209
Carlson, Gene H. 162
Carnahan, William L. 252
Cash, David Manfred 12, 15, 32, 35, 46
Chandler, Bruce "Tony" 200
Chu Chi 41
Cirrincione, Martin 158
Clark, Eugene 225
Clay, B.G. 73
Cleo, 1LT C. Hogan 47
Cleveland 12
Clifford Sims 6
Cluff, Keith A. 199
Collins, Rodney 200
Cooksley, Mike 158, 208
Cooper, Terry 200
Courtney, Jimmy Darrell 12, 15, 139
Cu Chi 39
Curtis, CPT Thomas M. 139, 141

# Index

## D

Daniels, Rex Martin 12, 239
Davis, Hubert L. 49, 56
Deland, James 34, 101
Delaney, Henrie L. 49, 56
Des Jarden, William 134
Dien, Phuoc 72
Division Reaction Force 233
Dodson, Compton T. 250
Dong Ap Bia 133
Dotson 172
Dunlap, Joe W. 46
Dunn, Robert 12, 109

## E

Eagle Beach 209
Eagle Beak 40
Eggles, Thomas J. 105
Eller, Lawrence William 12, 72
Englerth, William J. 134, 139
Erbach, CPT William W. 48, 51, 55
Ertel, Larry 199
Estevez, Jose R. 132
Evans, Eugene 204
Evers, Wayne 224

## F

FB Bastogne 90
FB Geronimo 67
FB Hardcore 73
FB Pinky 64, 79, 83
Feurer, Michael H. 102
Fish, Douglas 224
Fishe, Douglas 224
Fisher, Douglas 224
Flavin, CPT 253
Frick, John 106

## G

Gagne, PFC Brad (Gunship) 32, 44
Gagnon, Raymond 134
Gaines, Frankie 56

Gains, Frank D. 49, 75
Gaster, Drew 208
Gates, CPT Robert E., Jr. 131
German, LTC Robert L. 131, 139, 143
Gervasi, Bob 224
Gillard 12
Gillem, Denny 56
Gingery, John Bernard 12, 15, 34, 49, 56, 77
Godwin, Jack L. 200
Gould, Robert A. 46
Grant, Franklin, Jr. 69
Grant, Sylvester 134
Gravett, Jody 49, 56, 68
Gray, Tex W. 48, 49, 56
Grebinger, Charles 134
Green, George L. 140
Greene, Terry Willard 12, 239
Gregory, Eulas Fay 12, 34, 36, 68
Grelle, Paul 6
Griffin, Alto 211
Grimsley, LT Lee 12, 30, 53, 54
Grubidt, Ron 208
Guimond, Paul C. "Rat" 12. 15, 200

## H

Hacker, Bernard 35, 46
"Hamburger Hill" 133
Hanrahan, Warren P. 200
Hanrahan, Warren R. 200
Harter, 1Lt Terry Wayne 251
Hein, Robert Charles 12, 239
Heiserman, Lester 46
Heiter, LTC James A. 76, 94, 113
Hembree, SGT James Thomas, Jr. 12, 16, 200, 268, 270
Hendricks, Ronald 34, 46
Hennessey, M.G. John J. 165, 233
Henson, Darlene 7
Hill, Bobby G. 200
Hines, SFC 27
Hinz, William J. 35, 46
Hoffman, Gordon H. 128
Hogan, Cleo 6, 36, 50, 73
Hogenauer, Edward L. 105
Holgerson, Kenny 205
Holmes 12

Holmes, Ernest Paul  46
Holmes, Victor A.  49, 56
Hoof, Earnest  139
Hooper, SSgt Joe R.  6, 27, 30, 36, 47-49, 54, 56, 59, 165
Hopkins, Thomas A.  49, 56
Hue  32, 63, 81

## J

Jakes, David  104
James, Ava A.  49, 56
Jenkins, James  34, 46
Johnson, Lorin  34
Jones, William F.  12, 200

## K

Keister, John Lay. "Red"  12, 16, 146, 200
Kelley, Mark  158
Kelly, CPT John Edward, Jr.  137, 139
Kelly, John Edward, Jr.  16
Khe Sanh  30, 31
Kirk, Stephen  224
Kirkland, Steve  204
Knickerbocker  12
Kopay, Michael  46

## L

L., Harold Begody  45
Larson, Michael J.  132
Leaf, David  56
Leaf, David R.  49
Leshikar, Chuck  6, 101
Leuer, LTC Kenneth C.  242
Lewis, Willie J.  199
Livingston, LTC Otis T.  160, 165
Livingston, LtC Otis W.  214
Loffin, LT Dave  36
Loflin, LT  35
Loftin, William D.  32, 34, 36, 54, 70
Longbottom, Harry P.  104
Lovell, Larry  134
Lucas, Col.  208

## M

Marron  13
Martin, David W.  69

Martin, James L.  49, 56
Martin, Robert R.  134
Martinez, Alex Esequiel  13, 138
Marunchuck, Sp/4 Lawrence  32
Masunaga, Clifford N.  134
Maynard, Richard L.  13, 216
Mayor, Robert  109
McCarthy, Mike  144
McCreight, Kenneth W.  163
McGinnes, Charles Dennis  13, 16, 239
McGowans, Norman D.  163
McKenzie, Paul  13, 239, 242
McKieghan, David  33, 46
McKinney  13
McKinney, James B.  253
McKinney, Robert Dale  244
McManus, Ernest  49
McMenamy, C. Wayne  6, 21, 39, 46, 47
MEDCAP (Medical Civil Action Program)  79
Medina, Julio D.  35, 46
Mejia, John  119
Mercado, Jose E.  139
Michener, Dan  6
Miles, PFC  34
Miles, Roger  211
Miles, Thomas  49, 56
Miller, Bernard F.  134
Minh Tanh  30
Moore, Roy J.  273
Moore, Terry  6, 203, 205
Mount, Alfred M.  49, 56
Muncey, Jay Allen  13, 17, 211

## N

Nichols, Edward E.  134
Nissen, Gerald L.  134
Nordell Jr.  13

## O

Operation APACHE SNOW  132, 135
Operation APACHE SNOW  131
Operation CARENTAN II  71
Operation CLAIBORNE CHUTE  140, 142
Operation Eagle Thrust  39

Operation FULTON SQUARE 144
Operation JEB STUART 43, 71
Operation JEFFERSON GLEN/
    MONSOON PLAN 70 213
Operation KENTUCKY JUMPER
    125
Operation KENTUCKY JUMPER
    131
Operation MASSACHUSETTS
    STRIKER 131
Operation MASSACHUSETTS
    STRIKER 125
Operation NEVADA EAGLE 80, 125
Operation RANDOLPH GLEN
    146, 149, 157
Operation TEXAS STAR 157, 213

**P**

Padilla, Richard 224
Palm 13
Palm, John 5
Palm, Terry Alan 17, 158, 200, 268
Parker, George P. 30, 69, 83
Parker, PSG 53, 54
Pechacek, Glen 46
Peterson, Dwight E. 74
Phillips, Ronald 104
Phong Dien District 157
Phu Bai 30, 31, 39, 42
Phu Bai Airfield 165
Plenderleith, James 201
Pogue, Kenneth 256
Pohl Bridge 138
Pohlman, Larry 253
Policz, Erin Elizabeth 263
Poullard, James L. 199

**Q**

Quang Tri 31

**R**

Rachell, James C. 49, 56
Rainey, Barry 46
Rainwater, Robert 35, 46
Richardson, Larry 154
Riley, Stan T. 75
Robertson, Eugene 6, 34, 46

Robinson, Carl E. 199
Robinson, George (Rob) 224
Rockel, Noah N. 49, 56
Rollason, William David 13, 17, 209
Rufty, 1LT Joe Hearne 13, 17, 152,
    267, 270
Ryan, Richard 46

**S**

Saunders 13
Savage, Lee 158
Saxiones, Nicholas 69
Schaaf, Francis 224
Schneider, Gary Lee 13, 18, 201, 269
Schuelke, Top 169, 173
Scott, Arthur 22, 64
Scott, Ronald 107
Selvaggi, Ralph 200
Shannon, Carl 158, 166
Sharp, Herman 134
Sheldon 13
Shilling, Giles 224
Shipley, John 270
Simmons, Dennis C. 35, 46
Sims, Clifford Chester 13, 18, 47-49,
    56, 61
Sims, Robert J. 162
Sims, Sgt. Clifford 33-34, 36, 54
Sommer, Douglas 13, 134
Soubers, Rod 6
Spears, Lanny W. 160
Spivey, Alex D. "Doc" 33, 36, 46
Stearns 13
Stearns, Jerry Sheldon 13, 204, 239,
    242
Stewart, Garrett 158
Straub, CPT Christopher C. 153, 161,
    165, 169, 179
Sturgess, Craig 68

**T**

Tabet, Henry Marsial 13, 18, 46
Tallman, LTC 22,
    49, 51, 53, 54, 55, 76
Tan Hoa 41
Tarpley, M.G. Thomas M. 233
Terrel, CPT Douglas 131, 137
Terrell 13

# Index

Terrell, Robert Earl  18
Tet offensive  31
Thacher, Frank B.  134
Thackrey, Wade E., Jr.  13, 19, 34, 46
Thomas, Lonnie  49
Thompson, Bennie  260
Thompson, CPT John T.  141, 150, 153
Thon Duong Son  77
Thon Kim Doi  75
Thon Phuoc Dien  72
Thon Phuoc Yen  77
Thu Ben Regiment  76
Tomczuk, Richard S.  127
Tompkins, William G.  163
Torres, Jose Alicia  158
Trabert  82
Trujillo, Richard  160
Tucker, Kyle  34
Turman, James T.  132

## U

Urban, Dale  47-49, 56
Urban, Sgt Dale A.  47
Utah (Wunder) Beach  71, 73
Utter, Keith Edward  13, 19, 200

## V

Vandiver, Harry Melborn  13, 19, 258
Vaneych, Manuel E.  252

## W

Wagner  13
Wagner, David Frederick  13, 20
Walker, Kurtland  35, 46
Wall, 1LT Chris  150
Wallace, Davis  49, 56
Walters, Steven R.  134
Ward, William James  13, 239
Warner, Wilfred W.  13, 208
Warrick, Bruce E.  252
Washington, Robert B.  34, 69
Watson, LT Michael  32, 35, 53
Weaver, David L.  200
Wentworth, John  242

West, Charles  158
Wheat, John W.  46
White, Thomas L.  134
Williams  13
Williams, Arthur  107
Williams, Clifford Leroy  20, 69
Williams, Jr.  13
Williamson, Glenn  34
Wilson, LTC Joseph C.  131
Wilson, LTC Joseph O.  113
Wingo, Frank  108
Wright, M.G. John H.  165
Wunder Beach  74
Wyatt, SSgt. Charlie  26

## X, Z

Xam Thu Le  76
Zinn, Tommy D.  25